FROM THE CAVES AND JUNGLES OF HINDOSTAN

FROM THE CAVES AND JUNGLES OF HINDOSTAN

By

HELENA BLAVATSKY

GYAN

ISBN : 978-81-212-1586-2(HB)

First Published, 1883

Published, 2018

Published by

Gyan Publishing House
5, Ansari Road
Daryaganj, New Delhi-110002
Phone: 011-47034999, 9811692060
www.gyanbooks.com
E-mail: books@gyanbooks.com

Printed at: G. Print Process, Delhi.

TRANSLATOR'S PREFACE.

"YOU must remember," said Mme. Blavatsky, "that I never meant this for a scientific work. My letters to the *Russian Messenger*, under the general title: 'From the Caves and Jungles of Hindostan,' were written in leisure moments, more for amusement than with any serious design.

"Broadly speaking, the facts and incidents are true; but I have freely availed myself of an author's privilege to group, colour, and dramatize them, whenever this seemed necessary to the full artistic effect; though, as I say, much of the book is exactly true, I would rather claim kindly judgment for it, as a romance of travel, than incur the critical risks that haunt an avowedly serious work."

To this caution of the author's, the translator must add another; these letters, as Mme. Blavatsky says, were written in leisure moments, during 1879 and 1880, for the pages of the *Russki Vyestnik*, then edited by M. Katkoff. Mme. Blavatsky's manuscript was often incorrect; often obscure. The Russian compositors, though they did their best to render faithfully the Indian names and places, often produced, through their ignorance of Oriental tongues, forms which are strange, and sometimes unrecognizable.

The proof-sheets were never corrected by the author, who was then in India; and, in consequence, it has been impossible to restore all the local and personal names to their proper form.

A similar difficulty has arisen with reference to quotations and cited authorities, all of which have gone through a double process of refraction: first into Russian, then into English. The translator, also a Russian, and far from perfectly acquainted with English, cannot claim to possess the erudition necessary to verify and restore the many quotations to verbal accuracy; all that is hoped is that, by a careful rendering, the correct sense has been preserved.

The translator begs the indulgence of English readers for all imperfections of style and language; in the words of the Sanskrit proverb: "Who is to be blamed, if success be not reached after due effort?"

The translator's best thanks are due to Mr. John C. Staples, for valuable help in the early chapters.

London, July, 1892.

CONTENTS.

FROM THE CAVES AND JUNGLES OF HINDOSTAN.

IN BOMBAY.

LATE in the evening of the sixteenth of February, 1879, after a rough voyage which lasted thirty-two days, joyful exclamations were heard everywhere on deck. "Have you seen the lighthouse?" "There it is at last, the Bombay lighthouse."

Cards, books, music, everything was forgotten. Everyone rushed on deck. The moon had not risen as yet, and, in spite of the starry tropical sky, it was quite dark. The stars were so bright that, at first, it seemed hardly possible to distinguish, far away amongst them, a small fiery point lit by earthly hands. The stars winked at us like so many huge eyes in the black sky, on one side of which shone the Southern Cross. At last we distinguished the lighthouse on the distant horizon. It was nothing but a tiny fiery point diving in the phosphorescent waves. The tired travellers greeted it warmly. The rejoicing was general.

What a glorious daybreak followed this dark night! The sea no longer tossed our ship. Under the skilled guidance of the pilot, who had just arrived, and whose bronze form was so sharply defined against the pale sky, our steamer, breathing heavily with its broken machinery, slipped over the quiet, transparent waters of the Indian Ocean straight to the harbour. We were only four miles from Bombay, and, to us, who had trembled with cold only a few weeks ago in the Bay of Biscay, which has been so glorified by many poets and so heartily cursed by all sailors, our surroundings simply seemed a magical dream.

After the tropical nights of the Red Sea and the scorching hot days that had tortured us since Aden, we, people of the distant North, now experienced something strange and unwonted, as if the very fresh soft air had cast its spell over us. There was not a cloud in the sky, thickly strewn with dying stars. Even the moonlight, which till then had covered the sky with its silvery garb, was gradually vanishing; and the brighter grew the rosiness of dawn over the small island that lay before us in the East, the paler in the West grew the scattered rays of the moon that sprinkled with bright flakes of light the dark wake our ship left behind her, as if the glory of the West was bidding good-bye to us, while the light of the East welcomed the new-comers from far-off lands. Brighter and bluer grew the sky, swiftly absorbing the remaining pale stars one after the other, and we felt something touching in the sweet dignity with which the Queen of Night resigned her rights to the powerful usurper. At last, descending lower and lower, she disappeared completely.

And suddenly, almost without interval between darkness and light, the red-hot globe, emerging on the opposite side from under the cape, leant his golden chin on the lower rocks of the island and seemed to stop for a while, as if examining us. Then, with one powerful effort, the torch of day rose high over the sea and gloriously proceeded on its path, including in one mighty fiery embrace the blue waters of the bay, the shore and the islands with their rocks and cocoanut forests. His golden rays fell upon a crowd of Parsees, his rightful worshippers, who stood on shore raising their arms towards the mighty "Eye of Ormuzd." The sight was so impressive that everyone on deck became silent for a moment, even a red-nosed old sailor, who was busy quite close to us over the cable, stopped working, and, clearing his throat, nodded at the sun.

Moving slowly and cautiously along the charming but treacherous bay, we had plenty of time to admire the picture around us. On the right was a group of islands with Gharipuri or Elephanta, with its ancient temple, at their head. *Gharipuri* translated means "the town of caves" according to the Orientalists, and "the town of purification" according to the native Sanskrit scholars. This temple, cut out by an unknown hand in the very heart of a rock resembling porphyry, is a true apple of discord amongst the archæologists, of whom none can as yet fix, even approximately, its antiquity. Elephanta raises high its rocky brow, all overgrown with secular cactus, and right under it, at the foot of the rock, are hollowed out the chief temple and the two lateral ones. Like the serpent of our Russian fairy tales, it seems to be opening its fierce black mouth to swallow the daring mortal who comes to take possession of the secret mystery of Titan. Its two remaining teeth, dark with time, are formed by two huge pillars at the entrance, sustaining the palate of the monster.

How many generations of Hindus, how many races, have knelt in the dust before the Trimûrti, your threefold deity, O Elephanta? How many centuries were spent by weak man in digging out in your stone bosom this town of temples and carving your gigantic idols? Who can say? Many years have elapsed since I saw you last, ancient, mysterious temple, and still the same restless thoughts, the same recurrent questions vex me now as they did then, and still remain unanswered. In a few days we shall see each other again. Once more I shall gaze upon your stern image, upon your three huge granite faces, and shall feel as hopeless as ever of piercing the mystery of your being. This secret fell into safe hands three centuries before ours. It is not in vain that the old Portuguese historian Don Diego de Cuta boasts that "the big square stone fastened over the arch of the pagoda with a distinct inscription, having been torn out and sent as a present to the King Dom Juan III., disappeared *mysteriously* in the course of time . . . ," and adds, further, "Close to this big pagoda there stood another, and farther on even a third one, the most wonderful of all in beauty, incredible size, and richness of material. All those pagodas and caves have been built by the Kings of Kanada, (?) the most important of whom was Bonazur, and these buildings of Satan our (Portuguese) soldiers attacked with such vehemence that in a few years one stone was not left upon another. . . . ." And, worst of all, they left no inscriptions that might have given a clue to so much. Thanks to the fanaticism of Portuguese soldiers, the chronology of the Indian cave temples must remain for ever an enigma to the archæological world, beginning with the Brahmans, who say Elephanta is 374,000 years old, and ending with Fergusson, who tries to prove that it was carved only in the twelfth century of our era. Whenever one turns one's eyes to history, there is nothing to be found but hypotheses and darkness. And yet Gharipuri is mentioned in the epic *Mahâbhârata*, which was written, according to Colebrooke and Wilson, a good while before the reign of Cyrus. In another ancient legend it is said that the temple of Trimûrti was built on Elephanta by the sons of Pându, who took part in the war between the dynasties of the Sun and the Moon, and, belonging to the latter, were expelled at the end of the war. The Rajputs, who are the descendants of the first, still sing of this victory; but even in their popular songs there is nothing positive. Centuries have passed and will pass, and the ancient secret will die in the rocky bosom of the cave still unrecorded.

On the left side of the bay, exactly opposite Elephanta, and as if in contrast with all its antiquity and greatness, spreads the Malabar Hill, the residence of the modern Europeans and rich natives. Their brightly painted bungalows are bathed in the greenery of banyan, Indian fig, and various other trees, and the tall and straight trunks of cocoanut palms cover with the fringe of their leaves the whole ridge of the hilly headland. There, on the south-western end of the rock, you see the almost transparent, lace-like Government House surrounded on three sides by the ocean. This is the coolest and the most comfortable part of Bombay, fanned by three different sea breezes.

The island of Bombay, designated by the natives "Mambai," received its name from the goddess Mamba, in Mahrati Mahima, or Amba, Mama, and Amma, according to the dialect, a word meaning, literally, the Great Mother. Hardly one hundred years ago, on the site of the modern esplanade, there stood a temple consecrated to Mamba-Devi. With great difficulty and expense they carried it nearer to the shore, close to the fort, and erected it in front of Baleshwara the "Lord of the Innocent"—one of the names of the god Shiva. Bombay is part of a considerable group of islands, the most remarkable of which are Salsetta, joined to Bombay by a mole, Elephanta, so named by the Portuguese because of a huge rock cut in the shape of an elephant thirty-five feet long, and Trombay, whose lovely rock rises nine hundred feet above the surface of the sea. Bombay looks, on the maps, like an enormous cray-fish, and is at the head of the rest of the islands. Spreading far out into the sea its two claws, Bombay island stands like a sleepless guardian watching over his younger brothers. Between it and the Continent there is a narrow arm of a river, which gets gradually broader and then again narrower, deeply indenting the sides of both shores, and so forming a haven that has no equal in the world. It was not without reason that the Portuguese, expelled in the course of time by the English, used to call it "Buona Bahia."

In a fit of tourist exaltation some travellers have compared it to the Bay of Naples; but, as a matter of fact, the one is as much like the other as a lazzaroni is like a Kuli. The whole resemblance between the former consists in the fact that there is water in both. In Bombay, as well as in its harbour, everything is original and does not in the least remind one of Southern Europe. Look at those coasting vessels and native boats; both are built in the likeness of the sea bird "sat," a kind of kingfisher. When in motion these boats are the personification of grace, with their longs prows and rounded poops. They look as if they were gliding backwards, and one might mistake for wings the strangely shaped, long lateen sails, their narrow angles fastened upwards to a yard. Filling these two wings with the wind, and careening, so as almost to touch the surface of the water, these boats will fly along with astonishing swiftness. Unlike our European boats, they do not cut the waves, but glide over them like a sea-gull.

The surroundings of the bay transported us to some fairy land of the Arabian Nights. The ridge of the

Western Ghats, cut through here and there by some separate hills almost as high as themselves, stretched all along the Eastern shore. From the base to their fantastic, rocky tops, they are all overgrown with impenetrable forests and jungles inhabited by wild animals. Every rock has been enriched by the popular imagination with an independent legend. All over the slope of the mountain are scattered the pagodas, mosques, and temples of numberless sects. Here and there the hot rays of the sun strike upon an old fortress, once dreadful and inaccessible, now half ruined and covered with prickly cactus. At every step some memorial of sanctity. Here a deep *vihâra,* a cave cell of a Buddhist bhikshu saint, there a rock protected by the symbol of Shiva, further on a Jaina temple, or a holy tank, all covered with sedge and filled with water, once blessed by a Brahman and able to purify every sin, an indispensable attribute of all pagodas. All the surroundings are covered with symbols of gods and goddesses. Each of the three hundred and thirty millions of deities of the Hindu Pantheon has its representative in something consecrated to it, a stone, a flower, a tree, or a bird. On the West side of the Malabar Hill peeps through the trees Valakeshvara, the temple of the "Lord of Sand." A long stream of Hindus moves towards this celebrated temple; men and women, shining with rings on their fingers and toes, with bracelets from their wrists up to their elbows, clad in bright turbans and snow white muslins, with foreheads freshly painted with red, yellow, and white, holy sectarian signs.

The legend says that Râma spent here a night on his way from Ayodhya (Oudh) to Lanka (Ceylon) to fetch his wife Sîtâ who had been stolen by the wicked King Râvana. Râma's brother Lakshman, whose duty it was to send him daily a new lingam from Benares, was late in doing so one evening. Losing patience, Râma erected for himself a lingam of sand. When, at last, the symbol arrived from Benares, it was put in a temple, and the lingam erected by Râma was left on the shore. There it stayed during long centuries, but, at the arrival of the Portuguese, the "Lord of Sand" felt so disgusted with the feringhi (foreigners) that he jumped into the sea never to return. A little farther on there is a charming tank, called Vanattîrtha, or the "point of the arrow." Here Râma, the much worshipped hero of the Hindus, felt thirsty and, not finding any water, shot an arrow and immediately there was created a pond. Its crystal waters were surrounded by a high wall, steps were built leading down to it, and a circle of white marble dwellings was filled with dwija (twice born) Brahmans.

India is the land of legends and of mysterious nooks and corners. There is not a ruin, not a monument, not a thicket, that has no story attached to it. Yet, however they may be entangled in the cobweb of popular imagination, which becomes thicker with every generation, it is difficult to point out a single one that is not founded on fact. With patience and, still more, with the help of the learned Brahmans you can always get at the truth, when once you have secured their trust and friendship.

The same road leads to the temple of the Parsee fire-worshippers. At its altar burns an unquenchable fire, which daily consumes hundredweights of sandal wood and aromatic herbs. Lit three hundred years ago, the sacred fire has never been extinguished, notwithstanding many disorders, sectarian discords, and even wars. The Parsees are very proud of this temple of Zaratushta, as they call Zoroaster. Compared with it the Hindu pagodas look like brightly painted Easter eggs. Generally they are consecrated to Hanuman, the monkey-god and the faithful ally of Râma, or to the elephant headed Ganesha, the god of the occult wisdom, or to one of the Devis. You meet with these temples in every street. Before each there is a row of pipals (*Ficus religiosa*) centuries old, which no temple can dispense with, because these trees are the abode of the elementals and the sinful souls.

All this is entangled, mixed, and scattered, appearing to one's eyes like a picture in a dream. Thirty centuries have left their traces here. The innate laziness and the strong conservative tendencies of the Hindus, even before the European invasion, preserved all kinds of monuments from the ruinous vengeance of the fanatics, whether those memorials were Buddhist, or belonged to some other unpopular sect. The Hindus are not naturally given to senseless vandalism, and a phrenologist would vainly look for a bump of destructiveness on their skulls. If you meet with antiquities that, having been spared by time, are, nowadays, either destroyed or disfigured, it is not they who are to blame, but either Mussulmans, or the Portuguese under the guidance of the Jesuits.

At last we were anchored and, in a moment, were besieged, ourselves as well as our luggage, by numbers of naked skeleton-like Hindus, Parsees, Moguls, and various other tribes. All this crowd emerged, as if from the bottom of the sea, and began to shout, to chatter, and to yell, as only the tribes of Asia can. To get rid of this Babel confusion of tongues as soon as possible, we took refuge in the first bunder boat and made for the shore.

Once settled in the bungalow awaiting us, the first thing we were struck with in Bombay was the millions of crows and vultures. The first are, so to speak, the County Council of the town, whose duty it is to clean the streets, and to kill one of them is not only forbidden by the police, but would be very dangerous. By killing one you would rouse the vengeance of every Hindu, who is always ready to offer his own life in exchange for a crow's. The souls of the sinful forefathers transmigrate into crows and to kill one is to interfere with the law of Karma and to expose the poor ancestor to something still worse. Such is the firm belief, not only of Hindus, but of Parsees, even the most enlightened amongst them. The strange behaviour of the Indian crows explains, to a certain extent, this superstition. The vultures are, in a way, the grave-diggers of the Parsees and are under the personal protection of the Farvardania, the angel of death, who soars over the Tower of Silence, watching the occupations of the feathered workmen.

The deafening caw of the crows strikes every new comer as uncanny, but, after a while, is explained very simply. Every tree of the numerous cocoa-nut forests round Bombay is provided with a hollow pumpkin. The sap of the tree drops into it and, after fermenting, becomes a most intoxicating beverage, known in Bombay under the name of toddy. The naked toddy wallahs, generally half-caste Portuguese, modestly adorned with a single coral necklace, fetch this beverage twice a day, climbing the hundred and fifty feet high trunks like squirrels. The crows mostly build their nests on the tops of the cocoa-nut palms and drink incessantly out of the open pumpkins. The result of this is the chronic intoxication of the birds. As soon as we went out in the garden of our new habitation, flocks of crows came down heavily from every tree. The noise they make whilst jumping about everywhere is indescribable. There seemed to be something positively human in the positions of the slyly bent heads of the drunken birds, and a fiendish light shone in their eyes while they were examining us from foot to head.

We occupied three small bungalows, lost, like nests, in the garden, their roofs literally smothered in roses blossoming on bushes twenty feet high, and their windows covered only with muslin, instead of the usual panes of glass. The bungalows were situated in the native part of the town, so that we were transported, all at once, into the real India. We were living in India, unlike English people, who are only surrounded by India at a certain distance. We were enabled to study her character and customs, her religion, superstitions and rites, to learn her legends, in fact, to live among Hindus.

Everything in India, this land of the elephant and the poisonous cobra, of the tiger and the unsuccessful English missionary, is original and strange. Everything seems unusual, unexpected, and striking, even to one who has travelled in Turkey, Egypt, Damascus, and Palestine. In these tropical regions the conditions of nature are so various that all the forms of the animal and vegetable kingdoms must radically differ from what we are used to in Europe. Look, for instance, at those women on their way to a well through a garden, which is private and at the same time open to anyone, because somebody's cows are grazing in it. To whom does it not happen to meet with women, to see cows, and admire a garden? Doubtless these are among the commonest of all things. But a single attentive glance will suffice to show you the difference that exists between the same objects in Europe and in India. Nowhere more than in India does a human being feel his weakness and insignificance. The majesty of the tropical growth is such that our highest trees would look dwarfed compared with banyans and especially with palms. A European cow, mistaking, at first sight, her Indian sister for a calf, would deny the existence of any kinship between them, as neither the mouse-coloured wool, nor the straight goat-like horns, nor the humped back of the latter would permit her to make such an error. As to the women, each of them would make any artist feel enthusiastic about the gracefulness of her movements and drapery, but still, no pink and white, stout Anna Ivanovna would condescend to greet her. "Such a shame, God forgive me, the woman is entirely naked!"

This opinion of the modern Russian woman is nothing but the echo of what was said in 1470 by a distinguished Russian traveller, "the sinful slave of God, Athanasius son of Nikita from Tver," as he styles himself. He describes India as follows: "This is the land of India. Its people are naked, never cover their heads, and wear their hair braided. Women have babies every year. Men and women are black. Their prince wears a veil round his head and wraps another veil round his legs. The noblemen wear a veil on one shoulder, and the noblewomen on the shoulders and round the loins, but everyone is barefooted. The women walk about with their hair spread and their breasts naked. The children, boys and girls, never cover their shame until they are seven years old. . . ." This description is quite correct, but Athanasius Nikita's son is right only concerning the lowest and poorest classes. These really do "walk about" covered only with a veil, which often is so poor that, in fact, it is nothing but a rag. But still, even the poorest woman is clad in a piece of muslin at least ten yards long. One end serves as a sort of short petticoat, and the other covers the head and shoulders when out in the street, though the faces are always uncovered. The hair is erected into a kind of Greek chignon. The legs up to the knees, the arms, and the waist are never covered. There is not a single respectable woman who would consent to put on a pair of shoes. Shoes are the attribute and the prerogative of disreputable women. When, some time ago, the wife of the Madras governor thought of passing a law that should induce native women to cover their breasts, the place was actually threatened with a revolution. A kind of jacket is worn only by dancing girls. The Government recognized that it would be unreasonable to irritate women, who, very often, are more dangerous than their husbands and brothers, and the custom, based on the law of Manu, and sanctified by three thousand years' observance, remained unchanged.

For more than two years before we left America we were in constant correspondence with a certain learned Brahman, whose glory is great at present (1879) all over India. We came to India to study, under his guidance, the ancient country of Aryas, the *Vedas*, and their difficult language. His name is Dayanand Saraswati Swami. Swami is the name of the learned anchorites who are initiated into many mysteries unattainable by common mortals. They are monks who never marry, but are quite different from other mendicant brotherhoods, the so-called Sannyâsi and Hossein. This Pandit is considered the greatest Sanskritist of modern India and is an absolute enigma to everyone. It is only five years since he appeared on the arena of great reforms, but, till then, he lived, entirely secluded, in a jungle, like the ancient gymnosophists mentioned by the Greek and Latin authors. At this time he was studying the chief philosophical systems of the "Aryavârtta" and the occult meaning of the *Vedas* with the help of mystics and anchorites. All Hindus believe that on the Bhadrinath Mountains (22,000 feet above the level of the sea) there exist spacious caves, inhabited, now for many thousand years, by these anchorites. Bhadrinath is situated in the north of Hindustan on the river Bishegunj, and is celebrated for its temple of Vishnu right in the heart of the town. Inside the temple there are hot mineral springs, visited yearly by about fifty thousand pilgrims, who come to be purified by them.

From the first day of his appearance Dayanand Saraswati produced an immense impression and got the surname of the "Luther of India." Wandering from one town to another, to-day in the South, to-morrow in the North, and transporting himself from one end of the country to another with incredible quickness, he has visited every part of India, from Cape Comorin to the Himalayas, and from Calcutta to Bombay. He preaches the One Deity and, "*Vedas* in hand," proves that in the ancient writings there was not a word that could justify polytheism. Thundering against idol worship, the great orator fights with all his might against caste, infant marriages, and superstitions. Chastising all the evils grafted on India by centuries of casuistry and false interpretation of the *Vedas*, he blames for them the Brahmans, who, as he openly says before masses of people, are alone guilty of the humiliation of their country, once great and independent, now fallen and enslaved. And yet Great Britain has in him not an enemy, but rather an ally. He says openly—"If you expel the English, then, no later than to-morrow, you and I, and everyone who rises against idol worship will have our throats cut like mere sheep. The Mussulmans are stronger than the idol worshippers; but these last are stronger than we."

The Pandit held many a warm dispute with the Brahmans, those treacherous enemies of the people, and has almost always been victorious. In Benares secret assassins were hired to slay him, but the attempt did not succeed. In a small town of Bengal, where he treated fetishism with more than his usual severity, some fanatic threw on his naked feet a huge cobra. There are two snakes deified by the Brahman mythology: the one which surrounds the neck of Shiva on his idols is called Vasuki; the other, Ananta, forms the couch of Vishnu. So the worshipper of Shiva, feeling sure that his cobra, trained purposely for the mysteries of a Shivaite pagoda, would at once make an end of the offender's life, triumphantly exclaimed, "Let the god Vasuki himself show which of us is right!"

Dayanand jerked off the cobra twirling round his leg, and, with a single vigorous movement, crushed the reptile's head.

"Let him do so," he quietly assented. "Your god has been too slow. It is I who have decided the dispute. Now go," added he, addressing the crowd, "and tell everyone how easily perish the false gods."

Thanks to his excellent knowledge of Sanskrit the Pandit does a great service, not only to the masses, clearing their ignorance about the monotheism of the *Vedas*, but to science too, showing who, exactly, are the Brahmans, the only caste in India which, during centuries, had the right to study Sanskrit literature and comment on the *Vedas*, and which used this right solely for its own advantage.

Long before the time of such Orientalists as Burnouf, Colebrooke and Max Müller, there have been in India many reformers who tried to prove the pure monotheism of the Vedic doctrines. There have even been founders of new religions who denied the revelations of these scriptures; for instance, the Raja Ram Mohun Roy, and, after him, Babu Keshub Chunder Sen, both Calcutta Bengalees. But neither of them had much success. They did nothing but add new denominations to the numberless sects existing in India. Ram Mohun Roy died in England, having done next to nothing, and Keshub Chunder Sen, having founded the community of "Brahmo-Samaj," which professes a religion extracted from the depths of the Babu's own imagination, became a mystic of the most pronounced type, and now is only "a berry from the same field," as we say in Russia, as the Spiritualists, by whom he is considered to be a medium and a Calcutta Swedenborg. He spends his time in a dirty tank, singing praises to Chaitanya, Koran, Buddha, and his own person, proclaiming himself their prophet, and performs a mystical dance, dressed in woman's attire, which, on his part, is an attention to a "woman goddess" whom the Babu calls his "mother, father and eldest brother."

In short, all the attempts to re-establish the pure primitive monotheism of Aryan India have been a failure. They always got wrecked upon the double rock of Brahmanism and of prejudices centuries old. But lo! here appears unexpectedly the pandit Dayanand. None, even of the most beloved of his disciples, knows who he is and whence he comes. He openly confesses before the crowds that the name under which he is known is not his, but was given to him at the Yogi initiation.

The mystical school of Yogis was established by

Patanjali, the founder of one of the six philosophical systems of ancient India. It is supposed that the Neo-platonists of the second and third Alexandrian Schools were the followers of Indian Yogis, more especially was their theurgy brought from India by Pythagoras, according to the tradition. There still exist in India hundreds of Yogis who follow the system of Patanjali, and assert that they are in communion with Brahma. Nevertheless, most of them are do-nothings, mendicants by profession, and great frauds, thanks to the insatiable longing of the natives for miracles. The real Yogis avoid appearing in public, and spend their lives in secluded retirement and studies, except when, as in Dayanand's case, they come forth in time of need to aid their country. However, it is perfectly certain that India never saw a more learned Sanskrit scholar, a deeper metaphysician, a more wonderful orator, and a more fearless denunciator of every evil, than Dayanand, since the time of Sankharacharya, the celebrated founder of the Vedanta philosophy, the most metaphysical of Indian systems, in fact, the crown of pantheistic teaching. Then, Dayanand's personal appearance is striking. He is immensely tall, his complexion is pale, rather European than Indian, his eyes are large and bright, and his greyish hair is long. The Yogis and Dikshatas (initiated) never cut either their hair or beard. His voice is clear and loud, well calculated to give expression to every shade of deep feeling, ranging from a sweet childish caressing whisper to thundering wrath against the evil doings and falsehoods of the priests. All this taken together produces an indescribable effect on the impressionable Hindu. Wherever Dayanand appears crowds prostrate themselves in the dust over his footprints; but, unlike Babu Keshub Chunder Sen, he does not teach them a new religion, does not invent new dogmas. He only asks them to renew their half-forgotten Sanskrit studies, and, having compared the doctrines of their forefathers with what they have become in the hands of Brahmans, to return to the pure conceptions of Deity taught by the primitive Rishis—Agni, Vâyu, Aditya, and Anghira—the patriarchs who first gave the *Vedas* to humanity. He does not even claim that the *Vedas* are a heavenly revelation, but simply teaches that "every word in these scriptures belongs to the highest inspiration possible to the earthly man, an inspiration that is repeated in the history of humanity, and, when necessary, may happen to any nation. . . ."

During his five years of work Swami Dayanand made about two million proselytes, chiefly amongst the higher castes. Judging by appearances, they are all ready to sacrifice to him their lives and souls and even their earthly possessions, which are often more precious to them than their lives. But Dayanand is a real Yogi, he never touches money, and despises pecuniary affairs. He contents himself with a few handfuls of rice per day. One is inclined to think that this wonderful Hindu bears a charmed life, so careless is he of rousing the worst human passions, which are so dangerous in India. A marble statue could not be less moved by the raging wrath of the crowd. We saw him once at work. He sent away all his faithful followers and forbade them either to watch over him or to defend him, and stood alone before the infuriated crowd, facing calmly the monster ready to spring upon him and tear him to pieces.

Here a short explanation is necessary. A few years ago a society of well-informed, energetic people was formed in New York. A certain sharp-witted savant surnamed them "*La Société des Malcontents du Spiritisme.*" The founders of this club were people who, believing in the phenomena of spiritualism as much as in the possibility of every other phenomenon in Nature, still denied the theory of the "spirits." They considered that the modern psychology was a science still in the first stages of its development, in total ignorance of the nature of the psychic man, and denying, as do many other sciences, all that cannot be explained according to its own particular theories.

From the first days of its existence some of the most learned Americans joined the Society, which became known as the Theosophical Society. Its members differed on many points, much as do the members of any other Society, Geographical or Archæological, which fights for years over the sources of the Nile, or the Hieroglyphs of Egypt. But everyone is unanimously agreed that, as long as there is water in the Nile, its sources must exist somewhere. So much about the phenomena of spiritualism and mesmerism. These phenomena were still waiting their Champollion—but the Rosetta stone was to be searched for neither in Europe nor in America, but in the far-away countries where they still believe in magic, where wonders are performed daily by the native priesthood, and where the cold materialism of science has never yet reached—in one word, in the East.

The Council of the Society knew that the Lama-Buddhists, for instance, though not believing in God, and denying the personal immortality of the soul, are yet celebrated for their "phenomena," and that mesmerism was known and daily practised in China from time immemorial under the name of "gina." In India they fear and hate the very name of the spirits whom the Spiritualists venerate so deeply, yet many an ignorant fakir can perform "miracles" calculated to turn upside-down all the notions of a scientist and to be the despair of the most celebrated of European prestidigitateurs. Many members of the Society have visited India—many were born there and have themselves witnessed the "sorceries" of the Brahmans. The founders of the Club, well aware of the depth of modern ignorance in regard to the spiritual man, were most anxious that Cuvier's method of comparative anatomy should acquire rights of citizenship among metaphysicians, and, so, progress from regions physical to regions psychological on its own inductive and deductive foundation. "Otherwise," they thought, "psychology will be unable to move forward a single step, and may even obstruct every other branch of Natural History." Instances have not been wanting of physiology poaching on the preserves of purely metaphysical and abstract knowledge, all the time feigning to ignore the latter absolutely, and seeking to class psychology with the positive sciences, having first bound it to a Bed of Procrustes, where it refuses to yield its secret to its clumsy tormentors.

In a short time the Theosophical Society counted its members, not by hundreds, but by thousands. All the "malcontents" of American Spiritualism—and there were at that time twelve million Spiritualists in America—joined the Society. Collateral branches were formed in London, Corfu, Australia, Spain, Cuba, California, etc. Everywhere experiments were being performed, and the conviction that it is not spirits alone who are the causes of the phenomena was becoming general.

In course of time branches of the Society were formed in India and in Ceylon. The Buddhist and Brahmanical members became more numerous than the Europeans. A league was formed, and to the name of the Society was added the sub-title, "The Brotherhood of Humanity." After an active correspondence between the Arya-Samaj, founded by Swami Dayanand, and the Theosophical Society, an amalgamation was arranged between the two bodies. Then the Chief Council of the New York branch decided upon sending a special delegation to India, for the purpose of studying, on the spot, the ancient language of the *Vedas* and the manuscripts and the wonders of Yogism. On the 17th of December, 1878, the delegation, composed of two secretaries and two members of the council of the Theosophical Society, started from New York, to pause for a while in London, and then to proceed to Bombay, where it landed in February, 1879.

It may easily be conceived that, under these circumstances, the members of the delegation were better able to study the country and to make fruitful researches than might, otherwise, have been the case. To-day they are looked upon as brothers and aided by the most influential natives of India. They count among the members of their society pandits of Benares and Calcutta, and Buddhist priests of the Ceylon Vihâras—amongst others the learned Sumangala, mentioned by Minayeff in the description of his visit to Adam's Peak—and Lamas of Thibet, Burmah, Travancore and elsewhere. The members of the delegation are admitted to sanctuaries where, as yet, no European has set his foot. Consequently they may hope to render many services to Humanity and Science, in spite of the ill-will which the representatives of positive science bear to them.

As soon as the delegation landed, a telegram was despatched to Dayanand, as everyone was anxious to make his personal acquaintance. In reply, he said that he was obliged to go immediately to Hardwar, where hundreds of thousands of pilgrims were expected to assemble, but he insisted on our remaining behind, since cholera was certain to break out among the devotees. He appointed a certain spot, at the foot of the Himalayas, in the Punjab, where we were to meet in a month's time.

Alas! all this was written some time ago. Since then Swami Dayanand's countenance has changed completely toward us. He is, now, an enemy of the Theosophical Society and its two founders—Colonel Olcott and the author of these letters. It appeared that, on entering into an offensive and defensive alliance with the Society, Dayanand nourished the hope that all its members, Christians, Brahmans and Buddhists, would acknowledge his supremacy, and become members of the Arya Samaj. Needless to say, this was impossible. The Theosophical Society rests on the principle of complete non-interference with the religious beliefs of its members. Toleration is its basis and its aims are purely philosophical. This did not suit Dayanand. He wanted all the members, either to become his disciples, or to be expelled from the Society. It was quite clear that neither the President, nor the Council could assent to such a claim. Englishmen and Americans, whether they were Christians or Freethinkers, Buddhists, and especially Brahmans, revolted against Dayanand, and unanimously demanded that the league should be broken.

However, all this happened later. At the time of which I speak we were friends and allies of the Swami, and we learned with deep interest that the Hardwar "mela," which he was to visit, takes place every twelve years, and is a kind of religious fair, which attracts representatives from all the numerous sects of India.

Learned dissertations are read by the disputants in defence of their peculiar doctrines, and the debates are held in public. This year the Hardwar gathering was exceptionally numerous. The Sannyasis—the mendicant monks of India—alone numbered 35,000, and the cholera, foreseen by the Swami, actually broke out.

As we were not yet to start for the appointed meeting, we had plenty of spare time before us; so we proceeded to examine Bombay.

The Tower of Silence, on the heights of the Malabar Hill, is the last abode of all the sons of Zoroaster. It is, in fact, a Parsee cemetery. Here their dead, rich and poor, men, women and children, are all laid in a row, and in a few minutes nothing remains of them but bare skeletons. A dismal impression is made upon a foreigner by these towers, where absolute silence has reigned for centuries. This kind of building is very common in every place were ,Parsees live and die. In Bombay, of six towers, the largest was built 250 years ago, and the least but a short time since. With few exceptions, they are round or square in shape, from twenty to forty feet high, without roof, window, or door, but with a single iron gate opening towards the East, and so small that it is quite covered by a few bushes. The first corpse brought to a new tower—"dakhma"—must be the body of the innocent child of a mobed or priest. No one, not even the chief watcher, is allowed to approach within a distance of thirty paces of these towers. Of all living human beings "nassesalars"—corpse-carriers—alone enter and leave the "Tower of Silence." The life these men lead is simply wretched. No European executioner's position is worse. They live quite apart from the rest of the world, in whose eyes they are the most abject of beings. Being forbidden to enter the markets, they must get their food as they can. They are born, marry, and die, perfect strangers to all except their own class, passing through the streets only to fetch the dead and carry them to the tower. Even to be near one of them is a degradation. Entering the tower with a corpse, covered, whatever may have been its rank or position, with old white rags, they undress it and place it, in silence, on one of the three rows presently to be described. Then, still preserving the same silence, they come out, shut the gate, and burn the rags.

Amongst the fire-worshippers, Death is divested of all his majesty and is a mere object of disgust. As soon as the last hour of a sick person seems to approach, everyone leaves the chamber of death, as much to avoid impeding the departure of the soul from the body, as to shun the risk of polluting the living by contact with the dead. The mobed alone stays with the dying man for a while, and having whispered into his ear the Zend-Avesta precepts, "ashem-vóhu" and "Yato-Ahuvarie," leaves the room while the patient is still alive. Then a dog is brought and made to look straight into his face, This ceremony is called "sas-did," the "dog's-stare." A dog is the only living creature that the "Drux-nassu"—the evil one—fears, and that is able to prevent him from taking possession of the body. It must be strictly observed that no one's shadow lies between the dying man and the dog, otherwise the whole strength of the dog's gaze will be lost, and the demon will profit by the occasion. The body remains on the spot where life left it, until the nassesalars appear, their arms hidden to the shoulders under old bags, to take it away. Having deposited it in an iron coffin—the same for everyone—they carry it to the dakhma. If any one, who has once been carried thither, should happen to regain consciousness, the nassesalars are bound to kill him; for such a person, who has been polluted by one touch of the dead bodies in the dakhma, has thereby lost all right to return to the living, by doing so he would contaminate the whole community. As some such cases have occurred, the Parsees are trying to get a new law passed, that would allow the miserable ex-corpses to live again amongst their friends, and that would compel the nassesalars to leave the only gate of the dakhma unlocked, so that they might find a way of retreat open to them. It is very curious, but it is said that the vultures, which devour without hesitation the corpses, will never touch those who are only apparently dead, but fly away uttering loud shrieks. After a last prayer at the gate of the dakhma, pronounced from afar by the mobed, and repeated in chorus by the nassesalars, the dog ceremony is repeated. In Bombay there is a dog, trained for this purpose, at the entrance to the tower. Finally, the body is taken inside and placed on one or other of the rows, according to its sex and age.

We have twice been present at the ceremonies of dying, and once of burial, if I may be permitted to use such an incongruous term. In this respect the Parsees are much more tolerant than the Hindus, who are offended by the mere presence at their religious rites of an European. N. Bayranji, a chief official of the tower, invited us to his house to be present at the burial of some rich woman. So we witnessed all that was going on at a distance of about forty paces, sitting quietly on our obliging host's verandah. While the dog was staring into the dead woman's face, we were gazing, as intently, but with much more disgust, at the huge flock of vultures above the dakhma, that kept entering the tower, and flying out again with pieces of human flesh in their beaks. These birds, that build their nests in thousands round the Tower of Silence, have been purposely imported from Persia. Indian vultures proved to be too weak, and not sufficiently bloodthirsty, to perform the process of stripping the bones with the despatch prescribed by Zoroaster. We were told that the entire operation of denuding the bones occupies no more than a few minutes. As soon as the ceremony was over, we were led into another building, where a model of the dakhma was to be seen. We could now very easily imagine what was to take place presently inside the tower. In the centre there is a deep waterless well, covered with a grating like the opening into a drain. Around it are three broad circles, gradually sloping downwards. In each of them are coffin-like receptacles for the bodies. There are three hundred and sixty-five such places. The first and smallest row is destined for children, the second for women, and the third for men. This threefold circle is symbolical of three cardinal Zoroastrian virtues—pure thoughts, kind words, and good actions. Thanks to the vultures, the bones are laid bare in less than an hour, and, in two or three weeks, the tropical sun scorches them into such a state of fragility, that the slightest breath of wind is enough to reduce them to powder, and to carry them down into the pit. No smell is left behind, no source of plagues and epidemics. I do not know that this way may not be preferable to cremation, which leaves in the air about the Ghât a faint but disagreeable odour. The Ghât is a place by the sea, or river shore, where Hindus burn their dead. Instead of feeding the old Slavonic deity "Mother Wet Earth" with carrion, Parsees give to Armasti pure dust. Armasti means, literally, "fostering cow," and Zoroaster teaches that the cultivation of land is the noblest of all occupations in the eyes of God. Accordingly, the worship of Earth is so sacred among the Parsees, that they take all possible precautions against polluting the "fostering cow" that gives them "a hundred golden grains for every single grain." In the season of the Monsoon, when, during four months, the rain pours incessantly down and washes into the well everything that is left by the vultures, the water absorbed by the earth is filtered, for the bottom of the well, the walls of which are built of granite, is, to this end, covered with sand and charcoal.

The sight of the Pinjarapâla is less lugubrious and much more amusing. The Pinjarapâla is the Bombay Hospital for decrepit animals, but a similar institution exists in every town where Jainas dwell. Being one of the most ancient, this is also one of the most interesting, of the sects of India. It is much older than Buddhism, which took its rise about 543 to 477 B.C. Jainas boast that Buddhism is nothing more than a mere heresy of Jainism, Gautama, the founder of Buddhism, having been a disciple and follower of one of the Jaina Gurus. The customs, rites, and philosophical conceptions of Jainas place them midway between the Brahmanists and the Buddhists. In view of their social arrangements, they more closely resemble the former, but in their religion they incline towards the latter. Their caste divisions, their total abstinence from flesh, and their non-worship of the relics of the saints, are as strictly observed as the similar tenets of the Brahmans, but, like Buddhists, they deny the Hindu gods and the authority of the *Vedas*, and adore their own twenty-four Tirthankaras, or Jinas, who belong to the Host of the Blissful. Their priests, like the Buddhists', never marry, they live in isolated vihâras and choose their successors from amongst the members of any social class. According to them, Prakrit is the only sacred language, and is used in their sacred literature, as well as in Ceylon. Jainas and Buddhists have the same traditional chronology. They do not eat after sunset, and carefully dust any place before sitting down upon it, that they may not crush even the tiniest of insects. Both systems, or rather both schools of philosophy, teach the theory of eternal indestructible atoms, following the ancient atomistic school of Kanada. They assert that the universe never had a beginning and never will have an end. "The world and everything in it is but an illusion, a Mâyâ," say the Vedantists, the Buddhists, and the Jainas; but, whereas the followers of Sankaracharya preach Parabrahm (a deity devoid of will, understanding, and action, because "It is absolute understanding, mind and will"), and Ishwara emanating from It, the Jainás and the Buddhists believe in no Creator of the Universe, but teach only the existence of Swabhawati, a plastic, infinite, self-created principle in Nature. Still they firmly believe, as do all Indian sects, in the transmigration of souls. Their fear, lest, by killing an animal or an insect, they may, perchance, destroy the life of an ancestor, develops their love and care for every living creature to an almost incredible extent. Not only is there a hospital for invalid animals in every town and village, but their priests always wear a muslin muzzle, (I trust they will pardon the disrespectful expression!) in order to avoid destroying even the smallest animalcule, by inadvertence in the act of breathing. The same fear impels them to drink only filtered water. There are a few millions of Jainas in Gujerat, Bombay, Konkan, and some other places.

The Bombay Pinjarapâla occupies a whole quarter of

the town, and is separated into yards, meadows and gardens, with ponds, cages for beasts of prey, and enclosures for tame animals. This institution would have served very well for a model of Noah's Ark. In the first yard, however, we saw no animals, but, instead, a few hundred human skeletons—old men, women and children. They were the remaining natives of the, so-called, famine districts, who had crowded into Bombay to beg their bread. Thus, while, a few yards off, the official "Vets." were busily bandaging the broken legs of jackals, pouring ointments on the backs of mangy dogs, and fitting crutches to lame storks, human beings were dying, at their very elbows, of starvation. Happily for the famine-stricken, there were at that time fewer hungry animals than usual, and so they were fed on what remained from the meals of the brute pensioners. No doubt many of these wretched sufferers would have consented to transmigrate instantly into the bodies of any of the animals who were ending so snugly their earthly careers.

But even the Pinjarapâla roses are not without thorns. The graminivorous "subjects," of course, could not wish for anything better; but I doubt very much whether the beasts of prey, such as tigers, hyenas, and wolves, are content with the rules and the forcibly prescribed diet. Jainas themselves turn with disgust even from eggs and fish, and, in consequence, all the animals of which they have the care must turn vegetarians. We were present when an old tiger, wounded by an English bullet, was fed. Having sniffed at a kind of rice soup which was offered to him, he lashed his tail, snarled, showing his yellow teeth, and with a weak roar turned away from the food. What a look he cast askance upon his keeper, who was meekly trying to persuade him to taste his nice dinner! Only the strong bars of the cage saved the Jaina from a vigorous protest on the part of this veteran of the forest. A hyena, with a bleeding head and an ear half torn off, began by sitting in the trough filled with this Spartan sauce, and then, without any further ceremony, upset it, as if to show its utter contempt for the mess. The wolves and the dogs raised such disconsolate howls that they attracted the attention of two inseparable friends, an old elephant with a wooden leg and a sore-eyed ox, the veritable Castor and Pollux of this institution. In accordance with his noble nature, the first thought of the elephant concerned his friend. He wound his trunk round the neck of the ox, in token of protection, and both moaned dismally. Parrots, storks, pigeons, flamingoes—the whole feathered tribe—revelled in their breakfast. Monkeys were the first to answer the keeper's invitation and greatly enjoyed themselves. Further on we were shown a *holy* man, who was feeding insects with his own blood. He lay with his eyes shut, and the scorching rays of the sun striking full upon his naked body. He was literally covered with flies, mosquitoes, ants and bugs.

"All these are our brothers," mildly observed the keeper, pointing to the hundreds of animals and insects. "How can you Europeans kill and even devour them?"

"What would you do," I asked, "if this snake were about to bite you? Is it possible you would not kill it, if you had time?"

"Not for all the world. I should cautiously catch it, and then I should carry it to some deserted place outside the town, and there set it free."

"Nevertheless; suppose it bit you?"

"Then I should recite a mantram, and, if that produced no good result, I should be fain to consider it as the finger of Fate, and quietly leave this body for another."

These were the words of a man who was educated to a certain extent, and very well read. When we pointed out that no gift of Nature is aimless, and that the human teeth are all devouring, he answered by quoting whole chapters of Darwin's *Theory of Natural Selection* and *Origin of Species*. "It is not true," argued he, "that the first men were born with canine teeth. It was only in course of time, with the degradation of humanity,—only when the appetite for flesh food began to develop—that the jaws changed their first shape under the influence of new necessities."

I could not help asking myself, "*Où la science va-t'elle se fourrer?*"

The same evening, in Elphinstone's Theatre, there was given a special performance in honour of "the American Mission," as we are styled here. Native actors represented in Gujerati the ancient fairy drama *Sîtâ-Râma*, that has been adapted from the *Râmâyana*, the celebrated epic by Valmîki. This drama is composed of fourteen acts and no end of tableaux, in addition to transformation scenes. All the female parts, as usual, were acted by young boys, and the actors, according to the historical and national customs, were barefooted and half-naked. Still, the richness of the costumes, the stage adornments and transformations, were truly wonderful. For instance, even on the stages of large metropolitan theatres, it would have been difficult to give a better representation of the army of Râma's allies, who are nothing more than troops of monkeys under the leadership of Hanuman—the soldier, statesman, dramatist, poet, god, who is so celebrated in history (that of India s.v.p.). The oldest and best of all Sanskrit dramas, *Hanuman-Nâtak*, is ascribed to this talented forefather of ours.

Alas! gone is the glorious time when, proud of our white skin (which after all may be nothing more than the result of a fading, under the influences of our northern sky), we looked down upon Hindus and other "niggers" with a feeling of contempt well suited to our own magnificence. No doubt Sir William Jones's soft heart ached, when translating from the Sanskrit such humiliating sentences as the following: "Hanuman is said to be the forefather of the Europeans." Râma, being a hero and a demi-god, was well entitled to unite all the bachelors of his useful monkey army to the daughters of the Lanka (Ceylon) giants, the Râkshasas, and to present these Dravidian beauties with the dowry of all Western lands. After the mcst pompous marriage ceremonies, the monkey soldiers made a bridge, with the help of their own tails, and safely landed with their spouses in Europe, where they lived very happily and had a numerous progeny. This progeny are we, Europeans. Dravidian words found in some European languages, in Basque for instance, greatly rejoice the hearts of the Brahmans, who would gladly promote the philologists to the rank of demi-gods for this important discovery, which confirms so gloriously their ancient legend. But it was Darwin who crowned the edifice of proof with the authority of Western education and Western scientific literature. The Indians became still more convinced that we are the veritable descendants of Hanuman, and that, if one only took the trouble to examine carefully, our tails might easily be discovered. Our narrow breeches and long skirts only add to the evidence, however uncomplimentary the idea may be to us.

Still, if you consider seriously, what are we to say when Science, in the person of Darwin, concedes this hypothesis to the wisdom of ancient Aryas. We must perforce submit. And, really, it is better to have for a forefather Hanuman, the poet, the hero, the god, than any other monkey, even though it be a tail-less one. *Sîtâ-Râma* belongs to the category of mythological dramas, something like the tragedies of Æschylus. Listening to this production of the remotest antiquity, the spectators are carried back to the times when the gods, descending upon earth, took an active part in the everyday life of mortals. Nothing reminds one of a modern drama, though the exterior arrangement is the same. "From the sublime to the ridiculous there is but a step," and *vice versâ*. The goat, chosen for a sacrifice to Bacchus, presented the world with tragedy (Τράγος ᾠδη). The death bleatings and buttings of the quadrupedal offering of antiquity have been polished by the hands of time and of civilization, and, as a result of this process, we get the dying whisper of Rachel in the part of Adrienne Lecouvreur, and the fearfully realistic "kicking" of the modern Croisette in the poisoning scene of *The Sphinx*. But, whereas the descendants of Themistocles gladly receive, whether captive or free, all the changes and improvements considered as such by modern taste, thinking them to be a corrected and enlarged edition of the genius of Æschylus; Hindus, happily for archæologists and lovers of antiquity, have never moved a step since the times of our much honoured forefather Hanuman.

We awaited the performance of *Sîtâ-Râma* with the liveliest curiosity. Except ourselves and the building of the theatre, everything was strictly indigenous and nothing reminded us of the West. There was not the trace of an orchestra. Music was only to be heard from the stage, or from behind it. At last the curtain rose. The silence, which had been very remarkable before the performance, considering the huge crowd of spectators of both sexes, now became absolute. Râma is one of the incarnations of Vishnu and, as most of the audience were worshippers of Vishnu, for them the spectacle was not a mere theatrical performance, but a religious mystery, representing the life and achievements of their favourite and most venerated gods.

The prologue was laid in the epoch before creation began (it may safely be said that no dramatist would dare to choose an earlier one)—or, rather, before the last manifestation of the universe. All the philosophical sects of India, except Mussulmans, agree that the universe has always existed. But the Hindus divide the periodical appearances and vanishings into days and nights of Brahmâ. The nights, or withdrawals of the objective universe, are called Pralayas, and the days, or epochs of new awakening into life and light, are called Manvantaras, Yugas, or "centuries of the gods." These periods are also called, respectively, the inbreathings and outbreathings of Brahmâ. When Pralaya comes to an end Brahmâ awakens, and, with this awakening, the universe that rested in deity, in other words, that was reabsorbed in its subjective essence, emanates again from the divine principle and becomes visible. The gods, who died at the same time as the universe, begin slowly to return to life. The "Invisible" alone, the "Infinite," the "Lifeless," the One who is the unconditioned original "Life" itself, soars, surrounded by shoreless chaos. Its holy presence is not visible. It shows itself only in the periodical pulsation of chaos, represented by a dark mass of waters filling the whole stage. These waters are not, as yet, separated from the dry land, because Brahmâ, the creative spirit of Nârâyana, has not yet separated from the "Ever Unchanging." Then comes a heavy shock of the whole mass and the waters begin to acquire transparency. Rays, proceeding from a golden egg at the bottom, spread through the chaotic waters. Receiving life from the spirit of Nârâyana, the egg bursts and the awakened Brahmâ rises to the surface of the water in the shape of a huge lotus. Light clouds appear, at first transparent and web-like. They gradually become condensed, and transform themselves into Prajapatis, the ten personified creative powers of Brahma, the god of everything living, and sing a hymn of praise to the creator. Something naively poetical, to our unaccustomed ears, breathed in this uniform melody unaccompanied by any orchestra.

The hour of general revival has struck. Pralaya comes to an end. Everything rejoices, returning to life. The sky is separated from the waters and on it appear the Asuras and Gandharvas, the heavenly singers and musicians. Then Indra, Yama, Varuna, and Kuvera, the spirits presiding over the four cardinal points, or the four elements, water, fire, earth, and air, pour forth atoms, whence springs the serpent "Ananta." The monster swims to the surface of the waves and, bending its swanlike neck, forms a couch on which Vishnu reclines with the Goddess of Beauty, his wife Lakshmi, at his feet. "Swatha! Swatha! Swatha!" cries the choir of heavenly musicians, hailing the deity. In the Russian church service this is pronounced Swiat! Swiat! Swiat! and means holy! holy! holy!

In one of his future avatars Vishnu will incarnate in Râma, the son of a great king, and Lakshmi will become Sîtâ. The motive of the whole poem of *Râmâyana* is sung in a few words by the celestial musicians. Kâma, the God of Love, shelters the divine couple and, that very moment, a flame is lit in their hearts and the whole world is created.

Later there are performed the fourteen acts of the drama, which is well known to everybody, and in which several hundred personages take part. At the end of the prologue the whole assembly of gods come forward, one after another, and acquaint the audience with the contents and the epilogue of their performance, asking the public not to be too exacting. It is as though all these familiar deities, made of painted granite and marble, left the temples and came down to remind mortals of events long past and forgotten.

The hall was full of natives. We four alone were representatives of Europe. Like a huge flower bed, the women displayed the bright colours of their garments. Here and there, among handsome, bronze-like heads, were the pretty, dull white faces of Parsee women, whose beauty reminded me of the Georgians. The front rows were occupied by women only. In India it is quite easy to learn a person's religion, sect, and caste, and even whether a woman is married or single, from the marks painted in bright colours on everyone's forehead.

Since the time when Alexander the Great destroyed the sacred books of the Gebars, they have constantly been oppressed by the idol worshippers. King Ardeshir-Babechan restored fire worship in the years 229-243 A.C. Since then they have again been persecuted during the reign of one of the Shakpurs, either II., IX., or XI., of the Sassanids, but which of them is not known. It is, however, reported that one of them was a great protector of the Zartushta doctrines. After the fall of Yesdejird, the fire-worshippers emigrated to the island of Ormasd, and, some time later, having found a book of Zoroastrian prophecies, in obedience to one of them they set out for Hindustan. After many wanderings, they appeared, about 1,000 or 1,200 years ago, in the territory of Mahârâna-Jayadeva, a vassal of the Rajput King Champanir, who allowed them to colonize his land, but only on condition that they laid down their weapons, that they abandoned the Persian language for Hindi, and that their women put off their national dress and clothed themselves after the manner of Hindu women. He, however, allowed them to wear shoes, since this is strictly prescribed by Zoroaster. Since then very few changes have been made. It follows that the Parsee women could only be distinguished from their Hindu sisters by very slight differences. The almost white faces of the former were separated by a strip of smooth black hair from a sort of white cap, and the whole was covered with a bright veil. The latter wore no covering on their rich, shining hair, twisted into a kind of Greek chignon. Their foreheads were brightly painted, and their nostrils adorned with golden rings. Both are fond of bright, but uniform, colours, both cover their arms up to the elbow with bangles, and both wear saris.

Behind the women a whole sea of most wonderful turbans was waving in the pit. There were long-haired Rajputs with regular Grecian features and long beards parted in the middle, their heads covered with "pagris" consisting of, at least, twenty yards of finest white muslin, and their persons adorned with earrings and necklaces; there were Mahrata Brahmans, who shave their heads, leaving only one long central lock, and wear turbans of blinding red, decorated in front with a sort of golden horn of plenty; Bangas, wearing three-cornered helmets with a kind of cockscomb on the top;

Kachhis, with Roman helmets; Bhillis, from the borders of Râjastan, whose chins are wrapped three times in the ends of their pyramidal turbans, so that the innocent tourist never fails to think that they constantly suffer from toothache; Bengalis and Calcutta Babus, bare-headed all the year round, their hair cut after an Athenian fashion, and their bodies clothed in the proud folds of a white *toga-virilis,* in no way different from those once worn by Roman senators; Parsees, in their black, oil-cloth mitres; Sikhs, the followers of Nanaka, strictly monotheist and mystic, whose turbans are very like the Bhillis', but who wear long hair down to their waists; and hundreds of other tribes.

Proposing to count how many different headgears are to be seen in Bombay alone, we had to abandon the task as impracticable after a fortnight. Every caste, every trade, guild, and sect, every one of the thousand sub-divisions of the social hierarchy, has its own bright turban, often sparkling with gold lace and precious stones, which is laid aside only in case of mourning. But, as if to compensate for this luxury, even the members of the municipality, rich merchants, and Rai-Bahadurs, who have been created baronets by the Government, never wear any stockings, and leave their legs bare up to the knees. As for their dress, it chiefly consists of a kind of shapeless white shirt.

In Baroda some Gaikwars (a title of all the Baroda princes) still keep in their stables elephants and the less common giraffes, though the former are strictly forbidden in the streets of Bombay. We had an opportunity of seeing ministers, and even Rajas, mounted on these noble animals, their mouths full of pansupari (betel leaves), their heads drooping under the weight of the precious stones on their turbans, and each of their fingers and toes adorned with rich golden rings. While the evening I am describing lasted, however, we saw no elephants, no giraffes, though we enjoyed the company of Rajas and ministers. We had in our box the handsome ambassador and late tutor of the Mahârârana of Oodeypore. Our companion was a Raja and a pandit. His name was a Mohunlal-Vishnulal-Pandia. He wore a small pink turban sparkling with diamonds, a pair of pink barége trousers, and a white gauze coat. His raven black hair half covered his amber-coloured neck, which was surrounded by a necklace that might have driven any Parisian belle frantic with envy. The poor Rajput was awfully sleepy, but he stuck heroically to his duties, and, thoughtfully pulling his beard, led us all through the endless labyrinth of metaphysical entanglements of the *Râmâyana.* During the entr'actes we were offered coffee, sherbets, and cigarettes, which we smoked even during the performance, sitting in front of the stage in the first row. We were covered, like idols, with garlands of flowers, and the manager, a stout Hindu clad in transparent muslins, sprinkled us several times with rose-water.

The performance began at eight p.m. and, at half-past two, had only reached the ninth act. In spite of each of us having a punkah-wallah at our backs, the heat was unbearable. We had reached the limits of our endurance, and tried to excuse ourselves. This led to general disturbance, on the stage as well as in the auditorium. The airy chariot, on which the wicked king Râvana was carrying Sîtâ away, paused in the air. The king of the Nagas (serpents) ceased breathing flames, the monkey soldiers hung motionless on the trees, and Râma himself, clad in light blue and crowned with a diminutive pagoda, came to the front of the stage and pronounced in pure English a speech, in which he thanked us for the honour of our presence. Then new bouquets, pansu-paris, and rose-water, and, finally, we reached home about four a.m. Next morning we learned that the performance had ended at half-past six.

ON THE WAY TO KARLI.

It is an early morning near the end of March. A light breeze caresses with its velvety hand the sleepy faces of the pilgrims; and the intoxicating perfume of tuberoses mingles with the pungent odours of the bazaar. Crowds of barefooted Brahman women, stately and well-formed, direct their steps, like the biblical Rachel, to the well, with brass water pots bright as gold upon their heads. On our way lie numerous sacred tanks, filled with stagnant water, in which Hindus of both sexes perform their prescribed morning ablutions. Under the hedge of a garden somebody's tame mongoose is devouring the head of a cobra. The headless body of the snake convulsively, but harmlessly, beats against the thin flanks of the little animal, which regards these vain efforts with an evident delight. Side by side with this group of animals is a human figure; a naked *mâli* (gardener), offering betel and salt to a monstrous stone idol of Shiva, with the view of pacifying the wrath of the "Destroyer," excited by the death of the cobra, which is one of his favourite servants. A few steps before reaching the railway station, we meet a modest Catholic procession, consisting of a few newly converted pariahs and some of the native Portuguese. Under a baldachin is a litter, on which swings to and fro a dusky Madonna dressed after the fashion of the native goddesses, with a ring in her nose. In her arms she carries the holy Babe, clad in yellow pyjamas and a red Brahmanical turban. "Hari, hari, devaki!" ("Glory to the holy Virgin!") exclaim the converts, unconscious of any difference between the Devaki, mother of Krishna, and the Catholic Madonna. All they know is that, excluded from the temples by the Brahmans on account of their not belonging to any of the Hindu castes, they are admitted sometimes into the Christian pagodas, thanks to the "padris," a name adopted from the Portuguese *padre*, and applied indiscriminately to the missionaries of every European sect.

At last, our gharis—native two-wheeled vehicles drawn by a pair of strong bullocks—arrived at the station. English employés open wide their eyes at the sight of white-faced people travelling about the town in gilded Hindu chariots. But we are true Americans, and we have come hither to study, not Europe, but India and her products on the spot.

If the tourist casts a glance on the shore opposite to the port of Bombay, he will see a dark blue mass rising like a wall between himself and the horizon. This is Parbul, a flat-topped mountain 2,250 feet high. Its right slope leans on two sharp rocks covered with woods. The highest of them, Mataran, is the object of our trip. From Bombay to Narel, a station situated at the foot of this mountain, we are to travel four hours by railway, though, as the crow flies, the distance is not more than twelve miles. The railroad wanders round the foot of the most charming little hills, skirts hundreds of pretty lakes, and pierces with more than twenty tunnels the very heart of the rocky ghats.

We were accompanied by three Hindu friends. Two of them once belonged to a high caste, but were excommunicated from their pagoda for association and friendship with us, unworthy foreigners. At the station our party was joined by two more natives, with whom we had been in correspondence for many a year. All were members of our Society, reformers of the Young India school, enemies of Brahmans, castes, and prejudices, and were to be our fellow-travellers and visit with us the annual fair at the temple festivities of Karli, stopping on the way at Mataran and Khanduli. One was a Brahman from Poona, the second a moodeliar (landowner) from Madras, the third a Singalese from Kegalla, the fourth a Bengali Zemindar, and the fifth a gigantic Rajput, whom we had known for a long time by the name of Gulab-Lal-Sing, and had called simply Gulab-Sing. I shall dwell upon his personality more than on any of the others, because the most wonderful and diverse stories were in circulation about this strange man. It was asserted that he belonged to the sect of Raj-Yogis, and was an initiate of the mysteries of magic, alchemy, and various other occult sciences of India. He was rich and independent, and rumour did not dare to suspect him of deception, the more so because, though quite full of these sciences, he never uttered a word about them in public, and carefully concealed his knowledge from all except a few friends.

He was an independent Takur from Rajistan, a province the name of which means the land of kings. Takurs are, almost without exception, descended from the Surya (sun), and are accordingly called Surya-vansa. They are prouder than any other nation in the world. They have a proverb, "The dirt of the earth cannot stick to the rays of the sun." They do not despise any sect, except the Brahmans, and honour only the bards who sing their military achievements. Of the latter Colonel Tod writes somewhat as follows,* "The mag-

* In nearly every instance the passages quoted from various authorities have been re-translated from the Russian. As the time and labour needful for verification would be too great, the sense only of these passages is given here. They do not pretend to be textual.—Translator.

nificence and luxury of the Rajput courts in the early periods of history were truly wonderful, even when due allowance is made for the poetical license of the bards. From the earliest times Northern India was a wealthy country, and it was precisely here that was situated the richest satrapy of Darius. At all events, this country abounded in those most striking events which furnish history with her richest materials. In Rajistan every small kingdom had its Thermopylæ, and every little town has produced its Leonidas. But the veil of the centuries hides from posterity events that the pen of the historian might have bequeathed to the everlasting admiration of the nations. Somnath might have appeared as a rival of Delphi, the treasures of Hind might outweigh the riches of the King of Lydia, while compared with the army of the brothers Pandu, that of Xerxes would seem an inconsiderable handful of men, worthy only to rank in the second place."

England did not disarm the Rajputs, as she did the rest of the Indian nations, so Gulab-Sing came accompanied by vassals and shield-bearers.

Possessing an inexhaustible knowledge of legends, and being evidently well acquainted with the antiquities of his country, Gulab-Sing proved to be the most interesting of our companions.

"There, against the blue sky," said Gulab-Lal-Sing, "you behold the majestic Bhao Mallin. That deserted spot was once the abode of a holy hermit; now it is visited yearly by crowds of pilgrims. According to popular belief the most wonderful things happen there—miracles. At the top of the mountain, two thousand feet above the level of the sea, is the platform of a fortress. Behind it rises another rock two hundred and seventy feet in height, and at the very summit of this peak are to be found the ruins of a still more ancient fortress, which for seventy-five years served as a shelter for this hermit. Whence he obtained his food will for ever remain a mystery. Some think he ate the roots of wild plants, but upon this barren rock there is no vegetation. The only mode of ascent of this perpendicular mountain consists of a rope, and holes, just big enough to receive the toes of a man, cut out of the living rock. One would think such a pathway accessible only to acrobats and monkeys. Surely fanaticism must provide wings for the Hindus, for no accident has ever happened to any of them. Unfortunately, about forty years ago, a party of Englishmen conceived the unhappy thought of exploring the ruins, but a strong gust of wind arose and carried them over the precipice. After this, General Dickinson gave orders for the destruction of all means of communication with the upper fortress, and the lower one, once the cause of so many losses and so much bloodshed, is now entirely deserted, and serves only as a shelter for eagles and tigers."

Listening to these tales of olden times, I could not help comparing the past with the present. What a difference!

"Kali-Yug!" cry old Hindus with grim despair. "Who can strive against the Age of Darkness?"

This fatalism, the certainty that nothing good can be expected now, the conviction that even the powerful god Shiva himself can neither appear nor help them are all deeply rooted in the minds of the old generation. As for the younger men, they receive their education in high schools and universities, learn by heart Herbert Spencer, John Stuart Mill, Darwin and the German philosophers, and entirely lose all respect, not only for their own religion, but for every other in the world.

The young "educated" Hindus are materialists almost without exception, and often achieve the last limits of Atheism. They seldom hope to attain to anything better than a situation as "chief mate of the junior clerk," as we say in Russia, and either become sycophants, disgusting flatterers of their present lords, or, which is still worse, or at any rate sillier, begin to edit a newspaper full of cheap liberalism, which gradually develops into a revolutionary organ.

But all this is only *en passant*. Compared with the mysterious and grandiose *past* of India, the ancient Aryavarta, her *present* is a natural Indian ink background, the black shadow of a bright picture, the inevitable evil in the cycle of every nation. India has become decrepit and has fallen down, like a huge memorial of antiquity, prostrate and broken to pieces. But the most insignificant of these fragments will for ever remain a treasure for the archæologist and the artist, and, in the course of time, may even afford a clue to the philosopher and the psychologist. "Ancient Hindus built like giants and finished their work like goldsmiths," says Archbishop Heber, describing his travels in India. In his description of the Taj-Mahal of Agra, that veritable eighth wonder of the world, he calls it "a poem in marble." He might have added that it is difficult to find in India a ruin, in the least state of preservation, that cannot speak, more eloquently than whole volumes, of the past of India, her religious aspirations, her beliefs and hopes.

There is not a country of antiquity, not even excluding the Egypt of the Pharaohs, where the development of the subjective ideal into its demonstration by an objective symbol has been expressed more graphically, more skilfully, and artistically, than in India. The whole pantheism of the Vedânta is contained in the symbol of the bisexual deity Ardhanârî. It is surrounded by the double triangle, known in India under the name of the sign of Vishnu. By his side lie a lion, a bull, and an eagle. In his hands there rests a full moon, which is reflected in the waters at his feet. The Vedânta has taught for thousands of years what some of the German philosophers began to preach at the end of last century and the beginning of this one, namely, that everything objective in the world, as well as the world itself, is no more than an illusion, a Mâyâ, a phantom created by our imagination, and as unreal as the reflection of the moon upon the surface of the waters. The phenomenal world, as well as the subjectivity of our conception concerning our Egos, are nothing but, as it were, a mirage. The true sage will never submit to the temptations of illusion. He is well aware that man will attain to self-knowledge, and become a real Ego, only after the entire union of the personal fragment with the All, thus becoming an immutable, infinite, universal Brahma. Accordingly, he considers the whole cycle of birth, life, old-age, and death as the sole product of imagination.

Generally speaking, Indian philosophy, split up as it is into numerous metaphysical teachings, possesses, when united to Indian ontological doctrines, such a well developed logic, such a wonderfully refined psychology, that it might well take the first rank when contrasted with the schools, ancient and modern, idealist or positivist, and eclipse them all in turn. That positivism expounded by Lewis, that makes each particular hair on the heads of Oxford theologians stand on end, is ridiculous child's play compared with the atomistic school of Vaisheshika, with its world divided, like a chess-board, into six categories of everlasting atoms, nine substances, twenty-four qualities, and five motions. And, however difficult, and even impossible may seem the exact representation of all these abstract ideas, idealistic, pantheistic, and, sometimes, purely material, in the condensed shape of allegorical symbols, India, nevertheless, has known how to express all these teachings more or less successfully. She has immortalized them in her ugly, four-headed idols, in the geometrical, complicated forms of her temples, and even in the entangled lines and spots on the foreheads of her sectaries.

We were discussing this and other topics with our Hindu fellow-travellers when a Catholic *padre*, a teacher in the Jesuit College of St. Xavier in Bombay, entered our carriage at one of the stations. Soon he could contain himself no longer, and joined in our conversation. Smiling and rubbing his hands, he said that he was curious to know on the strength of what sophistry our companions could find anything resembling a philosophical explanation "in the fundamental idea of the four faces of this ugly Shiva, crowned with snakes," pointing with his finger to the idol at the entrance to a pagoda.

"It is very simple," answered the Bengali Babu. "You see that its four faces are turned towards the four cardinal points, South, North, West, and East—but all these faces are on one body and belong to one god."

"Would you mind explaining first the philosophical idea of the four faces and eight hands of your Shiva," interrupted the *padre*.

"With great pleasure. Thinking that our great Rudra (the Vedic name for this god) is omnipresent, we represent him with his face turned simultaneously in all directions. Eight hands indicate his omnipotence, and his single body serves to remind us that he is One, though he is everywhere, and nobody can avoid his all-seeing eye, or his chastising hand."

The *padre* was going to say something when the train stopped; we had arrived at Narel.

It is hardly twenty-five years since, for the first time, a white man ascended Mataran, a huge mass of various kinds of trap rock, for the most part crystalline in form. Though quite near to Bombay, and only a few miles from Khandala, the summer residence of the Europeans, the threatening heights of this giant were long considered inaccessible. On the north, its smooth, almost vertical face rises 2,450 feet over the valley of the river Pen, and, further on, numberless separate rocks and hillocks, covered with thick vegetation, and divided by valleys and precipices, rise up to the clouds. In 1854, the railway pierced one of the sides of Mataran, and now has reached the foot of the last mountain, stopping at Narel, where, not long ago, there was nothing but a precipice. From Narel to the upper plateau is but eight miles, which you may travel on a pony, or in an open or closed palanquin, as you choose.

Considering that we arrived at Narel about six in the evening, this course was not very tempting. Civilization has done much with inanimate nature, but, in spite of all its despotism, it has not yet been able to conquer tigers and snakes. Tigers, no doubt, are banished to the more remote jungles, but all kinds of snakes, especially cobras and coralillos, which last by preference inhabit trees, still abound in the forests of Mataran as in days of old, and wage a regular guerilla warfare against the invaders. Woe betide the belated pedestrian, or even horseman, if he happens to pass under a tree which forms the ambuscade of a coralillo snake! Cobras and other reptiles seldom attack men, and will generally try to avoid them, unless accidentally trodden upon, but these guerilleros of the forest, the tree serpents, lie in wait for their victims. As soon as the head of a man comes under the branch which shelters the coralillo, this enemy of man, coiling its tail round the branch, dives down into space with all the length of its body, and strikes with its fangs at the man's forehead. This curious fact was long considered to be a mere fable, but it has now been verified, and belongs to the natural history of India. In these cases the natives see in the snake the envoy of Death, the fulfiller of the will of the bloodthirsty Kâli, the spouse of Shiva.

But evening, after the scorchingly hot day, was so tempting, and held out to us from the distance such promise of delicious coolness, that we decided upon risking our fate. In the heart of this wondrous nature one longs to shake off earthly chains, and unite oneself with the boundless life, so that death itself has its attractions in India.

Besides, the full moon was about to rise at eight p.m. Three hours' ascent of the mountain, on such a moonlit, tropical night as would tax the descriptive powers of the greatest artists, was worth any sacrifice. *Apropos*, among the few artists who can fix upon canvas the subtle charm of a moonlit night in India public opinion, begins to name our own V. V. Vereshtchagin.

Having dined hurriedly in the dâk bungalow we asked for our sedan chairs, and, drawing our roof-like topees over our eyes, we started. Eight coolies, clad, as usual, in vine-leaves, took possession of each chair and hurried up the mountain, uttering the shrieks and yells no true Hindu can dispense with. Each chair was accompanied besides by a relay of eight more porters. So we were sixty-four, without counting the Hindus and their servants—an army sufficient to frighten any stray leopard or jungle tiger, in fact any animal, except our fearless cousins on the side of our great-grandfather Hanuman. As soon as we turned into a thicket at the foot of the mountain, several dozens of these kinsmen joined our procession. Thanks to the achievements of Râma's ally, monkeys are sacred in India. The Government, emulating the earlier wisdom of the East India Company, forbids everyone to molest them, not only when met with in the forests, which in all justice belong to them, but even when they invade the city gardens. Leaping from one branch to another, chattering like magpies, and making the most formidable grimaces, they followed us all the way, like so many midnight spooks. Sometimes they hung on the trees in full moonlight, like forest nymphs of Russian mythology; sometimes they preceded us, awaiting our arrival at the turns of the road as if showing us the way. They never left us. One monkey babe alighted on my knees. In a moment the authoress of his being, jumping without any ceremony over the coolies' shoulders, came to his rescue, picked him up, and, after making the most ungodly grimace at me, ran away with him.

"Bandras (monkeys) bring luck with their presence," remarked one of the Hindus, as if to console me for the loss of my crumpled topee. "Besides," he added, "seeing them here we may be sure that there is not a single tiger for ten miles round."

Higher and higher we ascended by the steep winding path, and the forest grew perceptibly thicker, darker, and more impenetrable. Some of the thickets were as dark as graves. Passing under hundred-year-old banyans it was impossible to distinguish one's own finger at the distance of two inches. It seemed to me that in certain places it would not be possible to advance without feeling our way, but our coolies never made a false step, but hastened onwards. Not one of us uttered a word. It was as if we had agreed to be silent at these moments. We felt as though wrapped in the heavy veil of darkness, and no sound was heard but the short, irregular breathing of the porters, and the cadence of their quick, nervous footsteps upon the stony soil of the path. One felt sick at heart and ashamed of belonging to that human race, one part of which makes of the other mere beasts of burden. These poor wretches are paid for their work four annas a day all the year round. Four annas for going eight miles upwards and eight miles downwards not less than twice a day; altogether thirty-two miles up and down a mountain 1,500 feet high, carrying a burden of two hundredweight! However, India is a country where everything is adjusted to never changing customs, and four annas a day is the pay for unskilled labour of any kind.

Gradually open spaces and glades became more frequent and the light grew as intense as by day. Millions of grasshoppers were shrilling in the forest, filling the air with a metallic throbbing, and flocks of frightened parrots rushed from tree to tree. Sometimes the thundering, prolonged roars of tigers rose from the bottom of the precipices thickly covered with all kinds of vegetation. Shikaris assure us that, on a quiet night, the roaring of these beasts can be heard for many miles around. The panorama, lit up, as if by Bengal fires, changed at every turn. Rivers, fields, forests, and rocks, spread out at our feet over an enormous distance, moved and trembled, iridescent, in the silvery moonlight, like the tides of a mirage. The fantastic character of the pictures made us hold our breath. Our heads grew giddy if, by chance, we glanced down into the depths by the flickering moonlight. We felt that the precipice, 2,000 feet deep, was fascinating us. One of our American fellow travellers, who had begun the voyage on horseback, had to dismount, afraid of being unable to resist the temptation to dive head foremost into the abyss.

Several times we met with lonely pedestrians, men and young women, coming down Mataran on their way home after a day's work. It often happens that some of them never reach home. The police unconcernedly report that the missing man has been carried off by a tiger, or killed by a snake. All is said, and he is soon entirely forgotten. One person, more or less, out of the two hundred and forty millions who inhabit India does not matter much! But there exists a very strange superstition in the Deccan about this mysterious, and only partially explored, mountain. The natives assert that, in spite of the considerable number of victims, there has never been found a single skeleton. The corpse, whether intact or mangled by tigers, is immediately carried away by the monkeys, who, in the latter case, gather the scattered bones, and bury them so skilfully in deep holes, that no traces ever remain. Englishmen laugh at this superstition, but the policemen do not deny the fact of the entire disappearance of the bodies. When the sides of the mountain were excavated, in the course of the construction of the railway, separate bones, with the marks of tigers' teeth upon them, broken bracelets, and other adornments, were found at an incredible depth from the surface. The fact of these things being broken showed clearly that they were not buried by men, because, neither the religion of the Hindus, nor their greed, would allow them to break and bury silver and gold. Is it possible, then, that, as amongst men one hand washes the other, so in the animal kingdom one species conceals the crimes of another?

Having spent the night in a Portuguese inn, woven like an eagle's nest out of bamboos, and clinging to the almost vertical side of a rock, we rose at daybreak, and, having visited all the *points de vue* famed for their beauty, made our preparations to return to Narel. By daylight the panorama was still more splendid than by night; volumes would not suffice to describe it. Had it not been that on three sides the horizon was shut out by rugged ridges of mountain, the whole of the Deccan plateau would have appeared before our eyes. Bombay was so distinct that it seemed quite near to us, and the channel that separates the town from Salsetta shone like a tiny silvery streak. It winds like a snake on its way to the port, surrounding Kanari and other islets, which look the very image of green peas scattered on the white cloth of its bright waters, and, finally, joins the blinding line of the Indian Ocean in the extreme distance. On the other side is the northern Konkan, terminated by the Tal-Ghats, the needle-like summits of the Jano-Maòli rocks, and, lastly, the battlemented ridge of Funell, whose bold silhouette stands out in strong relief against the distant blue of the dim sky, like a giant's castle in some fairy tale. Further on looms Parbul, whose flat summit, in the days of old, was the seat of the gods, whence, according to the legends, Vishnu spoke to mortals. And there below, where the defile widens into a valley, all covered with huge separate rocks, each of which is crowded with historical and mythological legends, you may perceive the dim blue ridge of mountains, still loftier and still more strangely shaped. That is Khandala, which is overhung by a huge stone block, known by the name of the Duke's Nose. On the opposite side, under the very summit of the mountain, is situated Karli, which, according to the unanimous opinion of archæologists, is the most ancient and best preserved of Indian cave temples.

One who has traversed the passes of the Caucasus again and again; one who, from the top of the Cross Mountain, has beheld beneath her feet thunderstorms and lightnings; who has visited the Alps and the Rigi; who is well acquainted with the Andes and Cordilleras, and knows every corner of the Catskills in America, may be allowed, I hope, the expression of a humble opinion. The Caucasian Mountains, I do not deny, are more majestic than the Ghats of India, and their splendour cannot be dimmed by comparison with these; but their beauty is of a classical type, if I may use this expression. At their sight one experiences true delight, but at the same time a sensation of awe. One feels like a pigmy before these Titans of nature. But in India, the Himalayas excepted, mountains produce quite a different impression. The highest summits of the Deccan, as well as of the triangular ridge that fringes Northern Hindostan, and of the Eastern Ghats, do not exceed 3,000 feet. Only in the Western Ghats of the Malabar coast, from Cape Comorin to the river Surat, are there heights of 7,000 feet above the surface of the sea. So that no comparison can be drawn between these and the hoary-headed patriarch Elbruz, or Kasbek, which exceeds 18,000 feet. The chief and original charm of Indian mountains consists in their wonderfully capricious shapes. Sometimes these mountains, or, rather, separate volcanic peaks standing in a row, form chains; but it is more common to find them scattered, to the great perplexity of geologists, without visible cause, in places where the formation seems quite unsuitable. Spacious valleys, surrounded by high walls of rock, over the very ridge of which passes the railway, are common. Look below, and it will seem to you that you are gazing upon the studio of some whimsical Titanic sculptor, filled with half finished groups, statues, and monuments. Here is a dream-land bird, seated upon the head of a monster six hundred feet high, spreading its wings and widely gaping its dragon's mouth; by its side the bust of a man, surmounted by a helmet, battlemented like the walls of a feudal castle; there, again, new monsters devouring each other, statues with broken limbs, disorderly heaps of huge balls, lonely fortresses with loopholes, ruined towers and bridges. All this scattered and intermixed with shapes changing incessantly like the dreams of delirium. And the chief attraction is that nothing here is the result of art, everything is the pure sport of nature, which, however, has occasionally been turned to account by ancient builders. The art of man in India is to be sought in the interior of the earth, not on its surface. Ancient Hindus seldom built their temples otherwise than in the bosom of the earth, as though they were ashamed of their efforts, or did not dare to rival the sculpture of nature. Having chosen, for instance, a pyramidal rock, or a cupola shaped hillock like Elephanta, or Karli, they scraped away inside, according to the Purânas, for centuries, planning on so grand a style that no modern architecture has been able to conceive anything to equal it. Fables (?) about the Cyclops seem truer in India than in Egypt.

The marvellous railroad from Narel to Khandala reminds one of a similar line from Genoa up the Apennines. One may be said to travel in the air, not on land. The railway traverses a region 1,400 feet above Konkan, and, in some places, while one rail is laid on the sharp edge of the rock, the other is supported on vaults and arches. The Mali Khindi viaduct is 163 feet high. For two hours we hastened on between sky and earth, with abysses on both sides thickly covered with mango trees and bananas. Truly English engineers are wonderful builders.

The pass of Bhor-Ghat is safely accomplished and we are in Khandala. Our bungalow here is built on the very edge of a ravine, which nature herself has carefully concealed under a cover of the most luxuriant vegetation. Everything is in blossom, and, in this unfathomed recess, a botanist might find sufficient material to occupy him for a life-time. Palms have disappeared; for the most part they grow only near the sea. Here they are replaced by banyans, mango trees, pipals (*ficus religiosa*), fig trees, and thousands of other trees and shrubs, unknown to such outsiders as ourselves. The Indian flora is too often slandered and misrepresented as being full of beautiful, but scentless, flowers. At some seasons this may be true enough, but, as long as jasmines, the various balsams, white tuberoses, and golden champa (champaka or frangipani) are in blossom, this statement is far from being true. The aroma of champa alone is so powerful as to make one almost giddy. For size, it is the king of flowering trees, and hundreds of them were in full bloom, just at this time of year, on Mataran and Khandala.

We sat on the verandah, talking and enjoying the surrounding views, until well-nigh midnight. Everything slept around us.

Khandala is nothing but a big village, situated on the flat top of one of the mountains of the Sahiadra range, about 2,200 feet above the sea level. It is surrounded by isolated peaks, as strange in shape as any we have seen.

One of them, straight before us, on the opposite side of the abyss, looked exactly like a long, one-storied building, with a flat roof and a battlemented parapet. The Hindus assert that, somewhere about this hillock, there exists a secret entrance, leading into vast interior halls, in fact to a whole subterranean palace, and that there still exist people who possess the secret of this abode. A holy hermit, Yogi, and Magus, who had inhabited these caves for "many centuries," imparted this secret to Sivaji, the celebrated leader of the Mahratta armies. Like Tanhauser, in Wagner's opera, the unconquerable Sivaji spent seven years of his youth in this mysterious abode, and therein acquired his extraordinary strength and valour.

Sivaji is a kind of Indian Ilia Moorometz, though his epoch is much nearer to our times. He was the hero and the king of the Mahrattas in the seventeenth century, and the founder of their shortlived empire. It is to him that India owes the weakening, if not the entire destruction, of the Mussulman yoke. No taller than an ordinary woman, and with the hand of a child, he was, nevertheless, possessed of wonderful strength, which, of course, his compatriots ascribed to sorcery. His sword is still preserved in a museum, and one cannot help wondering at its size and weight, and at the hilt, through which only a ten-year-old child could put his hand. The basis of this hero's fame is the fact that he, the son of a poor officer in the service of a Mogul emperor, like another David, slew the Mussulman Goliath, the formidable Afzul Khan. It was not, however, with a sling that he killed him, he used in this combat the formidable Mahratti weapon, *vaghnakh*, consisting of five long steel nails, as sharp as needles, and very strong. This weapon is worn on the fingers, and wrestlers use it to tear each other's flesh like wild animals. The Deccan is full of legends about Sivaji, and even the English historians mention him with respect. Just as in the fable respecting Charles V, one of the local Indian traditions asserts that Sivaji is not dead, but lives secreted in one of the Sahiadra caves. When the fateful hour strikes (and according to the calculations of the astrologers the time is not far off) he will reappear, and will bring freedom to his beloved country.

The learned and artful Brahmans, those Jesuits of India, profit by the profound superstition of the masses to extort wealth from them, sometimes to the last cow, the only food giver of a large family.

In the following passage I give a curious example of this. At the end of July, 1879, this mysterious document appeared in Bombay. I translate literally from the Mahratti copy, the original having been translated into all the dialects of India, of which there are 273.

"Shri!" (an untranslatable greeting). "Let it be known unto every one that this epistle, traced in the original in golden letters, came down from Indra-loka" (the heaven of Indra), "in the presence of holy Brahmans, on the altar of the Vishveshvara temple, which is in the sacred town of Benares.

"Listen and remember, O tribes of Hindustan, Rajistan, Punjab, etc., etc. On Saturday, the second day of the first half of the month Magha, 1809, of Shalivahan's era" (1887 A.D.), "the eleventh month of the Hindus, during the Ashwini Nakshatra" (the first of the twenty-seven constellations on the moon's path), "when the sun enters the sign Capricorn, and the time of the day will be near the constellation Pisces, that is to say, exactly one hour and thirty-six minutes after sunrise, the hour of the end of Kali-Yug will strike, and the much desired

Satya-Yug will commence" (that is to say, the end of the Maha-Yug, the great cycle that embraces the four minor Yugas). "This time Satya-Yug will last 1,100 years. During all this time a man's lifetime will be 128 years. The days will become longer and will consist of twenty hours and forty-eight minutes, and the nights of thirteen hours and twelve minutes, that is to say, instead of twenty-four hours we shall have exactly thirty-four hours and one minute. The first day of Satya-Yug will be very important for us, because it is then that will appear to us our new King with white face and golden hair, who will come from the far North. He will become the autonomous Lord of India. The Mâyâ of human unbelief, with all the heresies over which it presides, will be thrown down to Patâla" (signifying at once hell and the antipodes), "and the Mâyâ of the righteous and pious will abide with them, and will help them to enjoy life in Mretinloka" (our earth).

"Let it also be known to everyone that, for the dissemination of this divine document, every separate copy of it will be rewarded by the forgiveness of as many sins as are generally forgiven when a pious man sacrifices to a Brahman one hundred cows. As for the disbelievers and the indifferent, they will be sent to Naraka" (hell). "Copied out and given, by the slave of Vishnu, Madlau Shriram, on Saturday, the 7th day of the first half of Shravan" (the fifth month of the Hindu year), "1801, of Shalivahan's era" (that is, 26th July, 1879).

The further career of this ignorant and cunning epistle is not known to me. Probably the police put a stop to its distribution; however, this only concerns the wise administrators. But it splendidly illustrates, from one side, the credulity of the populace, drowned in superstition, and from the other the unscrupulousness of the Brahmans.

Concerning the word Patâla, which literally means the opposite side, a recent discovery of Swami Dayanand Saraswati, whom I have already mentioned in the preceding letters, is interesting, especially if this discovery can be accepted by philologists, as the facts seem to promise. Dayanand tries to show that the ancient Aryans knew, and even visited, America, which in ancient MSS. is called Patâla, and out of which popular fancy constructed, in the course of time, something like the Greek Hades. He supports his theory by many quotations from the oldest MSS., especially from the legends about Krishna and his favourite disciple Arjuna. In the history of the latter it is mentioned that Arjuna, one of the five Pandavas, descendants of the moon dynasty, visited Patâla on his travels, and there married the widowed daughter of King Nagual, called Illupl. Comparing the names of father and daughter we reach the following considerations, which speak strongly in favour of Dayanand's supposition.

(1) Nagual is the name by which the sorcerers of Mexico, Indians and aborigines of America, are still designated. Like the Assyrian and Chaldean Nargals, chiefs of the Magi, the Mexican Nagual unites in his person the functions of priest and of sorcerer, being served in the latter capacity by a demon in the shape of some animal, generally a snake or a crocodile. These Naguals are thought to be the descendants of Nagua, the king of the snakes. Abbé Brasseur de Bourbourg devotes a considerable amount of space to them in his book about Mexico, and says that the Naguals are servants of the evil one, who, in his turn, renders them but a temporary service. In Sanskrit, likewise, snake is

Nâga, and the "King of the Nagas" plays an important part in the history of Buddha; and in the *Purânas* there exists a tradition that it was Arjuna who introduced snake worship into Patala. The coincidence, and the identity of the names are so striking that our scientists really ought to pay some attention to them.

(2) The name of Arjuna's wife Illupl is purely old Mexican, and if we reject the hypothesis of Swami Dayanand it will be perfectly impossible to explain the actual existence of this name in Sanskrit manuscripts long before the Christian era. Of all ancient dialects and languages it is only in those of the American aborigines that you constantly meet with such combinations of consonants as *pl*, *tl*, etc. They are abundant especially in the language of the Toltecs, or Nahuatl, whereas, neither in Sanskrit nor in ancient Greek are they ever found at the end of a word. Even the words *Atlas* and *Atlantis* seem to be foreign to the etymology of the European languages. Wherever Plato may have found them, it was not he who invented them. In the Toltec language we find the root *atl*, which means water and war, and directly after America was discovered Columbus found a town called Atlan, at the entrance of the Bay of Uraga. It is now a poor fishing village called Aclo. Only in America does one find such names as Itzcoatl, Zempoaltecatl, and Popocatepetl. To attempt to explain such coincidences by the theory of blind chance would be too much, consequently, as long as science does not seek to deny Dayanand's hypothesis, which, as yet, it is unable to do, we think it reasonable to adopt it, be it only in order to follow out the axiom "one hypothesis is equal to another." Amongst other things Dayanand points out that the route that led Arjuna to America five thousand years ago was by Siberia and Behring's Straits.

It was long past midnight, but we still sat listening to this legend and others of a similar kind. At length the innkeeper sent a servant to warn us of the dangers that threatened us if we lingered too long on the verandah on a moonlit night. The programme of these dangers was divided into three sections—snakes, beasts of prey, and dacoits. Besides the cobra and the "rock-snake," the surrounding mountains are full of a kind of very small mountain snake, called furzen, the most dangerous of all. Their poison kills with the swiftness of lightning. The moonlight attracts them, and whole parties of these uninvited guests crawl up to the verandahs of houses, in order to warm themselves. Here they are more snug than on the wet ground. The verdant and perfumed abyss below our verandah happened, too, to be the favourite resort of tigers and leopards, who come thither to quench their thirst at the broad brook which runs along the bottom, and then wander until daybreak under the windows of the bungalow. Lastly, there were the mad dacoits, whose dens are scattered in mountains inaccessible to the police, who often shoot Europeans simply to afford themselves the pleasure of sending *ad patres* one of the hateful *bellatis* (foreigners). Three days before our arrival the wife of a Brahman disappeared, carried off by a tiger, and two favourite dogs of the commandant were killed by snakes. We declined to wait for further explanations, but hurried to our rooms. At daybreak we were to start for Karli, six miles from this place.

IN THE KARLI CAVES.

AT five o'clock in the morning we had already arrived at the limit, not only of driveable, but, even, of rideable roads. Our bullock-cart could go no further. The last half mile was nothing but a rough sea of stones. We had either to give up our enterprise, or to climb on all-fours up an almost perpendicular slope two hundred feet high. We were utterly at our wits' end, and meekly gazed at the historical mass before us, not knowing what to do next. Almost at the summit of the mountain, under the overhanging rocks, were a dozen black openings. Hundreds of pilgrims were crawling upwards, looking, in their holiday dresses, like so many green, pink, and blue ants. Here, however, our faithful Hindu friends came to our rescue. One of them, putting the palm of his hand to his mouth, produced a strident sound something between a shriek and a whistle. This signal was answered from above by an echo, and the next moment several half naked Brahmans, hereditary watchmen of the temple, began to descend the rocks as swiftly and skilfully as wild cats. Five minutes later they were with us, fastening round our bodies strong leathern straps, and rather dragging than leading us upwards. Half an hour later, exhausted but perfectly safe, we stood before the porch of the chief temple, which until then had been hidden from us by giant trees and cactuses.

This majestic entrance, resting on four massive pillars which form a quadrangle, is fifty-two feet wide and is covered with ancient moss and carvings. Before it stands the "lion column," so-called from the four lions carved as large as nature, and seated back to back, at its base. Over the principal entrance, its sides covered with colossal male and female figures, is a huge arch, in front of which three gigantic elephants are sculptured in relief, with heads and trunks that project from the wall. The shape of the temple is oval. It is 128 feet long and forty-six feet wide. The central space is separated on each side from the aisles by forty-two pillars, which sustain the cupola-shaped ceiling. Further on is an altar, which divides the first dome from a second one which rises over a small chamber, formerly used by the ancient Aryan priests for an inner, secret altar. Two side passages leading towards it come to a sudden end, which suggests that, once upon a time, either doors or walls were there which exist no longer. Each of the forty-two pillars has a pedestal, an octagonal shaft, and a capital, described by Fergusson as "of the most exquisite workmanship, representing two kneeling elephants surmounted by a god and a goddess." Fergusson further says that this temple, or *chaitya*, is older and better preserved than any other in India, and may be assigned to a period about 200 years B.C., because Prinsep, who has read the inscription on the Silastamba pillar, asserts that the lion pillar was the gift of Ajmitra Ukasa, son of Saha Ravisobhoti, and another inscription shows that the temple was visited by Dathama Hara, otherwise Dathahamini, King of Ceylon, in the twentieth year of his reign, that is to say, 163 years before our era. For some reason or other, Dr. Stevenson points to seventy years B.C. as the date, asserting that Karlen, or Karli, was built by the Emperor Devobhuti, under the supervision of Dhanu-Kákata. But how can this be maintained in view of the above-mentioned perfectly authentic inscriptions? Even Fergusson, the celebrated defender of the Egyptian antiquities and hostile critic of those of India, insists that Karli belongs to the erections of the third century B.C., adding that "the disposition of the various parts of its architecture is identical with the architecture of the choirs of the Gothic period, and the polygonal apsides of cathedrals."

Above the chief entrance is found a gallery, which reminds one of the choirs, where, in Catholic churches, the organ is placed. Besides the chief entrance there are two lateral entrances, leading to the aisles of the temple, and over the gallery there is a single spacious window in the shape of a horseshoe, so that the light falls on the *daghopa* (altar) entirely from above, leaving the aisles, sheltered by the pillars, in obscurity, which increases as you approach the further end of the building. To the eyes of a spectator standing at the entrance, the whole daghopa shines with light, and behind it is nothing but impenetrable darkness, where no profane footsteps were permitted to tread. A figure on the daghopa, from the summit of which "Raja priests" used to pronounce verdicts to the people, is called Dharma-Raja, from Dharma, the Hindu Minos. Above the temple are two stories of caves, in each of which are wide open galleries formed by huge carved pillars, and from these galleries an opening leads to roomy cells and corridors, sometimes very long, but quite useless, as they invariably come to an abrupt termination at solid walls, without the trace of an issue of any kind. The guardians of the temple have either lost the secret of further caves, or conceal them jealously from Europeans.

Besides the Vihâras already described, there are many others, scattered over the slope of the mountain. These temple-monasteries are all smaller than the first, but, according to the opinion of some archæologists, they are much older. To what century or epoch they belong is not known except to a few Brahmans, who keep silence. Generally speaking, the position of a European archæologist in India is very sad. The masses, drowned in superstition, are utterly unable to be of any use to him, and the learned Brahmans, initiated into the mysteries of secret libraries in pagodas, do all they can to prevent archæological research. However, after all that has happened, it would be unjust to blame the conduct of the Brahmans in these matters. The bitter experience of many centuries has taught them that their only weapons are distrust and circumspection, without these their national history and the most sacred of their treasures would be irrevocably lost. Political *coups d'état* which have shaken their country to its foundation, Mussulman invasions that proved so fatal to its welfare, the all-destructive fanaticism of Mussulman vandals and of Catholic *padres*, who are ready for anything in order to secure manuscripts and destroy them—all these form a good excuse for the action of the Brahmans. However, in spite of these manifold destructive tendencies, there exist in many places in India vast libraries capable of pouring a bright and new light, not only on the history of India itself, but also on the darkest problems of universal history. Some of these libraries, filled with the most precious manuscripts, are in the possession of native princes and of pagodas attached to their territories, but the greater part is in the hands of the Jainas (the oldest of Hindu sects) and of the Rajputana Takurs, whose ancient hereditary castles are scattered all over Rajistan, like so many eagles' nests on high rocks. The existence of the celebrated collections in Jassulmer and Patana is not unknown to the Government, but they remain wholly beyond its reach. The manuscripts are written in an ancient and now completely forgotten language, intelligible only to the high priests and their initiated librarians. One thick folio is so sacred and inviolable that it rests on a heavy golden chain in the centre of the temple of Chintamani in Jassulmer, and is taken down only to be dusted and rebound at the advent of each new pontiff. This is the work of Somaditya Suru Acharya, a great priest of the pre-Mussulman time, well-known in history. His mantle is still preserved in the temple, and forms the robe of initiation of every new high priest. Colonel James Tod, who spent so many years in India and gained the love of the people as well as of the Brahmans—a most uncommon trait in the biography of any Anglo-Indian—has written the only true history of India, but even he was never allowed to touch this folio. Natives commonly believe that he was offered initiation into the mysteries at the price of the adoption of their religion. Being a devoted archæologist he almost resolved to do so, but, having to return to England on account of his health, he left this world before he could return to his adopted country, and thus the enigma of this new book of the sibyl remains unsolved.

The Takurs of Rajputana, who are said to possess some of the underground libraries, occupy in India a position similar to the position of European feudal barons of the Middle Ages. Nominally they are dependent on some of the native princes or on the British Government; but *de facto* they are perfectly independent. Their castles are built on high rocks, and besides the natural difficulty of entering them, their possessors are made doubly unreachable by the fact that long secret passages exist in every such castle, known only to the present owner and confided to his heir only at his death. We have visited two such underground halls, one of them big enough to contain a whole village. No torture would ever induce the owners to disclose the secret of their entrances, but the Yogis and the initiated Adepts come and go freely, entirely trusted by the Takurs.

A similar story is told concerning the libraries and subterranean passages of Karli. As for the archæologists, they are unable even to determine whether this temple was built by Buddhists or Brahmans. The huge daghopa that hides the holy of holies from the eyes of the worshippers is sheltered by a mushroom-shaped roof, and resembles a low minaret with a cupola. Roofs of this description are called "umbrellas," and usually shelter the statues of Buddha and of the Chinese sages. But, on the other hand, the worshippers of Shiva, who possess the temple nowadays, assert that this low building is nothing but a lingam of Shiva. Besides, the carvings of gods and goddesses cut out of the rock forbid one to think that the temple is the production of the Buddhists. Fergusson writes, "What is this monument of antiquity? Does it belong to the Hindus, or to the Buddhists? Has it been built upon plans drawn since the death of Sakya Sing, or does it belong to a more ancient religion?"

That is the question. If Fergusson, being bound by facts existing in inscriptions to acknowledge the antiquity of Karli, will still persist in asserting that Elephanta is of much later date, he will scarcely be able to solve this dilemma, because the two styles are exactly the same, and the carvings of the latter are still more magnificent. To ascribe the temples of Elephanta and Kanari to the Buddhists, and to say that their respective periods correspond to the fourth and fifth centuries in the first case, and the tenth in the second, is to introduce into history a very strange and unfounded anachronism. After the first century A.D. there was not left a single influential Buddhist in India. Conquered and persecuted by the Brahmans, they emigrated by thousands to Ceylon and the trans-Himalayan districts. After the death of King Asoka, Buddhism speedily broke down, and in a short time was entirely displaced by the theocratic Brahmanism.

Fergusson's hypothesis that the followers of Sakya Sing, driven out by intolerance from the continent, probably sought shelter on the islands that surround Bombay, would hardly sustain critical analysis. Elephanta and Salsetta are quite near to Bombay, two and five miles distant respectively, and they are full of ancient Hindu temples. Is it credible, then, that the Brahmans, at the culminating point of their power, just before the Mussulman invasions, fanatical as they were, and mortal enemies of the Buddhists, would allow these hated heretics to build temples within their possessions in general and on Gharipuri in particular, this latter being an island consecrated to their Hindu pagodas? It is not necessary to be either a specialist, an architect, or an eminent archæologist, in order to be convinced at the first glance that such temples as Elephanta are the work of Cyclopses, requiring centuries and not years for their construction. Whereas in Karli everything is built and carved after a perfect plan, in Elephanta it seems as if thousands of different hands had wrought at different times, each following its own ideas and fashioning after its own device. All three caves are dug out of a hard porphyry rock. The first temple is practically a square, 130 feet 6 inches long and 130 feet wide. It contains twenty-six thick pillars and sixteen pilasters.

Between some of them there is a distance of 12 or 16 feet, between others 15 feet 5 inches, 13 feet 3½ inches, and so on. The same lack of uniformity is found in the pedestals of the columns, the finish and style of which is constantly varying.

Why, then, should we not pay some attention to the explanations of the Brahmans? They say that this temple was begun by the sons of Pandu, after "the great war," Mahabharata, and that after their death every true believer was bidden to continue the work according to his own notions. Thus the temple was gradually built during three centuries. Every one who wished to redeem his sins would bring his chisel and set to work. Many were the members of royal families, and even kings, who personally took part in these labours.

On the right hand side of the temple there is a corner stone, a lingam of Shiva in his character of Fructifying Force, which is sheltered by a small square chapel with four doors. Round this chapel are many colossal human figures. According to the Brahmans, these are statues representing the royal sculptors themselves; they being doorkeepers of the holy of holies, Hindus of the highest caste. Each of the larger figures leans upon a dwarf representative of the lower castes, which have been promoted by the popular fancy to the rank of demons (Pisachas). Moreover, the temple is full of unskilful work. The Brahmans hold that such a holy place could not be deserted if men of the preceding and present generations had not become unworthy of visiting it. As to Kanari or Kanhari, and some other cave temples, there is not the slightest doubt that they were all erected by Buddhists. In some of them were found inscriptions in a perfect state of preservation, and their style does not remind one in the least of the symbolical buildings of the Brahmans. Archbishop Heber thinks the Kanari caves were built in the first or second centuries B.C. But Elephanta is much older and must be classed among prehistoric monuments, that is to say, its date must be assigned to the epoch that immediately followed the "great war," Mahabharata. Unfortunately the date of this war is a point of disagreement between European scientists; the celebrated and learned Dr. Martin Haug thinks it is almost antediluvian, while the no less celebrated and learned Professor Max Müller places it as near the first century of our era as possible.

The fair was at its culmination when, having finished visiting the cells, climbing over all the stories, and examining the celebrated "hall of wrestlers," we descended, not by way of the stairs, of which there is no trace to be found, but after the fashion of pails bringing water out of a deep well, that is to say, by the aid of ropes. A crowd of about three thousand persons had assembled from the surrounding villages and towns. Women were there adorned from the waist down in brilliant-hued saris, with rings in their noses, their ears, their lips, and on all parts of their limbs that could hold a ring. Their raven-black hair which was smoothly combed back, shone with cocoanut oil, and was adorned with crimson flowers, which are sacred to Shiva and to Bhavani, the feminine aspect of this god.

Before the temple there were rows of small shops and of tents, where could be bought all the requisites for the usual sacrifices—aromatic herbs, incense, sandal wood, rice, gulab, and the red powder with which the pilgrim sprinkles first the idol and then his own face. Fakirs, bairagis, hosseins, the whole body of the mendicant brotherhood, was present among the crowd. Wreathed in chaplets, with long uncombed hair twisted at the top of the head into a regular chignon, and with bearded faces, they presented a very funny likeness to naked apes. Some of them were covered with wounds and bruises due to mortification of the flesh. We also saw some bunis, snake-charmers, with dozens of various snakes round their waists, necks, arms, and legs—models well worthy of the brush of a painter who intended to depict the image of a male Fury. One jadugar was especially remarkable. His head was crowned with a turban of cobras. Expanding their hoods and raising their leaf-like dark green heads, these cobras hissed furiously and so loudly that the sound was audible a hundred paces off. Their "stings" quivered like lightning, and their small eyes glittered with anger at the approach of every passer-by. The expression, "the sting of a snake," is universal, but it does not describe accurately the process of inflicting a wound. The "sting" of a snake is perfectly harmless. To introduce the poison into the blood of a man, or of an animal, the snake must pierce the flesh with its fangs, not prick with its sting. The needle-like eye teeth of a cobra communicate with the poison gland, and if this gland is cut out the cobra will not live more than two days. Accordingly, the supposition of some sceptics, that the bunis cut out this gland, is quite unfounded. The term "hissing" is also inaccurate when applied to cobras. They do not hiss. The noise they make is exactly like the death-rattle of a dying man. The whole body of a cobra is shaken by this loud and heavy growl.

Here we happened to be the witnesses of a fact which I relate exactly as it occurred, without indulging in explanations or hypotheses of any kind. I leave to naturalists the solution of the enigma.

Expecting to be well paid, the cobra-turbaned buni sent us word by a messenger boy that he would like very much to exhibit his powers of snake-charming. Of course we were perfectly willing, but on condition that between us and his pupils there should be what Mr. Disraeli would call a "scientific frontier."* We selected a spot about fifteen paces from the magic circle. I will not describe minutely the tricks and wonders that we saw, but will proceed at once to the main fact. With the aid of a vaguda, a kind of musical pipe of bamboo, the buni caused all the snakes to fall into a sort of cataleptic sleep. The melody that he played, monotonous, low, and original to the last degree, nearly sent us to sleep ourselves. At all events we all grew extremely sleepy without any apparent cause. We were aroused from this half lethargy by our friend Gulab-Sing, who gathered a handful of a grass, perfectly unknown to us, and advised us to rub our temples and eyelids with it. Then the buni produced from a dirty bag a kind of round stone, something like a fish's eye, or an onyx with a white spot in the centre, not bigger than a ten-kopek bit. He declared that anyone who bought that stone would be able to charm any cobra (it would produce no effect on snakes of other kinds) paralyzing the creature and then causing it to fall asleep. Moreover, by his account, this stone is the only remedy for the bite of a cobra. You have only to place this talisman on the wound, where it will stick so firmly that it cannot be torn off until all the poison is absorbed into it, when it will fall off of itself, and all danger will be past.

Being aware that the Government gladly offers any premium for the invention of a remedy for the bite of the cobra, we did not show any unreasonable interest on

* Written in 1879.

the appearance of this stone. In the meanwhile, the buni began to irritate his cobras. Choosing a cobra eight feet long, he literally enraged it. Twisting its tail round a tree, the cobra arose and hissed. The buni quietly let it bite his finger, on which we all saw drops of blood. A unanimous cry of horror arose in the crowd. But master buni stuck the stone on his finger and proceeded with his performance.

"The poison gland of the snake has been cut out," remarked our New York colonel. "This is a mere farce."

As if in answer to this remark, the buni seized the neck of the cobra, and, after a short struggle, fixed a match into its mouth, so that it remained open. Then he brought the snake over and showed it to each of us separately, so that we all saw the death-giving gland in its mouth. But our colonel would not give up his first impression so easily. "The gland is in its place right enough," said he, "but how are we to know that it really does contain poison?"

Then a live hen was brought forward and, tying its legs together, the buni placed it beside the snake. But the latter would pay no attention at first to this new victim, but went on hissing at the buni, who teased and irritated it until at last it actually struck at the wretched bird. The hen made a weak attempt to cackle, then shuddered once or twice and became still. The death was instantaneous. Facts will remain facts, the most exacting critic and disbeliever notwithstanding. This thought gives me courage to write what happened further. Little by little the cobra grew so infuriated that it became evident the jadugar himself did not dare to approach it. As if glued to the trunk of the tree by its tail, the snake never ceased diving into space with its upper part and trying to bite everything. A few steps from us was somebody's dog. It seemed to attract the whole of the buni's attention for some time. Sitting on his haunches, as far as possible from his raging pupil, he stared at the dog with motionless glassy eyes, and then began a scarcely audible song. The dog grew restless. Putting his tail between his legs, he tried to escape, but remained, as if fastened to the ground. After a few seconds he crawled nearer and nearer to the buni, whining, but unable to tear his gaze from the charmer. I understood his object, and felt awfully sorry for the dog. But, to my horror, I suddenly felt that my tongue would not move. I was perfectly unable either to get up or even to raise my finger. Happily this fiendish scene was not prolonged. As soon as the dog was near enough, the cobra bit him. The poor animal fell on his back, made a few convulsive movements with his legs, and shortly died. We could no longer doubt that there was poison in the gland. In the meanwhile the stone had dropped from the buni's finger and he approached to show us the healed member. We all saw the trace of the prick, a red spot not bigger than the head of an ordinary pin.

Next he made his snakes rise on their tails, and, nolding the stone between his first finger and thumb, he proceeded to demonstrate its influence on the cobras. The nearer his hand approached to the head of the snake, the more the reptile's body recoiled. Looking steadfastly at the stone they shivered, and, one by one, dropped as if paralyzed. The buni then made straight for our sceptical colonel, and made him an offer to try the experiment himself. We all protested vigorously, but he would not listen to us, and chose a cobra of a very considerable size. Armed with the stone, the colonel bravely approached the snake. For a moment I positively felt petrified with fright. Inflating its hood, the cobra made an attempt to fly at him, then suddenly stopped short, and, after a pause, began following with all its body the circular movements of the colonel's hand. When he put the stone quite close to the reptile's head, the snake staggered as if intoxicated, its hissing grew weak, its hood dropped helplessly on both sides of its neck, and its eyes closed. Drooping lower and lower, the snake fell at last on the ground like a stick, and slept.

Only then did we breathe freely. Taking the sorcerer aside we expressed our desire to buy the stone, to which he easily assented, and, to our great astonishment, asked for it only two rupees. This talisman became my own property and I still keep it. The buni asserts, and our Hindu friends confirm the story, that it is not a stone but an excrescence. It is found in the mouth of one cobra in a hundred, between the bone of the upper jaw and the skin of the palate. This "stone" is not fastened to the skull, but hangs, wrapped in skin, from the palate, and so is very easily cut off; but after this operation the cobra is said to die. If we are to believe Bishu Nath, for that was our sorcerer's name, this excrescence confers upon the cobra who possesses it the rank of king over the rest of his kind.

"Such a cobra," said the buni, "is like a Brahman, a Dwija Brahman amongst Shudras, they all obey him. There exists, moreover, a poisonous toad that also, sometimes, possesses this stone, but its effect is much weaker. To destroy the effect of a cobra's poison you must apply the toad's stone not later than two minutes after the infliction of the wound; but the stone of a cobra is effectual to the last. Its healing power is certain as long as the heart of the wounded man has not ceased to beat."

Bidding us good-bye, the buni advised us to keep the stone in a dry place and never to leave it near a dead body, also, to hide it during the sun and moon eclipses, "otherwise," said he, "it will lose all its power." In case we were bitten by a mad dog, he said, we were to put the stone into a glass of water and leave it there during the night, next morning the sufferer was to drink the water and then forget all danger.

"He is a regular devil and not a man!" exclaimed our colonel, as soon as the buni had disappeared on his way to a Shiva temple, where, by the way, we were not admitted.

"As simple a mortal as you or I," remarked the Rajput with a smile, "and, what is more, he is very ignorant. The truth is, he has been brought up in a Shivaite pagoda, like all the real snake-charmers. Shiva is the patron god of snakes, and the Brahmans teach the bunis to produce all kinds of mesmeric tricks by empirical methods, never explaining to them the theoretical principles, but assuring them that Shiva is behind every phenomenon. So that the bunis sincerely ascribe to their god the honour of their 'miracles.'"

"The Government of India offers a reward for an antidote to the poison of the cobra. Why then do the bunis not claim it, rather than let thousands of people die helpless?"

"The Brahmans would never suffer that. If the Government took the trouble to examine carefully the statistics of deaths caused by snakes, it would be found that *no Hindu of the Shivaite sect* has ever died from the bite of a cobra. They let people of other sects die, but save the members of their own flock."

"But did we not see how easily he parted with his secret, notwithstanding we were foreigners. Why should not the English buy it as readily?"

"Because this secret is quite useless in the hands of Europeans. The Hindus do not try to conceal it, because they are perfectly certain that without their aid nobody can make any use of it. The stone will retain its wonderful power only when it is taken from a live cobra. In order to catch the snake without killing it, it must be cast into a lethargy, or, if you prefer the term, *charmed*. Who is there among the foreigners who is able to do this? Even amongst the Hindus, you will not find a single individual in all India who possesses this ancient secret, unless he be a disciple of the Shivaite Brahmans. Only Brahmans of this sect possess a monopoly of the secret, and not all even of them, only those, in short, who belong to the pseudo-Patanjali school, who are usually called Bhuta ascetics. Now there exist, scattered over the whole of India, only about half-a-dozen of their pagoda schools, and the inmates would rather part with their very lives than with their secret."

"We have paid only two rupees for a secret which proved as strong in the colonel's hands as in the hands of the buni. Is it then so difficult to procure a store of these stones?"

Our friend laughed.

"In a few days," said he, "the talisman will lose all its healing powers in your inexperienced hands. This is the reason why he let it go at such a low price, which he is, probably, at this moment sacrificing before the altar of his deity. I guarantee you a week's activity for your purchase, but after that time it will only be fit to be thrown out of the window."

We soon learned how true were these words. On the

following day we came across a little girl, bitten by a green scorpion. She seemed to be in the last convulsions. No sooner had we applied the stone than the child seemed relieved, and, in an hour, she was gaily playing about, whereas, even in the case of the sting of a common black scorpion, the patient suffers for two weeks. But when, about ten days later, we tried the experiment of the stone upon a poor coolie, just bitten by a cobra, it would not even stick to the wound, and the poor wretch shortly expired. I do not take upon myself to offer, either a defence, or an explanation of the virtues of the "stone." I simply state the facts and leave the future career of the story to its own fate. The sceptics may deal with it as they will. Yet I can easily find people in India who will bear witness to my accuracy.

In this connection I was told a funny story. When Dr. (now Sir J.) Fayrer, who lately published his *Thanatophidia*, a book on the venomous snakes of India, a work well known throughout Europe, he categorically stated in it his disbelief in the wondrous snake-charmers of India. However, about a fortnight or so after the book appeared amongst the Anglo-Indians, a cobra bit his own cook. A buni, who happened to pass by, readily offered to save the man's life. It stands to reason that the celebrated naturalist could not accept such an offer. Nevertheless, Major Kelly and other officers urged him to permit the experiment. Declaring that in spite of all, in less than an hour his cook would be no more, he gave his consent. But it happened that in less than an hour the cook was quietly preparing dinner in the kitchen, and, it is added, Dr. Fayrer seriously thought of throwing his book into the fire.

The day grew dreadfully hot. We felt the heat of the

rocks in spite of our thick-soled shoes. Besides, the general curiosity aroused by our presence, and the unceremonious persecutions of the crowd, were becoming tiring. We resolved to "go home," that is to say, to return to the cool cave, six hundred paces from the temple, where we were to spend the evening and to sleep. We would wait no longer for our Hindu companions, who had gone to see the fair, and so we started by ourselves

---

On approaching the entrance of the temple we were struck by the appearance of a young man, who stood apart from the crowd and was of an ideal beauty. He was a member of the Sadhu sect, a "candidate for saintship," to use the expression of one of our party.

The Sadhus differ greatly from every other sect. They never appear unclothed, do not cover themselves with damp ashes, wear no painted signs on their faces, or foreheads, and do not worship idols. Belonging to the Adwaiti section of the Vedantic school, they believe only in Parabrahm (the great spirit). The young man looked quite decent in his light yellow costume, a kind of nightgown without sleeves. He had long hair, and his head was uncovered. His elbow rested on the back of a cow, which was itself well calculated to attract attention, for, in addition to her four perfectly shaped legs, she had a fifth growing out of her hump. This wonderful freak of nature used its fifth leg as if it were a hand and arm, hunting and killing tiresome flies, and scratching its head with the hoof. At first we thought it was a trick to attract attention, and even felt offended with the animal, as well as with its handsome owner, but, coming nearer, we saw that it was no trick, but an actual sport of mischievous Nature. From the young man we learned that the cow had been presented to him by the Maharaja Holkar, and that her milk had been his only food during the last two years.

Sadhus are aspirants to the Raj Yoga, and, as I have said above, usually belong to the school of the Vedanta. That is to say, they are disciples of initiates who have entirely resigned the life of the world, and lead a life of monastic chastity. Between the Sadhus and the Shivaite bunis there exists a mortal enmity, which manifests itself by a silent contempt on the side of the Sadhus, and on that of the bunis by constant attempts to sweep their rivals off the face of the earth. This antipathy is as marked as that between light and darkness, and reminds one of the dualism of the Ahura-Mazda and Ahriman of the Zoroastrians. Masses of people look up to the first as to Magi, sons of the sun and of the Divine Principle, while the latter are dreaded as dangerous sorcerers. Having heard most wonderful accounts of the former, we were burning with anxiety to see some of the "miracles" ascribed to them by some even among the Englishmen. We eagerly invited the Sadhu to visit our vihâra during the evening. But the handsome ascetic sternly refused, for the reason that we were staying within the temple of the idol-worshippers, the very air of which would prove antagonistic to him. We offered him money, but he would not touch it, and so we parted.

A path, or rather a ledge cut along the perpendicular face of a rocky mass 200 feet high, led from the chief temple to our vihâra. A man needs good eyes, sure feet, and a very strong head to avoid sliding down the precipice at the first false step. Any help would be quite out of the question, for, the ledge being only two feet wide, no one could walk side by side with another. We had to walk one by one, appealing for aid only to the whole of our personal courage. But the courage of many of us was gone on an unlimited furlough. The position of our American colonel was the worst, for he was very stout and short-sighted, which defects, taken together, caused him frequent vertigos. To keep up our spirits we indulged in a choral performance of the duet from *Norma*, "Moriam' insieme," holding each other's hands the while, to ensure our being spared by death or dying all four in company. But the colonel did not fail to frighten us nearly out of our lives. We were already half way up to the cave when he made a false step, staggered, lost hold of my hand, and rolled over the edge. We three, having to clutch the bushes and stones, were quite unable to help him. A unanimous cry of horror escaped us, but died away as we perceived that he had succeeded in clinging to the trunk of a small tree, which grew on the slope a few steps below us. Fortunately, we knew that the colonel was good at athletics, and remarkably cool in danger. Still the moment was a critical one. The slender stem of the tree might give way at any moment. Our cries of distress were answered by the sudden appearance of the mysterious Sadhu with his cow.

They were quietly walking along about twenty feet below us, on such invisible projections of the rock that a child's foot could barely have found room to rest there, and they both travelled as calmly, and even carelessly, as if a comfortable causeway were beneath their feet, instead of a vertical rock. The Sadhu called out to the colonel to hold on, and to us to keep quiet. He patted the neck of his monstrous cow, and untied the rope by which he was leading her. Then, with both hands he turned her head in our direction, and clucking with his tongue, he cried "Chal!" (go). With a few wild goat-like bounds the animal reached our path, and stood before us motionless. As for the Sadhu himself, his movements were as swift and as goat-like. In a moment he had reached the tree, tied the rope round the colonel's body, and put him on his legs again; then, rising higher, with one effort of his strong hand he hoisted him up to the path. Our colonel was with us once more, rather pale, and with the loss of his *pince-nez*, but not of his presence of mind.

An adventure that had threatened to become a tragedy ended in a farce.

"What is to be done now?" was our unanimous inquiry. "We cannot let you go alone any further."

"In a few moments it will be dark and we shall be lost," said Mr. Y——, the colonel's secretary.

And, indeed, the sun was dipping below the horizon, and every moment was precious. In the meanwhile, the Sadhu had fastened the rope round the cow's neck again and stood before us on the pathway, evidently not understanding a word of our conversation. His tall, slim figure seemed as if suspended in the air above the precipice. His long, black hair, floating in the breeze, alone showed that in him we beheld a living being and not a magnificent statue of bronze. Forgetting our recent danger and our present awkward situation, Miss X——, who was a born artist, exclaimed: "Look at the majesty of that pure profile; observe the pose of that man. How beautiful are his outlines seen against the golden and blue sky. One would say, a Greek Adonis, not a Hindu!"

But the "Adonis" in question put a sudden stop to her ecstasy. He glanced at Miss X—— with half-pitying, half-kindly, laughing eyes, and said with his ringing voice in Hindi—

"Bara-Sahib cannot go any further without the help

of someone else's eyes. Sahib's eyes are his enemies. Let the Sahib ride on my cow. She cannot stumble."

"I! Ride on a cow, and a five-legged one at that? Never!" exclaimed the poor colonel, with such a helpless air, nevertheless, that we burst out laughing,

"It will be better for Sahib to sit on a cow than to lie on a chitta" (the pyre on which dead bodies are burned), remarked the Sadhu with modest seriousness. "Why call forth the hour which has not yet struck?"

The colonel saw that argument was perfectly useless, and we succeeded in persuading him to follow the Sadhu's advice, who carefully hoisted him on the cow's back, then, recommending him to hold on by the fifth leg, he led the way. We all followed to the best of our ability.

In a few minutes more we were on the verandah of our vihâra, where we found our Hindu friends, who had arrived by another path. We eagerly related all our adventures, and then looked for the Sadhu, but, in the meanwhile, he had disappeared together with his cow.

"Do not look for him, he is gone by a road known only to himself," remarked Gulab-Sing carelessly. "He knows you are sincere in your gratitude, but he would not take your money. He is a Sadhu, not a buni," added he proudly.

We remembered that it was reported this proud friend of ours also belonged to the Sadhu sect. "Who can tell," whispered the colonel in my ear, "whether these reports are mere gossip, or the truth?"

Sadhu-Nânaka must not be confounded with Guru-Nânaka, a leader of the Sikhs. The former are Adwaitas, the latter monotheists. The Adwaitas believe only in an impersonal deity named Parabrahm.

In the chief hall of the vihâra was a life-sized statue

of Bhavani, the feminine aspect of Shiva. From the bosom of this *devaki* streams forth the pure cold water of a mountain spring, which falls into a reservoir at her feet. Around it lay heaps of sacrificial flowers, rice, betel leaves and incense. This hall was, in consequence, so damp that we preferred to spend the night on the verandah in the open air, hanging, as it were, between sky and earth, and lit from below by numerous fires kept burning all the night by Gulab-Sing's servants, to scare away wild beasts, and, from above, by the light of the full moon. A supper was arranged after the Eastern fashion, on carpets spread upon the floor, and with thick banana leaves for plates and dishes. The noiselessly gliding steps of the servants, more silent than ghosts, their white muslins and red turbans, the limitless depths of space, lost in waves of moonlight, before us, and behind, the dark vaults of ancient caves, dug out by unknown races, in unknown times, in honour of an unknown, prehistoric religion—all these, our surroundings, transported us into a strange world, and into distant epochs far different from our own.

We had before us representatives of five different peoples, five different types of costume, each quite unlike the others. All five are known to us in ethnography under the generic name of Hindus. Similarly eagles, condors, hawks, vultures, and owls are known to ornithology as "birds of prey," but the analogous differences are as great. Each of these five companions, a Rajput, a Bengali, a Madrasi, a Sinhalese and a Mahratti, is a descendant of a race, the origin of which European scientists have discussed for over half a century without coming to any agreement.

Rajputs are called Hindus and are said to belong to

the Aryan race; but they call themselves Suryà-vansa, that is to say, descendants of Surya or the sun.

The Brahmans derive their origin from Indu, the moon, and are called Indu-vansa; Indu, Soma, or Chandra, meaning moon in Sanskrit. If the first Aryans, appearing in the prologue of universal history, are Brahmans, that is to say, the people who, according to Max Müller, having crossed the Himalayas conquered the country of the five rivers, then the Rajputs are no Aryans; and if they are Aryans they are not Brahmans, as all their genealogies and sacred books (*Purânas*) show that they are much older than the Brahmans; and, in this case, moreover, the Aryan tribes had an actual existence in other countries of our globe than the much renowned district of the Oxus, the cradle of the Germanic race, the ancestors of Aryans and Hindus, in the fancy of the scientist we have named and his German school.

The "moon" line begins with Pururavas (see the genealogical tree prepared by Colonel Tod from the MS. *Purânas* in the Oodeypore archives), that is to say, two thousand two hundred years before Christ, and much later than Ikshvâku, the patriarch of the Surya-vansa. The fourth son of Pururavas, Rech, stands at the head of the line of the moon-race, and only in the fifteenth generation after him appears Harita, who founded the Kanshikagotra, the Brahman tribe.

The Rajputs hate the latter. They say the children of the sun and Rama have nothing in common with the children of the moon and Krishna. As for the Bengalis, according to their traditions and history, they are aborigines. The Madrasis and the Sinhalese are Dravidians. They have, in turn, been said to belong to the Semites, the Hamites, the Aryans, and, lastly, they have been given up to the will of God, with the conclusion drawn that the Sinhalese, at all events, must be Mongolians of Turanian origin. The Mahrattis are aborigines of the West of India, as the Bengalis are of the East; but to what group of tribes belong these two nationalities no ethnographer can define, save perhaps a German. The traditions of the people themselves are generally denied, because they are not in harmony with foregone conclusions. The meaning of ancient manuscripts is disfigured, and, in fact, sacrificed to fiction, if only the latter proceeds from the mouth of some favourite oracle.

The ignorant masses are often blamed and found to be guilty of superstition for creating idols in the spiritual world. Is not, then, the educated man, the man who craves after knowledge, who is enlightened, still more inconsistent than these masses, when he deals with his favourite authorities? Are not half a dozen laurel-crowned heads allowed by him to do whatever they like with facts, to draw their own conclusions, according to their own liking, and does he not stone every one who would dare to rise against the decisions of these quasi-infallible specialists, and brand him as an ignorant fool?

Let us remember the case in point of Louis Jacolliot, who spent twenty years in India, who actually knew the language and the country to perfection, and who, nevertheless, was rolled in the mud by Max Müller, whose foot never touched Indian soil.

The oldest peoples of Europe are mere babes compared with the tribes of Asia, and especially of India. And oh! how poor and insignificant are the genealogies of the oldest European families compared with those of some Rajputs. In the opinion of Colonel Tod, who for over twenty years studied these genealogies on the spot, they are the completest and most trustworthy of the records of the peoples of antiquity. They date from 1,000 to 2,200 years B.C., and their authenticity may often be proved by reference to Greek authors. After long and careful research and comparison with the text of the *Purānas*, and various monumental inscriptions, Colonel Tod came to the conclusion that in the Oodeypore archives (now hidden from public inspection), not to mention other sources, may be found a clue to the history of India in particular, and to universal ancient history in general. Colonel Tod advises the earnest seeker after this clue not to think, with some flippant archæologists who are insufficiently acquainted with India, that the stories of Rama, the Mahabharata, Krishna, and the five brothers Pandu, are mere allegories. He affirms that he who seriously considers these legends will very soon become thoroughly convinced that all these so-called "fables" are founded on historical facts, by the actual existence of the descendants of the heroes, by tribes, ancient towns, and coins still extant; that to acquire the right to pronounce a final opinion one must read first the inscriptions on the Inda-Prestha pillars of Purag and Mevar, on the rocks of Junagur, in Bijoli, on Aravuli and on all the ancient Jaina temples scattered throughout India, where are to be found numerous inscriptions in a language utterly unknown, in comparison with which the hieroglyphs will seem a mere toy.

Yet, nevertheless, Professor Max Müller, who, as already mentioned, was never in India, sits as a judge and corrects chronological tables as is his wont, and Europe, taking his words for those of an oracle, endorses his decisions. *Et c'est ainsi que s'écrit l'histoire.*

Talking of the venerable German Sanskritist's chronology, I cannot resist the desire to show, be it only to Russia, on what a fragile basis are founded his scientific discussions, and how little he is to be trusted when he pronounces upon the antiquity of this or that manuscript. These pages are of a superficial and descriptive nature, and, as such, make no pretence to profound learning, so that what follows may seem incongruous. But it must be remembered that in Russia, as elsewhere in Europe, people estimate the value of this philological light by the points of exclamation lavished upon him by his admiring followers, and that no one reads the *Veda Bhashya* of Swami Dayanand. It may even be that I shall not be far from the truth in saying that the very existence of this work is ignored, which may perhaps be a fortunate fact for the reputation of Professor Max Müller. I shall be as brief as possible. When Professor Max Müller states, in his *Sahitya-Grantha*, that the Aryan tribe in India acquired the notion of God step by step and very slowly, he evidently wishes to prove that the *Vedas* are far from being as old as is supposed by some of his colleagues. Having presented, in due course, some more or less valuable evidence to prove the truth of this new theory, he ends with a fact which, in his opinion, is indisputable. He points to the word *hiranya-garbha* in the mantrams, which he translates by the word "gold," and adds that, as the part of the *Vedas* called chanda appeared 3,100 years ago, the part called mantrams could not have been written earlier than 2,900 years ago. Let me remind the reader that the *Vedas* are divided into two parts: chandas—slokas, verses, etc.; and mantrams—prayers and rhythmical hymns, which are, at the same time, incantations used in white magic. Professor Max Müller divides the mantram ("Agnihi Poorwebhihi," etc.) philologically and chronologically, and, finding in it the word *hiranya-garbha,* he denounces it as an anachronism. The ancients, he says, had no knowledge of gold, and, therefore, if gold is mentioned in this mantram it means that the mantram was composed at a comparatively modern epoch, and so on.

But here the illustrious Sanskritist is very much mistaken. Swami Dayanand and other pandits, who sometimes are far from being Dayanand's allies, maintain that Professor Max Müller has completely misunderstood the meaning of the term *hiranya.* Originally it did not mean, and, when united to the word *garbha,* even now does not mean, gold. So all the Professor's brilliant demonstrations are labour in vain. The word *hiranya* in this mantram must be translated "divine light"—mystically a symbol of knowledge; analogically the alchemists used the term "sublimated gold" for "light," and hoped to compose the objective metal out of its rays. The two words, *hiranya-garbha,* taken together, mean, literally, the "radiant bosom," and, when used in the *Vedas,* designate the first principle, in whose bosom, like gold in the bosom of the earth, rests the light of divine knowledge and truth, the essence of the soul liberated from the sins of the world. In the mantrams, as in the chandas, one must always look for a double meaning; (1) a metaphysical one, purely abstract, and (2) one as purely physical; for everything existing upon the earth is closely bound to the spiritual world, from which it proceeds and by which it is reabsorbed. For instance Indra, the god of thunder, Surya, the sun-god, Vayu, god of the wind, and Agni, god of fire, all four depending on this first divine principle, expand, according to the mantram from *hiranya-garbha,* the radiant bosom. In this case the gods are the personifications of the forces of Nature. But the initiated Adepts of India understand very clearly that the god Indra, for instance, is nothing more than a mere sound, born of the shock of electrical forces, or simply electricity itself. Surya is not the god of the sun, but simply the centre of fire in our system, the *essence whence come fire, warmth, light,* and so on; the very thing, namely, which no European scientist, steering an even course between Tyndall and Schröpfer, has, as yet, defined. This concealed meaning has totally escaped Professor Max Müller's attention, and this is why, clinging to the dead letter, he never hesitates before cutting a Gordian knot. How then can he be permitted to pronounce upon the antiquity of the *Vedas,* when he is so far from the right understanding of the language of these ancient writings.

The above is a *resumé* of Dayanand's argument, and to him the Sanskritists must apply for further particulars, which they will certainly find in his Rigvedadi Bhashya Bhoomika.

In the cave, every one slept soundly round the fire except myself. None of my companions seemed to mind in the least either the hum of the thousand voices of the fair, or the prolonged, far-away roar of the tigers rising from the valley, or even the loud prayers of the pilgrims who passed to and fro all night long, never fearing to cross the steep passage which, even by daylight, caused us such perplexity. They came in parties of twos and threes, and sometimes there appeared a lonely unescorted woman. They could not reach the large vihâra, because we occupied the verandah at its entrance, and so, after grumbling a little, they entered a small lateral cave something like a chapel, containing a statue of Devaki-Mata, above a tank full of water. Each pilgrim prostrated himself for a time, then placed his offering at the feet of the goddess and bathed in the "holy waters of purification," or, at the least, sprinkled some water over his forehead, cheeks, and breast. Lastly, retreating backwards, he knelt again at the door and disappeared in the darkness with a final invocation: "Mata, maha mata!"—Mother, O great mother!

Two of Gulab-Sing's servants, with traditional spears and shields of rhinoceros skin, who had been ordered to protect us from wild beasts, sat on the steps of the verandah. I was unable to sleep, and so watched with increasing curiosity everything that was going on. The Takur, too, was sleepless. Every time I raised my eyes, heavy with fatigue, the first object upon which they fell was the gigantic figure of our mysterious friend.

Having seated himself after the Eastern fashion, with his feet drawn up and his arms round his knees, the Rajput sat on a bench cut in the rock at one end of the verandah, gazing out into the silvery atmosphere. He was so near the abyss that the least incautious movement would expose him to great danger. But the granite goddess, Bhavani herself, could not be more immovable. The light of the moon before him was so strong that the black shadow under the rock which sheltered him was doubly impenetrable, shrouding his face in absolute darkness. From time to time the flame of the sinking fires leaping up shed its hot reflection on the dark bronze face, enabling me to distinguish its sphinx-like lineaments and its shining eyes, as unmoving as the rest of the features.

"What am I to think? Is he simply sleeping, or is he in that strange state, that temporary annihilation of bodily life? . . . Only this morning he was telling us how the initiate Raj-yogis were able to plunge into this state at will. . . . . Oh, if I could only go to sleep. . . ."

Suddenly a loud prolonged hissing, quite close to my ear, made me start, trembling with indistinct reminiscences of cobras. The sound was strident and evidently came from under the hay upon which I rested. Then it struck one! two! It was our American alarum-clock, which always travelled with me. I could not help laughing at myself, and, at the same time, feeling a little ashamed of my involuntary fright.

But neither the hissing, nor the loud striking of the clock, nor my sudden movement, that made Miss X—— raise her sleepy head, awakened Gulab-Sing, who still hung over the precipice. Another half hour passed. The far-away roar of the festivity was still heard, but everything round me was calm and still. Sleep fled further and further from my eyes. A fresh, strong wind arose, before the dawn, rustling the leaves and then shaking the tops of the trees that rose above the abyss. My attention became absorbed by the group of three Rajputs before me—by the two shield bearers and their master. I cannot tell why I was specially attracted at this moment by the sight of the long hair of the servants, which was waving in the wind, though the place they occupied was comparatively sheltered. I turned my eyes upon their Sahib, and the blood in my veins stood still. The veil of somebody's topi, which hung beside him, tied to a pillar, was simply whirling in the wind, while the hair of the Sahib himself lay as still as if it had been glued to his shoulders, not a hair moved, nor a single fold of his light muslin garment. No statue could be more motionless.

What is this then? I said to myself. Is it delirium? Is this a hallucination, or a wonderful inexplicable reality? I shut my eyes, telling myself I must look no longer. But a moment later I again looked up, startled by a crackling sound from above the steps. The long, dark silhouette of some animal appeared at the entrance, clearly outlined against the pale sky. I saw it in profile. Its long tail was lashing to and fro. Both the servants rose swiftly and noiselessly and turned their heads towards Gulab-Sing, as if asking for orders. But where was Gulab-Sing? In the place which, but a moment ago, he occupied, there was no one. There lay only the topi, torn from the pillar by the wind. I sprang up: a tremendous roar deafened me, filling the vihâra, wakening the slumbering echoes, and resounding, like the softened rumbling of thunder, over all the borders of the precipice. Good heavens! A tiger!

Before this thought had time to shape itself clearly in my mind, the sleepers sprang up and the men all seized their guns and revolvers, and then we heard the sound of crashing branches, and of something heavy sliding down into the precipice. The alarm was general.

"What is the matter now?" said the calm voice of Gulab-Sing, and I again saw him on the stone bench. "Why should you be so frightened?"

"A tiger! Was it not a tiger?" came in hasty, questioning tones from Europeans and Hindus.

Miss X—— trembled like one stricken with fever.

"Whether it was a tiger, or something else, matters very little to us now. Whatever it was, it is, by this time, at the bottom of the abyss," answered the Rajput yawning.

"I wonder the Government does not destroy all these horrid animals," sobbed poor Miss X——, who evidently believed firmly in the omnipotence of her Executive.

"But how did you get rid of the 'striped one'?" insisted the colonel. "Has any one fired a shot?"

"You Europeans think that shooting is, if not the only, at least the best way to get rid of wild animals. We possess other means, which are sometimes more efficacious than guns," explained Babu Narendro-Das-Sen. "Wait until you come to Bengal, there you will have many opportunities to make acquaintance with the tigers."

It was now getting light, and Gulab-Sing proposed to us to descend and examine the rest of the caves and the ruins of a fortress before the day became too hot, so, at half-past three, we went by another and easier way to the valley, and, happily, this time we had no adventures. The Mahratti did not accompany us. He disappeared without informing us whither he was going.

We saw Logarh, a fortress which was captured by Sivaji from the Moguls in 1670, and the ruins of the hall, where the widow of Nana Farnavese, under the pretext of an English protectorate, became *de facto* the captive of General Wellesley in 1804, with a yearly pension of 12,000 rupees. We then started for the village of Vargaon, once fortified and still very rich. We were to spend the hottest hours of the day there, from nine in the morning until four in the afternoon, and proceed afterwards to the historical caves of Birsa and Badjah, about three miles from Karli.

At about two P.M. when, in spite of the huge punkahs waving to and fro, we were grumbling at the heat, appeared our friend the Mahratta Brahman, whom we thought we had lost on the way. Accompanied by half-a-dozen Daknis (inhabitants of the Dekhan plateau) he was slowly advancing, seated almost on the ears of his horse, which snorted and seemed very unwilling to move. When he reached the verandah and jumped down, we saw the reason of his disappearance. Across the saddle was tied a huge tiger, whose tail dragged in the dust. There were traces of dark blood in his half-opened mouth. He was taken from the horse and laid down by the doorstep.

Was it our visitor of the night before? I looked at Gulab-Sing. He lay on a rug in a corner, resting his head on his hand and reading. He knitted his brows slightly, but did not say a word. The Brahman who had just brought the tiger was very silent too, watching over certain preparations, as if making ready for some solemnity. We soon learned that, in the eyes of a superstitious people, what was about to happen was a solemnity indeed.

A bit of hair cut from the skin of a tiger that has been killed, neither by bullet, nor by knife, but by a "word," is considered the best of all talismans against his tribe.

"This is a very rare opportunity," explained the Mahratti. "It is very seldom that one meets with a man who possesses the *word*. Yogis and Sadhus do not generally kill wild animals, thinking it sinful to destroy any living creature, be it even a cobra or a tiger, so they simply keep out of the way of noxious animals. There exists only one brotherhood in India whose members possess all secrets, and from whom nothing in nature is concealed. Here is the body of the tiger to testify that the animal was not killed with a weapon of any kind, but simply by the *word* of Gulab-Lal-Sing. I found it, very easily, in the bushes exactly under our vihâra, at the foot of the rock over which the tiger had rolled, already dead. Tigers never make false steps. Gulab-Lal-Sing, you are a Raj-Yogi, and I salute you!" added the proud Brahman, kneeling before the Takur.

"Do not use vain words, Krishna Rao!" interrupted

Gulab-Sing. "Get up; do not play the part of a Shudra."

"I obey you, Sahib, but, forgive me, I trust my own judgment. No Raj-Yogi ever yet acknowledged his connection with the brotherhood, since the time Mount Abu came into existence."

And he began distributing bits of hair taken from the dead animal. No one spoke. I gazed curiously at the group of my fellow-travellers. The colonel, President of our Society, sat with downcast eyes, very pale. His secretary, Mr. Y——, lay on his back, smoking a cigar and looking straight above him, with no expression in his eyes. He silently accepted the hair and put it in his purse. The Hindus stood round the tiger, and the Sinhalese traced mysterious signs on its forehead. Gulab-Sing continued quietly reading his book.

The Birza cave, about six miles from Vargaon, is constructed on the same plan as Karli. The vault-like ceiling of the temple rests upon twenty-six pillars, eighteen feet high, and the portico on four, twenty-eight feet high; over the portico are carved groups of horses, oxen, and elephants, of the most exquisite beauty. The "Hall of Initiation" is a spacious, oval room, with pillars, and eleven very deep cells cut in the rock. The Bajah caves are older and more beautiful. Inscriptions may still be seen showing that all these temples were built by Buddhists, or, rather, by Jainas. Modern Buddhists believe in one Buddha only, Gautama, Prince of Kapilavastu (six centuries before Christ) whereas the Jainas recognize a Buddha in each of their twenty-four divine teachers (Tirthankaras) the last of whom was the Guru (teacher) of Gautama. This disagreement is very embarrassing when people try to conjecture the antiquity of this or that vihâra or chaitya. The origin of the Jaina sect is lost in the remotest, unfathomed antiquity, so the name of Buddha, mentioned in the inscriptions, may be attributed to the last of the Buddhas as easily as to the first, who lived (see Tod's genealogy) a long time before 2,200 B.C.

One of the inscriptions in the Baira cave, for instance, in cuneiform characters, says: "From an ascetic in Nassik to the one who is worthy, to the holy Buddha, purified from sins, heavenly and great."

This tends to convince scientists that the cave was cut out by Buddhists.

Another inscription, in the same cave, but over another cell, contains the following: "An agreeable offering of a small gift to the moving force [life], to the mind principle [soul], the well-beloved material body, fruit of Manu, priceless treasure, to the highest and here present, Heavenly."

Of course the conclusion is drawn that the building does not belong to the Buddhists, but to the Brahmans, who believe in Manu.

Here are two more inscriptions from Bajah caves.

"An agreeable gift of the symbol and vehicle of the purified Saka-Saka."

"Gift of the vehicle of Radha [wife of Krishna, symbol of perfection] to Sugata who is gone for ever."

Sugata, again, is one of the names of Buddha. A new contradiction!

It was somewhere here, in the neighbourhood of Vargaon, that the Mahrattis seized Captain Vaughan and his brother, who were hanged after the battle of Khirki.

Next morning we drove to Chinchor, or, as it is called here, Chinchood. This place is celebrated in the annals of the Dekkan. Here one meets with a repetition in miniature of what takes place on a larger scale at L'hassa in Tibet. As Buddha incarnates in every new Dalai-Lama, so, here, Gunpati (Ganesha, the god of wisdom with the elephant's head) is allowed by his father Shiva to incarnate in the eldest son of a certain Brahman family. There is a splendid temple erected in his honour, where the avatars (incarnations) of Gunpati have lived and received adoration for over two hundred years.

This is how it happened.

About 250 years ago a poor Brahman couple were promised, in sleep, by the god of wisdom that he would incarnate in their eldest son. The boy was named Maroba (one of the god's titles) in honour of the deity. Maroba grew up, married, and begot several sons, after which he was commanded by the god to relinquish the world and finish his days in the desert. There, during twenty-two years, according to the legend, Maroba wrought miracles and his fame grew day by day. He lived in an impenetrable jungle, in a corner of the thick forest that covered Chinchood in those days. Gunpati appeared to him once more, and promised to incarnate in his descendants for seven generations. After this there was no limit to his miracles, so that the people began to worship him, and ended by building a splendid temple for him.

At last Maroba gave orders to the people to bury him alive, in a sitting posture, with an open book in his hands, and never to open his grave again under penalty of his wrath and maledictions. After the burial of Maroba, Gunpati incarnated in his first-born, who began a conjuring career in his turn. So that Maroba-Deo I. was replaced by Chintaman-Deo I. This latter god had eight wives and eight sons. The tricks of the eldest of these sons, Narayan-Deo I., became so celebrated that his fame reached the ears of the Emperor Alamgir. In order to test the extent of his "deification," Alamgir sent him a piece of a cow's tail wrapped in rich stuffs and coverings. Now, to touch the tail of a dead cow is the worst of all degradations for a Hindu. On receiving it Narayan sprinkled the parcel with water, and, when the stuffs were unfolded, there was found enclosed in them a nosegay of white syringa, instead of the ungodly tail. This transformation rejoiced the Emperor so much that he presented the god with eight villages, to cover his private expenses. Narayan's social position and property were inherited by Chintaman-Deo II., whose heir was Dharmadhar, and, lastly, Narayan II. came into power. He drew down the malediction of Gunpati by violating the grave of Maroba. That is why his son, the last of the gods, is to die without issue.

When we saw him, he was an aged man, about ninety years old. He was seated on a kind of platform. His head shook and his eyes idiotically stared without seeing us, the result of his constant use of opium. On his neck, ears, and toes, shone precious stones, and all around were spread offerings. We had to take off our shoes before we were allowed to approach this half-ruined relic.

On the evening of the same day we returned to Bombay. Two days later we were to start on our long journey to the North-West Provinces, and our route promised to be very attractive. We were to see Nassik, one of the few towns mentioned by Greek historians, its caves, and the tower of Rama; to visit Allahabad, the ancient Prayâga, the metropolis of the moon dynasty, built at the confluence of the Ganges and Jumna; Benares, the town of five thousand temples and as many monkeys; Cawnpur, notorious for the bloody revenge of Nana Sahib; the remains of the city of the sun, destroyed, according to the computations of Colebrooke, six thousand years ago; Agra and Delhi; and then, having explored Rajistan with its thousand Takur castles, fortresses, ruins, and legends, we were to go to Lahore, the metropolis of the Punjab, and, lastly, to stay for a while in Amritsar. There, in the Golden Temple, built in the centre of the "Lake of Immortality," was to be held the first meeting of the members of our Society, Brahmans, Buddhists, Sikhs, etc.—in a word, the representatives of the one thousand and one sects of India, who all sympathized, more or less, with the idea of the Brotherhood of Humanity of our Theosophical Society.

VANISHED GLORIES.

BENARES, Prayâga (now Allahabad), Nassik, Hurdwar, Bhadrinath, Matura—these were the sacred places of prehistoric India which we were to visit one after the other; but to visit them, not after the usual manner of tourists, *à vol d'oiseau*, with a cheap guide-book in our hands and a cicerone to weary our brains, and wear out our legs. We were well aware that all these ancient places are thronged with traditions and overgrown with the weeds of popular fancy, like ruins of ancient castles covered with ivy; that the original shape of the building is destroyed by the cold embrace of these parasitic plants, and that it is as difficult for the archæologist to form an idea of the architecture of the once perfect edifice, judging only by the heaps of disfigured rubbish that cover the country, as for us to select from out the thick mass of legends good wheat from weeds. No, guides and no cicerone could be of any use whatever to us. The only thing they could do would be to point out to us places where once there stood a fortress, a castle, a temple, a sacred grove, or a celebrated town, and then to repeat legends which came into existence only lately, under the Mussulman rule. As to the undisguised truth, the original history of every interesting spot, we should have had to search for these by ourselves, assisted only by our own conjectures.

Modern India does not present a pale shadow of what it was in the pre-Christian era, nor even of the Hindostan of the days of Akbar, Shah-Jehan and Aurungzeb. The neighbourhood of every town that has been shattered by many a war, and of every ruined hamlet, is covered with round reddish pebbles, as if with so many petrified tears of blood. But, in order to approach the iron gate of some ancient fortress, it is not over natural pebbles that it is necessary to walk, but over the broken fragments of some older granite remains, under which, very often, rest the ruins of a third town, still more ancient than the last. Modern names have been given to them by Mussulmans, who generally built their towns upon the remains of those they had just taken by assault. The names of the latter are sometimes mentioned in the legends, but the names of their predecessors had completely disappeared from the popular memory even before the Mussulman invasion. Will a time ever come for these secrets of the centuries to be revealed?

Knowing all this beforehand, we resolved not to lose patience, even though we had to devote whole years to explorations of the same places, in order to obtain better historical information, and facts less disfigured than those obtained by our predecessors, who had to be contented with a choice collection of naïve lies, poured forth from the mouth of some frightened semi-savage, or some Brahman, unwilling to speak and desirous of disguising the truth. As for ourselves, we were differently situated. We were helped by a whole society of educated Hindus, who were as deeply interested in the same questions as ourselves. Besides, we had a promise of the revelation of some secrets, and the accurate translation of some ancient chronicles, that had been preserved as if by a miracle.

The history of India has long since faded from the memories of her sons, and is still a mystery to her conquerors. Doubtless it still exists, though, perchance, only partly, in manuscripts that are jealously concealed from every European eye. This has been shown by some pregnant words, spoken by Brahmans on their rare occasions of friendly expansiveness. Thus, Colonel Tod, whom I have already quoted several times, is said to have been told by a Mahant, the chief of an ancient pagoda-monastery: "Sahib, you lose your time in vain researches. The Bellati India [India of foreigners] is before you, but you will never see the Gupta India [secret India]. We are the guardians of her mysteries, and would rather cut out each other's tongues than speak."

Yet, nevertheless, Tod succeeded in learning a good deal. It must be borne in mind that no Englishman has ever been loved so well by the natives as this old and courageous friend of the Maharana of Oodeypur, who, in his turn, was so friendly towards the natives that the humblest of them never saw a trace of contempt in his demeanour. He wrote before ethnology had reached its present stage of development, but his book is still an authority on everything concerning Rajistan. Though the author's opinion of his work was not very high, though he stated that "it is nothing but a conscientious collection of materials for a future historian," still in this book is to be found many a thing undreamed of by any British civil servant.

Let our friends smile incredulously. Let our enemies laugh at our pretensions "to penetrate the world-mysteries of Aryavarta," as a certain critic recently expressed himself. However pessimistic may be our critics' views, yet, even in the event of our conclusions not proving more trustworthy than those of Fergusson, Wilson, Wheeler, and the rest of the archæologists and Sanskritists who have written about India, still, I hope, they will not be less susceptible of proof. We are daily reminded that, like unreasonable children, we have undertaken a task before which archæologists and historians, aided by all the influence and wealth of the Government, have shrunk dismayed; that we have taken upon ourselves a work which has proved to be beyond the capacities of the Royal Asiatic Society.

Let it be so.

Let everyone try to remember, as we ourselves remember, that not very long ago a poor Hungarian, who not only had no means of any kind but was almost a beggar, travelled on foot to Tibet through unknown and dangerous countries, led only by the love of learning and the eager wish to pour light on the historical origin of his nation. The result was that inexhaustible mines of literary treasures were discovered. Philology, which till then had wandered in the Egyptian darkness of etymological labyrinths, and was about to ask the sanction of the scientific world to one of the *wildest* of theories, suddenly stumbled on the clue of Ariadne. Philology discovered, at last, that the Sanskrit language is, if not the forefather, at least—to use the language of Max Müller—"the elder brother" of all classical languages. Thanks to the extraordinary zeal of Alexander Csoma de Körös, Tibet yielded a language the literature of which was totally unknown. He partly translated it and partly analyzed and explained it. His translations have shown the scientific world that (1) the originals of the *Zend-Avesta*, the sacred scriptures of the sun-worshippers, of *Tripitaka*, that of the Buddhists, and of *Aytareya-Brahmanam*, that of the Brahmans, were written in one and the same Sanskrit language; (2) that all these three languages—Zend, Nepalese, and the modern Brahman Sanskrit—are more or less dialects of the first; (3) that old Sanskrit is the origin of all the less ancient Indo-European languages, as well as of the modern European tongues and dialects; (4) that the three chief religions of heathendom—Zoroastrianism, Buddhism and Brahmanism—are mere heresies of the monotheistic teachings of the *Vedas*, which does not prevent them from being real ancient religions and not modern falsifications.

The moral of all this is evident. A poor traveller, without either money or protection, succeeded in gaining admittance to the Lamaseries of Tibet and to the sacred literature of the isolated tribe which inhabits it, probably because he treated the Mongolians and the Tibetans as his brothers and not as an inferior race—a feat which has never been accomplished by generations of scientists. One cannot help feeling ashamed of humanity and science when one thinks that he whose labours first gave to science such precious results, he who was the first sower of such an abundant harvest, remained, almost until the day of his death, a poor and obscure worker. On his way from Tibet he walked to Calcutta without a penny in his pocket. At last Csoma de Körös became known, and his name began to be pronounced with honour and praise whilst he was dying in one of the poorest parts of Calcutta. Being already very ill, he wanted to get back to Tibet, and started on foot again through Sikkhim. He succumbed to his illness on the road and was buried in Darhjeeling.

It is needless to say we are fully aware that what we have undertaken is simply impossible within the limits of ordinary newspaper articles. All we hope to accomplish is to lay the foundation stone of an edifice, whose further progress must be entrusted to future generations. In order to combat successfully the theories worked out by two generations of Orientalists, half a century of diligent labour would be required. And, in order to replace these theories with new ones, we must get new facts, facts founded not on the chronology and false evidence of scheming Brahmans, whose interest is to feed the ignorance of European Sanskritists (as, unfortunately, was the experience of Lieutenant Wilford and Louis Jacolliot), but on indubitable proofs that are to be found in inscriptions as yet undeciphered. The clue to these inscriptions Europeans do not possess, because, as I have already stated, it is guarded in MSS. which are as old as the inscriptions and which are almost out of reach. Even in case our hopes are realized and we obtain this clue, a new difficulty will arise before us. We shall have to begin a systematic refutation, page by page, of many a volume of *hypotheses* published by the Royal Asiatic Society. A work like this might be accomplished by dozens of tireless, never-resting Sanskritists—a class which, even in India, is almost as rare as white elephants.

Thanks to private contributions and the zeal of some educated Hindu patriots, two free classes of Sanskrit and Pali had already been opened—one in Bombay by the Theosophical Society, the other in Benares under the presidency of the learned Rama-Misra-Shastri. In the present year, 1882, the Theosophical Society has, altogether, fourteen schools in Ceylon and India.

Our heads full of thoughts and plans of this kind, we, that is to say, one American, three Europeans, and three natives, occupied a whole carriage of the Great Indian Peninsular Railroad on our way to Nassik, one of the oldest towns in India, as I have already mentioned, and the most sacred of all in the eyes of the inhabitants of the Western Presidency. Nassik borrowed its name from the Sanskrit word "Nasika," which means *nose.* An epic legend assures us that on this very spot Lakshman, the eldest brother of the deified King Rama, cut off the nose of the giantess Sarpnaka, sister of Ravana, who stole Sita, the "Helen of Troy" of the Hindus.

The train stops six miles from the town, so that we had to finish our journey in six two-wheeled, gilded chariots, called ekkas, and drawn by bullocks. It was one o'clock A.M., but, in spite of the darkness of the hour, the horns of the animals were gilded and adorned with flowers, and brass bangles tinkled on their legs. Our way lay through ravines overgrown with jungle, where, as our drivers hastened to inform us, tigers and other four-footed misanthropes of the forest played hide-and-seek. However, we had no opportunity of making the acquaintance of the tigers, but enjoyed instead a concert of a whole community of jackals. They followed us step by step, piercing our ears with shrieks, wild laughter and barking. These animals are annoying, but so cowardly that, though numerous enough to devour, not only all of us, but our gold-horned bullocks too, none of them dared to come nearer than the distance of a few steps. Every time the long whip, our weapon against snakes, alighted on the back of one of them, the whole horde disappeared with unimaginable noise. Nevertheless, the drivers did not dispense with a single one of their superstitious precautions against tigers. They chanted mantrams in unison, spread betel over the road as a token of their respect to the Rajas of the forest, and, after every couplet, made the bullocks kneel and bow their heads in honour of the great gods. Needless to say, the ekka, as light as a nutshell, threatened each time to fall with its passenger over the horns of the bullocks. We had to endure this agreeable way of travelling for five hours under a very dark sky. We reached the Inn of the Pilgrims in the morning at about six o'clock.

The real cause of Nassik's sacredness, however, is not the mutilated trunk of the giantess, but the situation of the town on the banks of the Godavari, quite close to the sources of this river which, for some reason or other, are called by the natives Ganga (Ganges). It is to this magic name, probably, that the town owes its numerous magnificent temples, and the selectness of the Brahmans who inhabit the banks of the river. Twice a year pilgrims flock here to pray, and on these solemn occasions the number of the visitors exceeds that of the inhabitants, which is only 35,000. Very picturesque, but equally dirty, are the houses of the rich Brahmans built on both sides of the way from the centre of the town to the Godavari. A whole forest of narrow pyramidal temples spreads on both sides of the river. All these new pagodas are built on the ruins of those destroyed by the fanaticism of the Mussulmans. A legend informs us that most of them rose from the ashes of the tail of the monkey god Hanuman. Retreating from Lanka, where the wicked Ravana, having anointed the brave hero's tail with some combustible stuff set it on fire, Hanuman, with a single leap through the air, reached Nassik, his fatherland. And here the noble adornment of the monkey's back, burned almost entirely during the voyage, crumbled into ashes, and from every sacred atom of these ashes, fallen to the ground, there rose a temple. . . . . And, indeed, when seen from the mountain, these numberless pagodas, scattered in a most curious disorderly way, look as if they had really been thrown down by handfuls from the sky. Not only the river banks and the surrounding country, but every little island, every rock peeping from the water is covered with temples. And not one of them is destitute of a legend of its own, different versions of which are told by every individual of the Brahmanical community according to his own taste—of course in the hope of a suitable reward.

Here, as everywhere else in India, Brahmans are divided into two sects—worshippers of Shiva and worshippers of Vishnu—and between the two there is rivalry and warfare centuries old. Though the neighbourhood of the Godavari shines with a twofold fame derived from its being the birthplace of Hanuman and the theatre of the first great deeds of Rama, the incarnation of Vishnu, it possesses as many temples dedicated to Shiva as to Vishnu. The material of which the pagodas consecrated to Shiva are constructed is black basalt. And it is, exactly, the colour of the material which is the apple of discord in this case. The black material is claimed by the Vaishnavas as their own, it being of the same colour as the burned tail of Rama's ally. They try to prove that the Shivaites have no right to it. From the first days of their rule the English inherited endless law-suits between the fighting sectarians, cases decided in one law-court only to be transferred on appeal to another, and always having their origin in this ill-omened tail and its pretensions. This tail is a mysterious *deus ex machina* that directs all the thoughts of the Nassik Brahmans *pro* and *contra*.

On the subject of this tail were written more reams of paper and petitions than in the quarrel about the goose between Ivan Ivanitch and Ivan Nikiphoritch; and more ink and bile were spilt than there was mud in Mirgorod, since the creation of the universe. The pig that so happily decided the famous quarrel in Gogol would be a priceless blessing to Nassik, and the struggle for the tail. But unhappily even the "pig" if it hailed from "Russia" would be of no avail in India; for the English would suspect it at once, and arrest it as a Russian spy!

Rama's bathing place is shown in Nassik. The ashes of pious Brahmans are brought hither from distant parts to be thrown into the Godavari, and so to mingle for ever with the sacred waters of Ganges. In an ancient MS. there is a statement of one of Rama's generals, who, somehow or other, is not mentioned in the *Ramayana*. This statement points to the river Godavari as the frontier between the kingdoms of Rama, King of Ayodya (Oude), and of Ravana, King of Lanka (Ceylon). Legends and the poem of *Ramayana* state that this was the spot where Rama, while hunting, saw a beautiful antelope, and, intending to make a present to his beloved Sita of its skin, entered the regions of his unknown neighbour. No doubt Rama, Ravana, and even Hanuman, promoted, for some unexplained reason, to the rank of a monkey, are historical personages who once had a real existence. About fifty years ago it was vaguely suspected that the Brahmans possessed priceless MSS. It was reported that one of these MSS. treats of the prehistoric epoch when the Aryans first invaded the country, and began an endless war with the dark aborigines of southern India. But the religious fanaticism of the Hindus never allowed the English Government to verify these reports.

The most interesting sights of Nassik are its cave-temples, about five miles from the town. The day before we started thither, I certainly did not dream that a "tail" would have to play an important part in our visit to Nassik, that, in this case, it would save me, if not from death, at least from disagreeable and perhaps dangerous bruises. This is how it happened.

As the difficult task of ascending a steep mountain lay before us, we decided to hire elephants. The best couple in the town was brought before us. Their owner assured us "that the Prince of Wales had ridden upon them and was very contented." To go there and back and have them in attendance the whole day—in fact the whole pleasure-trip—was to cost us two rupees for each elephant. Our native friends, accustomed from infancy to this way of riding, were not long in getting on the back of their elephant. They covered him like flies, with no predilection for this or that spot of his vast back. They held on by all kinds of strings and ropes, more with their toes than their fingers, and, on the whole, presented a picture of contentment and comfort. We Europeans had to use the lady elephant, as being the tamer of the two. On her back there were two little benches with sloping seats on both sides, and not the slightest prop for our backs. The wretched, undergrown youngsters seen in European circuses give no idea of the real size of this noble beast. The mahout, or driver, placed himself between the huge animal's ears whilst we gazed at the "perfected" seats ready for us with an uneasy feeling of distrust The mahout ordered his elephant to kneel, and it must be owned that in climbing on her back with the aid of a small ladder I felt what the French call *chair de poule*. Our she-elephant answered to the poetical name of "Chanchuli Peri," the Active Fairy, and really was the most obedient and the merriest of all the representatives of her tribe that I have ever seen. Clinging to each other we at last gave the signal for departure, and the mahout goaded the right ear of the animal with an iron rod. First the elephant raised herself on her fore-legs, which movement tilted us all back, then she heavily rose on her hind ones, too, and we rolled forwards, threatening to upset the mahout. But this was not the end of our misfortunes. At the very first steps of Peri we slipped about in all directions, like quivering fragments of blancmange.

The journey came to a sudden pause. We were picked up in a hasty way, replaced on our respective seats, during which proceeding Peri's trunk proved very active, and the journey continued. The very thought of the five miles before us filled us with horror, but we would not give up the excursion, and indignantly refused to be tied to our seats, as was suggested by our Hindu companions, who could not suppress their merry laughter. . . However, I bitterly repented this display of vanity. This unusual mode of locomotion was something incredibly fantastical, and, at the same time, ridiculous. A horse carrying our luggage trotted by Peri's side, and looked, from our vast elevation, no bigger than a donkey. At every mighty step of Peri we had to be prepared for all sorts of unexpected acrobatic feats, while jolted from one side to the other by her swinging gait. This experience, under the scorching sun, unavoidably induced a state of body and mind something between sea-sickness and a delirious nightmare. As a crown to our pleasures, when we began to ascend a tortuous little path over the stony slope of a deep ravine, our Peri stumbled. This sudden shock caused me to lose my balance altogether. I sat on the hinder part of the elephant's back, in the place of honour, as it is esteemed, and, once thoroughly shaken, rolled down like a log. No doubt, next moment I should have found myself at the bottom of the ravine, with some more or less sad loss to my bodily constitution, if it had not been for the wonderful dexterity and instinct of the clever animal. Having felt that something was wrong she twisted her tail round me, stopped instantaneously and began to kneel down carefully. But my natural weight was too much for the thin tail of this kind animal. Peri did not lose hold of me, but, having at last knelt down, she moaned plaintively, though discreetly, thinking probably that she had nearly lost her tail through being so generous. The mahout hurried to my rescue and then examined the damaged tail of his animal.

We now witnessed a scene that clearly showed us the coarse cunning, greediness and cowardice of a low-class Hindu, of an outcast, as they are denominated here.

The mahout very indifferently and composedly examined Peri's tail, and even pulled it several times to make sure, and was already on the point of hoisting himself quietly into his usual place, when I had the unhappy thought of muttering something that expressed my regret and compassion. My words worked a miraculous transformation in the mahout's behaviour. He threw himself on the ground, and rolled about like a demoniac, uttering horrible wild groans. Sobbing and crying he kept on repeating that the Mam-Sahib had torn off his darling Peri's tail, that Peri was damaged for ever in everybody's estimation, that Peri's husband, the proud Airavati, lineal descendant of Indra's own favourite elephant, having witnessed her shame, would renounce his spouse, and that she had better die. . . . Yells and bitter tears were his only answer to all remonstrances of our companions. In vain we tried to persuade him that the "proud Airavati" did not show the slightest disposition to be so cruel, in vain we pointed out to him that all this time both elephants stood quietly together, Airavati even at this critical moment rubbing his trunk affectionately against Peri's neck, and Peri not looking in the least discomfited by the accident to her tail. All this was of no avail! Our friend Narayan lost his patience at last. He was a man of extraordinary muscular strength and took recourse to a last original means. With one hand he threw down a silver rupee, with the other he seized the mahout's muslin garment and hurled him after the coin. Without giving a thought to his bleeding nose, the mahout jumped at the rupee with the greediness of a wild beast springing upon its prey. He prostrated himself in the dust before us repeatedly, with endless "salaams," instantly changing his deep sorrow into mad joy. He gave another pull at the unfortunate tail and gladly declared that, thanks to the "prayers of the sahib," it really was safe; to demonstrate which he hung on to it, till he was torn away and put back on his seat.

"Is it possible that a single, miserable rupee can have been the cause of all this?" we asked each other in utter bewilderment.

"Your astonishment is natural enough," answered the Hindus. "We need not express how ashamed and how disgusted we all feel at this voluntary display of humiliation and greed. But do not forget that this wretch, who certainly has a wife and children, serves his employer for twelve rupees a year, instead of which he often gets nothing but a beating. Remember also the long centuries of tyrannical treatment from Brahmans, from fanatical Mussulmans, who regard a Hindu as nothing better than an unclean reptile, and, nowadays, from the average Englishman, and maybe you will pity this wretched caricature of humanity."

But the "caricature" in question evidently felt perfectly happy and not in the least conscious of a humiliation of any kind. Sitting on the roomy forehead of his Peri, he was telling her of his unexpected wealth, reminding her of her "divine" origin, and ordering her to salute the "sahibs" with her trunk. Peri, whose spirits had been raised by the gift of a whole stick of sugar-cane from me, lifted her trunk backwards and playfully blew into our faces.

On the threshold of the Nassik caves we bid good-bye to the modern pigmy India, to the petty things of her everyday life, and to her humiliations. We re-entered the unknown world of India, the great and the mysterious.

The main caves of Nassik are excavated in a mountain bearing the name of Pandu-Lena, which points again to the undying, persistent, primæval tradition that ascribes all such buildings to the five mythical (?) brothers of prehistoric times. The unanimous opinion of archæologists esteems these caves more interesting and more important than all the caves of Elephanta and Karli put together. And, nevertheless—is it not strange?—with the exception of the learned Dr. Wilson, who, it may be, was a little too fond of forming hasty opinions, no archæologist has, as yet, made so bold as to decide to what epoch they belong, by whom they were erected, and which of the three chief religions of antiquity was the one professed by their mysterious builders.

It is evident, however, that those who wrought here did not all belong either to the same generation or to the same sect. The first thing which strikes the attention is the roughness of the primitive work, its huge dimensions, and the decline of the sculpture on the solid walls, whereas the sculpture and carvings of the six colossi which prop the chief cave on the second floor, are magnificently preserved and very elegant. This circumstance would lead one to think that the work was begun many centuries before it was finished. But when? One of the Sanskrit inscriptions of a comparatively recent epoch (on the pedestal of one of the colossi) clearly points to 453 B.C. as the year of the building. At all events, Barth, Stevenson, Gibson, Reeves, and some other scientists, who being Westerns can have none of the prejudices proper to the native Pundits, have formed this conjecture on the basis of some astronomical data. Besides, the conjunction of the planets stated in the inscription leaves no doubt as to the dates, it must be either 453 B.C., or 1734 of our era, or 2640 B.C., which last is impossible, because Buddha and Buddhist monasteries are mentioned in the inscription. I translate some of the most important sentences:

"To the most Perfect and the Highest! May this be agreeable to Him! The son of King Kshaparata, Lord of the Kshatriya tribe and protector of people, the Ruler of Dinik, bright as the dawn, sacrifices a hundred thousand cows that graze on the river Banasa, together with the river, and also the gift of gold by the builder of this holy shelter of gods, the place of the curbing of the Brahmans' passions. There is no more desirable place than this place, neither in Prabhâsa, where accumulate hundreds of thousands of Brahmans repeating the sacred verse, nor in the sacred city Gaya, nor on the steep mountain near Dashatura, nor on the Serpents' Field in Govardhana, nor in the city Pratisraya where stands the monastery of Buddhists, nor even in the edifice erected by Depanakara on the shores of the fresh water [?] sea. This place, giving incomparable favours, is agreeable and useful in all respects to the spotted deerskin of an ascetic. A safe boat given also by him who built the gratuitous ferry daily transports to the well-guarded shore. By him also who built the house for travellers and the public fountain, a gilded lion was erected by the ever-assaulted gate of this Govardhana, also another [lion] by the ferry-boat, and another by Ramatirtha. Various kinds of food will always be found here by the scanty flock; for this flock more than a hundred kinds of herbs and thousands of mountain roots are stored by this generous giver. In the same Govardhana, in the luminous mountain, this second cave was dug by the order of the same beneficent person, *during the very year when the Sun, Shukra and Rahu, much respected by men, were in the full glory of their rise;* it was in this year that the gifts were offered. Lakshmi, Indra and Yama having blessed them, returned with shouts of triumph to their chariot, kept on the way free from obstacles [the sky], by the force of mantrams. When they [the gods] all left, poured a heavy shower. . . " and so on.

Rahu and Kehetti are the fixed stars which form the head and the tail of the constellation of the Dragon. Shukra is Venus. Lakshmi, Indra and Yama stand here for the constellations of Virgo, Aquarius and Taurus, which are subject and consecrated to these three among the twelve higher deities.

The first caves are dug out in a conical hillock about two hundred and eighty feet from its base. In the chief of them stand three statues of Buddha; in the lateral ones a lingam and two Jaina idols. In the top cave there is a statue of Dharma Raja, or Yudhshtira, the eldest of the Pandus, who is worshipped in a temple erected in his honour between Pent and Nassik. Farther on is a whole labyrinth of cells, where Buddhist hermits probably lived, a huge statue of Buddha in a reclining posture, and another as big, but surrounded with pillars adorned with figures of various animals. Styles, epochs and sects are here as much mixed up and entangled as different trees in a thick forest.

It is very remarkable that almost all the cave temples of India are to be found inside conical rocks and mountains. It is as though the ancient builders looked for such natural pyramids purposely. I noticed this peculiarity in Karli, and it is to be met with only in India. Is it a mere coincidence, or is it one of the rules of the religious architecture of the remote past? And which are the imitators—the builders of the Egyptian pyramids, or the unknown architects of the underground caves of India? In pyramids as well as in caves everything seems to be calculated with geometrical exactitude. In neither case are the entrances ever at the bottom, but always at a certain distance from the ground. It is well known that nature does not imitate art, and, as a rule, art tries to copy certain forms of nature. And if, even in this similarity of the symbols of Egypt and India, nothing is to be found but a coincidence, we shall have to own that coincidences are sometimes very extraordinary. Egypt has borrowed many things from India. We must not forget that nothing is known about the origin of the Pharaohs, and that the few facts science has succeeded in discovering, far from contradicting our theory, suggest India as the cradle of the Egyptian race. In the days of remote antiquity Kalluka-Bhatta wrote: "During the reign of Visvamitra, first king of the Somâ-Vansha dynasty, after a five days battle, Manu-Vena, the heir of ancient kings, was abandoned by the Brahmans, and emigrated with his army, and, having traversed Arya and Barria, at last reached the shores of Masra. . . . ."

Arya is Iran or Persia; Barria is an ancient name of

Arabia; Masr or Masra is a name of Cairo, disfigured by Mussulmans into Misro and Musr.

Kalluka-Bhatta is an ancient writer. Sanskritists still quarrel over his epoch, wavering between 2,000 years B.C., and the reign of the Emperor Akbar (the time of John the Terrible and Elizabeth of England). On the grounds of this uncertainty, the evidence of Kalluka-Bhatta might be objected to. In this case, there are the words of a modern historian, who has studied Egypt all his life, not in Berlin or London, like some other historians, but in Egypt, deciphering the inscriptions of the oldest sarcophagi and papyri, that is to say, the words of Henry Brugsch-Bey:

". . . I repeat, my firm conviction is that the Egyptians came from Asia long before the historical period, having traversed the Suez promontory, that bridge of all the nations, and found a new fatherland on the banks of the Nile."

An inscription on a Hammamat rock says that Sankara, the last Pharaoh of the eleventh dynasty, sent a nobleman to Punt: "I was sent on a ship to Punt, to bring back some aromatic gum, gathered by the princes of the Red Land."

Commenting on this inscription, Brugsch-Bey explains that "under the name of Punt the ancient inhabitants of Chemi meant a distant land surrounded by a great ocean, full of mountains and valleys, and rich in ebony and other expensive woods, in perfumes, precious stones and metals, in wild beasts, giraffes, leopards and big monkeys." The name of a monkey in Egypt was Kaff, or Kafi, in Hebrew Koff, in Sanskrit Kapi.

In the eyes of the ancient Egyptians, this Punt was a sacred land, because Punt or Pa-nuter was "the original land of the gods, who left it under the leadership of

A-Mon [Manu-Vena of Kalluka-Bhatta?] Hor and Hator, and duly arrived in Chemi."

Hanuman has a decided family likeness to the Egyptian Cynocephalus, and the emblem of Osiris and Shiva is the same. *Qui vivra verra!*

Our return journey was very agreeable. We had adapted ourselves to Peri's movements, and felt ourselves first-rate jockeys. But for a whole week afterwards we could hardly walk.

A CITY OF THE DEAD.

WHAT would be your choice if you had to choose between being blind and being deaf? Nine people out of ten answer this question by positively preferring deafness to blindness. And one whose good fortune it has been to contemplate, even for a moment, some fantastic fairy-like corner of India, this country of lace-like marble palaces and enchanting gardens, would willingly add to deafness, lameness of both legs, rather than lose such sights.

We are told that Saadi, the great poet, bitterly complained of his friends looking tired and indifferent while he praised the beauty and charm of his lady-love. "If the happiness of contemplating her wonderful beauty," remonstrated he, "was yours, as it is mine, you could not fail to understand my verses, which, alas, describe in such meagre and inadequate terms the rapturous feelings experienced by every one who sees her even from a distance!"

I fully sympathize with the enamoured poet, but cannot condemn his friends who never saw his lady-love, and that is, why I tremble lest my constant rhapsodies on India should bore my readers as much as Saadi bored his friends. But what, I pray you, is the poor narrator to do, when new, undreamed-of charms are daily discovered in the lady-love in question? Her darkest aspects, abject and immoral as they are, and sometimes of such a nature as to excite your horror—even these aspects are full of some wild poetry, of originality, which cannot be met with in any other country. It is not unusual for a European novice to shudder with disgust at some features of local everyday life; but at the same time these very sights attract and fascinate the attention like a horrible nightmare. We had plenty of these experiences whilst our *école buissonière* lasted. We spent these days far from railways and from any other vestige of civilization. Happily so, because European civilization does not suit India any better than a fashionable bonnet would suit a half naked Peruvian maiden, a true "daughter of Sun," of Cortes' time.

All the day long we wandered across rivers and jungles, passing villages and ruins of ancient fortresses, over local-board roads between Nassik and Jubblepore, travelling with the aid of bullock cars, elephants, horses, and very often being carried in *palks*. At nightfall we put up our tents and slept anywhere. These days offered us an opportunity of seeing that man decidedly can surmount trying and even dangerous conditions of climate, though, perhaps, in a passive way, by mere force of habit. In the afternoons, when we, white people, were very nearly fainting with the roasting heat, in spite of thick cork *topis* and such shelter as we could procure, and even our native companions had to use more than the usual supplies of muslin round their heads—the Bengali Babu travelled on horseback endless miles, under the vertical rays of the hot sun, *bareheaded*, protected only by his thick crop of hair. The sun has no influence whatever on Bengali skulls. They are covered only on solemn occasions, in cases of weddings and great festivities. Their turbans are useless adornments, like flowers in a European lady's hair.

Bengali Babus are born clerks; they invade all railroad stations, post and telegraph offices and Government law courts. Wrapped in their white muslin *toga virilis*, their legs bare up to the knees, their heads unprotected, they proudly loaf on the platforms of railway stations, or at the entrances of their offices, casting contemptuous glances on the Mahrattis, who dearly love their numerous rings and lovely earrings in the upper part of their right ears. Bengalis, unlike the rest of the Hindus, do not paint sectarian signs on their foreheads. The only trinket they do not completely despise is an expensive necklace; but even this is not common. Contrary to all expectations, the Mahrattis, with all their little effeminate ways, are the bravest tribe of India, gallant and experienced soldiers, a fact which has been demonstrated by centuries of fighting; but Bengal has never as yet produced a single soldier out of its sixty-five million inhabitants. Not a single Bengali is to be found in the native regiments of the British army. This is a strange fact, which I refused to believe at first, but which has been confirmed by many English officers and by Bengalis themselves. But with all this, they are far from being cowardly. Their wealthy classes do lead a somewhat effeminate life, but their zemindars and peasantry are undoubtedly brave. Disarmed by their present Government, the Bengali peasants go out to meet the tiger, which in their country is more ferocious than elsewhere, armed only with a club, as composedly as they used to go with rifles and swords.

Many out-of-the-way paths and groves which most probably had never before been trodden by a European foot, were visited by us during these short days. Gulab-Lal-Sing was absent, but we were accompanied by a trusted servant of his, and the welcome we met with almost everywhere was certainly the result of the magic influence of his name. If the wretched, naked peasants shrank from us and shut their doors at our approach, the Brahmans were as obliging as could be desired.

The sights around Kandesh, on the way to Thalner and Mhau, are very picturesque. But the effect is not entirely due to Nature's beauty. Art has a good deal to do with it, especially in Mussulman cemeteries. Now they are all more or less destroyed and deserted, owing to the increase of the Hindu inhabitants around them, and to the Mussulman princes, once the rightful lords of India, being expelled. Mussulmans of the present day are badly off and have to put up with more humiliations than even the Hindus. But still they have left many memorials behind them, and, amongst others, their cemeteries. The Mussulman fidelity to the dead is a very touching feature of their character. Their devotion to those that are gone is always more demonstrative than their affection for the living members of their families, and almost entirely concentrates itself on their last abodes. In proportion as their notions of paradise are coarse and material, the appearance of their cemeteries is poetical, especially in India. One may pleasantly spend whole hours in these shady, delightful gardens, amongst their white monuments crowned with turbans, covered with roses and jessamine and sheltered with rows of cypresses. We often stopped in such places to sleep and dine. A cemetery near Thalner is especially attractive. Out of several mausoleums in a good state of preservation the most magnificent is the monument of the family of Kiladar, who was hanged on the city tower by the order of General Hislop in 1818. Four other mausoleums attracted our attention and we learned that one of them is celebrated throughout India. It is a white marble octagon, covered from top to bottom with carving, the like of which could not be found even in Père La Chaise. A Persian inscription on its base records that it cost one hundred thousand rupees.

By day, bathed in the hot rays of the sun, its tall minaret-like outline looks like a block of ice against the blue sky. By night, with the aid of the intense, phosphorescent moonlight proper to India, it is still more dazzling and poetical. The summit looks as if it were covered with freshly fallen snow-crystals. Raising its slender profile above the dark background of bushes, it suggests some pure midnight apparition, soaring over this silent abode of destruction and lamenting what will never return. Side by side with these cemeteries rise the Hindu ghâts, generally by the river bank. There really is something grand in the ritual of burning the dead. Witnessing this ceremony the spectator is struck with the deep philosophy underlying the fundamental idea of this custom. In the course of an hour nothing remains of the body but a few handfuls of ashes. A professional Brahman, like a priest of death, scatters these ashes to the winds over a river. The ashes of what once lived and felt, loved and hated, rejoiced and wept, are thus given back again to the four elements: to *Earth*, which fed it during such a long time and out of which it grew and developed; to *Fire*, emblem of purity, that has just devoured the body in order that the spirit may be rid of everything impure, and may freely gravitate to the new sphere of posthumous existence, where every sin is a stumbling block on the way to "Moksha," or infinite bliss; to *Air*, which it inhaled and through which it lived, and to *Water*, which purified it physically and spiritually, and is now to receive its ashes into her pure bosom.

The adjective "pure" must be understood in the figurative sense of the mantram. Generally speaking, the rivers of India, beginning with the thrice sacred Ganges, are dreadfully dirty, especially near villages and towns.

In these rivers about two hundred millions of people daily cleanse themselves from the tropical perspiration and dirt. The corpses of those who are not worth burning are thrown in the same rivers, and their number is great, because it includes all Shudras, pariahs, and various other outcasts, as well as Brahman children under three years of age.

Only rich and high-born people are buried pompously. It is for them that the sandal-wood fires are lit after sunset; it is for them that mantrams are chanted, and for them that the gods are invoked. But Shudras must not listen on any account to the divine words dictated at the beginning of the world by the four Rishis to Veda-Vyasa, the great theologian of Aryavarta. No fires for them, no prayers. As during his life a Shudra never approaches a temple nearer than seven steps, so even after death he cannot be put on the same level with the "twice-born."

Brightly burn the fires, extending like a fiery serpent along the river. The dark outlines of strange, wildly-fantastical figures silently move amongst the flames. Sometimes they raise their arms towards the sky, as if in a prayer, sometimes they add fuel to the fires and poke them with long iron pitchforks. The dying flames rise high, creeping and dancing, sputtering with melted human fat and shooting towards the sky whole showers of golden sparks, which are instantly lost in the clouds of black smoke.

This on the right side of the river. Let us now see what is going on on the left. In the early hours of the morning, when the red fires, the black clouds of miasmas, and the thin figures of the fakirs grow dim and vanish little by little, when the smell of burned flesh is blown away by the fresh wind which rises at the approach of the dawn, when, in a word, the right side of the river with its ghotas plunges into stillness and silence, to be reawakened when the evening comes, processions of a different kind appear on the left bank. We see groups of Hindu men and women in sad, silent trains. They approach the river quietly. They do not cry, and have no rituals to perform. We see two men carrying something long and thin, wrapped in an old red rug. Holding it by the head and feet they swing it into the dirty, yellowish waves of the river. The shock is so violent that the red rug flies open and we behold the face of a young woman tinged with dark green, who quickly disappears in the river. Further on another group; an old man and two young women. One of them, a little girl of ten, small, thin, hardly fully developed, sobs bitterly. She is the mother of a still-born child, whose body is to be thrown in the river. Her weak voice monotonously resounds over the shore, and her trembling hands are not strong enough to lift the poor little corpse that is more like a tiny brown kitten than a human being. The old man tries to console her, and, taking the body in his own hands, enters the water and throws it right in the middle. After him both the women get into the river, and, having plunged seven times to purify themselves from the touch of a dead body, they return home, their clothes dripping with wet. In the meanwhile vultures, crows and other birds of prey gather in thick clouds and considerably retard the progress of the bodies down the river. Occasionally some half-stripped skeleton is caught by the reeds, and stranded there helplessly for weeks, until an outcast, whose sad duty it is to busy himself all his life long with such unclean work, takes notice of it, and catching it by the ribs with his long hook, restores it to its highway towards the ocean.

But let us leave the river bank, which is unbearably hot in spite of the early hour. Let us bid good-bye to the watery cemetery of the poor. Disgusting and heart-rending are such sights in the eyes of a European! And unconsciously we allow the light wings of reverie to transport us to the far North, to the peaceful village cemeteries where there are no marble monuments crowned with turbans, no sandal-wood fires, no dirty rivers to serve the purpose of a last resting place, but where humble wooden crosses stand in rows, sheltered by old birches. How peacefully our dead repose under the rich green grass! None of them ever saw these gigantic palms, sumptuous palaces and pagodas covered with gold. But on their poor graves grow violets and lilies of the valley, and in the spring evenings nightingales sing to them in the old birch-trees.

No nightingales ever sing for me, either in the neighbouring groves, or in my own heart. The latter least of all.

Let us stroll along this wall of reddish stone. It will lead us to a fortress once celebrated and drenched with blood, now harmless and half ruined, like many another Indian fortress. Flocks of green parrots, startled by our approach, fly from under every cavity of the old wall, their wings shining in the sun like so many flying emeralds. This territory is accursed by Englishmen. This is Chandvad, where, during the Sepoy mutiny, the Bhils streamed from their ambuscades like a mighty mountain torrent, and cut many an English throat.

Tatva, an ancient Hindu book, treating of the geography of the times of King Asoka (250-300 B.C.), teaches us that the Mahratti territory spreads up to the wall of Chandvad or Chandor, and that the Kandesh country begins on the other side of the river. But English people do not believe in *Tatva* or in any other authority and want us to learn that Kandesh begins right at the foot of Chandor hillocks.

Twelve miles south-east from Chandvad there is a whole town of subterranean temples, known under the name of Enkay-Tenkay. Here, again, the entrance is a hundred feet from the base, and the hill is pyramidal. I must not attempt to give a full description of these temples, as this subject must be worked out in a way quite impossible in a newspaper article. So I shall only note that here all the statues, idols, and carvings are ascribed to Buddhist ascetics of the first centuries after the death of Buddha. I wish I could content myself with this statement. But, unfortunately, *messieurs les archeologues* meet here with an unexpected difficulty, and a more serious one than all the difficulties brought on them by the inconsistencies of all other temples put together. In these temples there are more idols designated Buddhas than anywhere else. They cover the main entrance, sit in thick rows along the balconies, occupy the inner walls of the cells, watch the entrances of all the doors like monster giants, and two of them sit in the chief tank, where spring water washes them century after century without any harm to their granite bodies. Some of these Buddhas are decently clad, with pyramidal pagodas as their head gear; others are naked; some sit, others stand; some are real colossi, some tiny, some of middle size. However, all this would not matter; we may go so far as to overlook the fact of Gautama's or Siddhartha-Buddha's reform consisting precisely in his earnest desire to tear up by the roots the Brahmanical idol-worship. Though, of course, we cannot help remembering that his religion remained pure from idol-worship of any kind during centuries, until the Lamas of Tibet, the Chinese, the Burmese, and the Siamese taking it into their lands disfigured it, and spoilt it with heresies. We cannot forget that, persecuted by conquering Brahmans, and expelled from India, it found, at last, a shelter in Ceylon where it still flourishes like the legendary aloe, which is said to blossom once in its lifetime and then to die, as the root is killed by the exuberance of blossom, and the seeds cannot produce anything but weeds. All this we may overlook, as I said before. But the difficulty of the archæologists still exists, if not in the fact of idols being ascribed to early Buddhists, then in the physiognomies, in the *type* of all these Enkay-Tenkay Buddhas. They all, from the tiniest to the hugest, are *Negroes*, with flat noses, thick lips, forty-five degrees of the facial angle, and curly hair! There is not the slightest likeness between these negro faces and any of the Siamese or Tibetan Buddhas, which all have purely Mongolian features and perfectly straight hair. This unexpected African type, unheard of in India, upsets the antiquarians entirely. This is why the archæologists avoid mentioning these caves. Enkay-Tenkay is a worse difficulty for them than even Nassik; they find it as hard to conquer as the Persians found Thermopylæ.

We passed by Maleganva and Chikalval, where we examined an exceedingly curious ancient temple of the Jainas. No cement was used in the building of its outer walls, they consist entirely of square stones, which are so well wrought and so closely joined that the blade of the thinnest knife cannot be pushed between two of them; the interior of the temple is richly decorated.

On our way back we did not stop in Thalner, but went straight on to Ghara. There we had to hire elephants again to visit the splendid ruins of Mandu, once a strongly fortified town, about twenty miles due north-east of this place. This time we got there speedily and safely. I mention this place because some time later I witnessed in its vicinity a most curious sight, offered by the branch of the numerous Indian rites, which is generally called "devil worship."

Mandu is situated on the ridge of the Vindhya Mountains, about two thousand feet above the surface of the sea. According to Malcolm's statement, this town was built in A.D. 313, and for a long time was the capital of the Hindu Rajas of Dhara. The historian Ferishtah points to Mandu as the residence of Dilivan-Khan-Ghuri, the first King of Malwa, who flourished in 1387-1405. In 1526 the town was taken by Bahadur-Shah, King of Gujerat, but in 1570 Akbar won this town back, and a marble slab over the town gate still bears his name and the date of his visit.

On entering this vast city in its present state of solitude (the natives call it the "dead town") we all experienced a peculiar feeling, not unlike the sensation of a man who enters Pompeii for the first time. Everything shows that Mandu was once one of the wealthiest towns of India. The town wall is thirty-seven miles long. Streets ran whole miles, on their sides stand ruined palaces, and marble pillars lie on the ground. Black excavations of the subterranean halls, in the coolness of which rich ladies spent the hottest hours of the day, peer from under dilapidated granite walls. Further on are broken stairs, dry tanks, waterless fountains, endless empty yards, marble platforms, and disfigured arches of majestic porches. All this is overgrown with creepers and shrubs, hiding the dens of wild beasts. Here and there a well-preserved wall of some palace rises high above the general wreck, its empty windows fringed with parasitic plants blinking and staring at us like sightless eyes, protesting against troublesome intruders. And still further, in the very centre of the ruins, the heart of the dead town sends forth a whole crop of broken cypresses, an untrimmed grove on the place where heaved once so many breasts and clamoured so many passions.

In 1570 this town was called *Shadiabad*, the abode of happiness. The Franciscan missionaries, Adolf Aquaviva, Antario de Moncerotti, and others, who came here in that very year as an embassy from Goa to seek various privileges from the Mogul Government, described it over and over again. At this epoch it was one of the greatest cities of the world, whose magnificent streets and luxurious ways used to astonish the most pompous courts of India. It seems almost incredible that in such a short period nothing should remain of this town but the heaps of rubbish, amongst which we could hardly find room enough for our tent. At last we decided to pitch it in the only building which remained in a tolerable state of preservation, in Yami-Masjid, the cathedral-mosque, on a granite platform about twenty-five steps higher than the square. The stairs, constructed of pure marble like the greater part of the town buildings, are broad and almost untouched by time, but the roof has entirely disappeared, and so we were obliged to put up with the stars for a canopy.

All round this building runs a low gallery supported by several rows of thick pillars. From a distance it reminds one, in spite of its being somewhat clumsy and lacking in proportion, of the Acropolis of Athens. From the stairs, where we rested for a while, there was a view of the mausoleum of Gushanga-Guri, King of Malwa, in whose reign the town was at the culmination of its brilliancy and glory. It is a massive, majestic, white marble edifice, with a sheltered peristyle and finely carved pillars. This peristyle once led straight to the palace, but now it is surrounded with a deep ravine, full of broken stones and overgrown with cacti. The interior of the mausoleum is covered with golden lettering of inscriptions from the Koran, and the sarcophagus of the sultan is placed in the middle. Close by it stands the palace of Baz-Bahadur, all broken to pieces—nothing now but a heap of dust covered with trees.

We spent the whole day visiting these sad remains, and returned to our sheltering place a little before sunset, exhausted with hunger and thirst, but triumphantly carrying on our sticks three huge snakes, killed on our way home. Tea and supper were waiting for us. To our great astonishment we found visitors in the tent. The Patel of the neighbouring village—something between a tax-collector and a judge—and two zemindars (land owners) rode over to present us their respects and to invite us and our Hindu friends, some of whom they had known previously, to accompany them to their houses. On hearing that we intended to spend the night in the "dead town" they grew awfully indignant. They assured us it was highly dangerous and utterly impossible. Two hours later hyenas, tigers, and other beasts of prey were sure to come out from under every bush and every ruined wall, without mentioning thousands of jackals and wild cats. Our elephants would not stay, and if they did stay no doubt they would be devoured. We ought to leave the ruins as quickly as possible and go with them to the nearest village, which would not take us more than half an hour. In the village everything had been prepared for us, and our friend the Babu was already there, and getting impatient at our delay.

Only on hearing this did we become aware that our bareheaded and cautious friend was conspicuous by his absence. Probably he had left some time ago, without consulting us, and made straight to the village where he evidently had friends. Sending for us was a mere trick of his. But the evening was so sweet, and we felt so comfortable, that the idea of upsetting all our plans for the morning was not at all attractive. Besides, it seemed quite ridiculous to think that the ruins, amongst which we had wandered several hours without meeting anything more dangerous than a snake, swarmed with wild animals. So we smiled and returned thanks, but would not accept the invitation.

"But you positively must not dare to stay here," insisted the fat Patel. "In case of accident, I shall be responsible for you to the Government. Is it possible you do not dread a sleepless night spent in fighting jackals, if not something worse? You do not believe that you are surrounded with wild animals. . . . It is true they are invisible until sunset, but nevertheless they are dangerous. If you do not believe us, believe the instinct of your elephants, who are as brave as you, but a little more reasonable. Just look at them!"

We looked. Truly, our grave, philosophic-looking elephants behaved very strangely at this moment. Their lifted trunks looked like huge points of interrogation. They snorted and stamped restively. In another minute one of them tore the thick rope, with which he was tied to a broken pillar, made a sudden *volte-face* with all his heavy body, and stood against the wind, sniffing the air. Evidently he perceived some dangerous animal in the neighbourhood.

The colonel stared at him through his spectacles and whistled very meaningly.

"Well, well," remarked he, "what shall we do if tigers really assault us?"

"What shall we do indeed?" was my thought. "Takur Gulab-Lal-Sing is not here to protect us."

Our Hindu companions sat on the carpet after their oriental fashion, quietly chewing betel. On being asked their opinion, they said they would not interfere with our decision, and were ready to do exactly as we liked. But as for the European portion of our party, there was no use concealing the fact that we were frightened, and we speedily prepared to start. Five minutes later we mounted the elephants, and, in a quarter of an hour, just when the sun disappeared behind the mountain and heavy darkness instantaneously fell, we passed the gate of Akbar and descended into the valley.

We were hardly a quarter of a mile from our abandoned camping place when the cypress grove resounded with shrieking howls of jackals, followed by a well-known mighty roar. There was no longer any possibility of doubting. The tigers were disappointed at our escape. Their discontentment shook the very air, and cold perspiration stood on our brows. Our elephant sprang forward, upsetting the order of our procession and threatening to crush the horses and their riders before us. We ourselves, however, were out of danger. We sat in a strong *howdah*, locked as in a dungeon.

"It is useless to deny that we have had a narrow escape!" remarked the colonel, looking out of the window at some twenty servants of the Patel, who were busily lighting torches.

BRAHMANIC HOSPITALITIES.

In an hour's time we stopped at the gate of a large bungalow, and were welcomed by the beaming face of our bareheaded Bengali. When we were all safely gathered on the verandah, he explained to us that, knowing beforehand that our "American pigheadedness" would not listen to any warning, he had dodged up this little scheme of his own and was very glad he had been successful.

"Now let us go and wash our hands, and then to supper. And," he added, addressing me, "was it not your wish to be present at a real Hindu meal? This is your opportunity. Our host is a Brahman, and you are the first Europeans who ever entered the part of his house inhabited by the family."

Who amongst Europeans ever dreamed of a country where every step, and the least action of everyday life, especially of the family life, is controlled by religious rites and *cannot* be performed except according to a certain programme? India is this country. In India all the important incidents of a man's life, such as birth, reaching certain periods of a child's life, marriage, fatherhood, old age and death, as well as all the physical and physiological functions of everyday routine, like morning ablutions, dressing, eating, *et tout ce qui s'en suit*, from a man's first hour to his last sigh, everything must be performed according to a certain Brahmanical ritual, on penalty of expulsion from his caste. The Brahmans may be compared to the musicians of an orchestra in which the different musical instruments are the numerous sects of their country. They are all of a different shape and of a different *timbre;* but still every one of them obeys the same leader of the band. However widely the sects may differ in the interpretation of their sacred books, however hostile they may be to each other, striving to put forward their particular deity, every one of them, obeying blindly the ancient custom, must follow like musicians the same directing wand, the laws of Manu. This is the point where they all meet and form a unanimous, single-minded community, a strongly united mass. And woe to the one who breaks the symphony by a single discordant note! The elders and the caste or sub-caste councils (of these there are any number), whose members hold office for life, are stern rulers. There is no appeal against their decisions, and this is why expulsion from the caste is a calamity, entailing truly formidable consequences. The excommunicated member is worse off than a leper, the solidarity of the castes in this respect being something phenomenal. The only thing that can bear any comparison with it is the solidarity of the disciples of Loyola. If members of two different castes, united by the sincerest feelings of respect and friendship, may not intermarry, may not dine together, are forbidden to accept a glass of water from each other, or to offer each other a hookah, it becomes clear how much more severe all these restrictions must be in the case of an excommunicated person. The poor wretch must literally die to everybody, to the members of his own family as to strangers. His own household, his father, wife, children, are all bound to turn their faces from him, under the penalty of being excommunicated in their turn. There is no hope for his sons and daughters of getting married, however innocent they may be of the sin of their father.

From the moment of "excommunication" the Hindu must totally disappear. His mother and wife must not feed him, must not let him drink from the family well. No member of any existing caste dares to sell him his food or cook for him. He must either starve or buy eatables from outcasts and Europeans, and so incur the dangers of further pollution. When the Brahmanical power was at its zenith, such acts as deceiving, robbing and even killing this wretch were encouraged, as he was beyond the pale of the laws. Now, at all events, he is free from the latter danger, but still, even now, if he happens to die before he is forgiven and received back into his caste, his body may not be burned, and no purifying mantrams will be chanted for him; he will be thrown into the water, or left to rot under the bushes like a dead cat.

This is a passive force, and its passiveness only makes it more formidable. Western education and English influence can do nothing to change it. There exists only one course of action for the excommunicated; he must show signs of repentance and submit to all kinds of humiliations, often to the total loss of all his worldly possessions. Personally, I know several young Brahmans, who, having brilliantly passed the university examinations in England, have had to submit to the most repulsive conditions of purification on their return home; these purifications consisting chiefly in shaving off half their moustaches and eyebrows, crawling in the dust round pagodas, clinging during long hours to the tail of a sacred cow, and, finally, swallowing the excrements of this cow. The latter ceremony is called "Pancha-Gavya," literally, the five products of the cow: milk, curds, butter, etc. The voyage over Kalapani, the black water, that is to say the sea, is considered the worst of all the sins. A man who commits it is considered as polluting himself continually, from the first moment of his going on board the bellati (foreign) ship.

Only a few days ago a friend of ours, who is an LL.D., had to undergo this "purgation," and it nearly cost him his reason. When we remonstrated with him, pointing out that in his case it was simply foolish to submit, he being a materialist by conviction and not caring a straw for Brahmanism, he replied that he was bound to do so for the following reasons:

"I have two daughters," he explained, "one five, the other six years old. If I do not find a husband for the eldest of them in the course of the coming year, she will grow too old to get married, nobody will think of espousing her. Suppose I suffer my caste to excommunicate me, both my girls will be dishonoured and miserable for the rest of their lives. Then, again, I must take into consideration the superstitions of my old mother. If such a misfortune befell me, it would simply kill her. . . ."

But why should he not free himself from every bond to Brahmanism and caste? Why not join, once for all, the ever-growing community of men who are guilty of the same offence? Why not ask all his family to form a colony and join the civilization of the Europeans?

All these are very natural questions, but unfortunately there is no difficulty in finding reasons for answering them in the negative.

There were thirty-two reasons given why one of Napoleon's marshals refused to besiege a certain fortress, but the first of these reasons was the absence of gunpowder, and so it excluded the necessity of discussing the remaining thirty-one. Similarly the first reason why a Hindu cannot be Europeanized is quite sufficient, and does not call for any additional ones. This reason is that by doing so a Hindu *would not improve his position.* Were he such an adept of science as to rival Tyndall, were he such a clever politician as to eclipse the genius of Disraeli and Bismarck, as soon as he actually had given up his caste and kinsmen, he would indubitably find himself in the position of Mahomet's coffin; metaphorically speaking, he would hang half-way between the earth and the sky.

It would be an utter injustice to suppose that this state of things is the result of the policy of the English Government; that the said Government is afraid of giving a chance to natives who may be suspected of being hostile to the British rule. In reality, the Government has little or nothing to do with it. This state of things must be attributed entirely to the social ostracism, to the contempt felt by a "superior" for an "inferior" race, a contempt deeply rooted in some members of the Anglo-Indian society and displayed at the least provocation. This question of racial "superiority" and "inferiority" plays a more important part than is generally believed, even in England. Nevertheless, the natives (Mussulmans included) do not deserve contempt, and so the gulf between the rulers and the ruled widens with every year, and long centuries would not suffice to fill it up.

I have to dwell upon all this to give my readers a clear idea on the subject. And so it is no wonder the ill-fated Hindus prefer temporary humiliations and the physical and moral sufferings of the "purification," to the prospect of general contempt until death. These were the questions we discussed with the Brahmans during the two hours before dinner.

Dining with foreigners and people belonging to different castes is, no doubt, a dangerous breach of Manu's sacred precepts. But this time, for once, it was easily explained. First, the stout Patel, our host, was the head of his caste, and so was beyond the dread of ex-communication; secondly, he had already taken all the prescribed and advisable precautions against being polluted by our presence. He was a free-thinker in his own way, and a friend of Gulab-Lal-Sing, and so he rejoiced at the idea of showing us how much skilful sophistry and strategical circumspection can be used by adroit Brahmans to avoid the law in some circumstances, while adhering at the same time to its dead letter. Besides, our good-natured, well-favoured host evidently desired to obtain a diploma from our Society, being well aware that the collector of his district was enrolled amongst our members.

These, at any rate, were the explanations of our Babu when we expressed our astonishment; so it was our concern to make the most of our chance, and to thank Providence for this rare opportunity. And this we accordingly did.

Hindus take their food only twice a day, at ten o'clock in the morning and at nine in the evening. Both meals are accompanied by complicated rites and ceremonies. Even very young children are not allowed to eat at odd times, eating without the prescribed performance of certain exorcisms being considered a sin. Thousands of educated Hindus have long ceased to believe in all these superstitious customs, but, nevertheless, they are daily practised.

Sham Rao Bahunathji, our host, belonged to the ancient caste of Patarah Prabhus, and was very proud of his origin. Prabhu means lord, and this caste descends from the Kshatriyas. The first of them was Ashvapati (700 B.C.), a lineal descendant of Rama and Prithu, who, as is stated in the local chronology, governed India in the Dvapara and Treta Yugas, which is a good while ago! The Patarah Prabhus are the only caste within which Brahmans have to perform certain purely Vedic rites, known under the name of the "Kshatriya rites." But this does not prevent their being *Patans*, instead of *Patars*, Patan meaning the fallen one. This is the fault of King Ashvapati. Once, when distributing gifts to holy anchorites, he inadvertently forgot to give his due to the great Bhrigu. The offended prophet and seer declared to him that his reign was drawing near its end, and that all his posterity would perish. The king, throwing himself on the ground, implored the prophet's pardon. But his curse had worked its fulfilment already. All that he could do to stop the mischief consisted in a solemn promise not to let the king's descendants disappear completely from the earth. However, the Patars soon lost their throne and their power. Since then they have had to "live by their pens," in the employment of many successive governments, to exchange their name of Patars for Patans, and to lead a humbler life than many of their late subjects. Happily for our talkative Amphitryon, his forefathers became Brahmans, that is to say "went through the golden cow."

The expression "to live by their pens" alludes, as we learned later on, to the fact of the Patans occupying all the small Government posts in the Bombay Presidency, and so being dangerous rivals of the Bengali Babus since the time of British rule. In Bombay the Patan clerks reach the considerable figure of five thousand. Their complexion is darker than the complexion of Konkan Brahmans, but they are handsomer and brighter. As to the mysterious expression, "went through the golden cow," it illustrates a very curious custom. The Kshatriyas, and even the much-despised Shudras, may become a sort of left-hand Brahmans. This metamorphosis depends on the will of the real Brahmans, who may, if they like, sell this right for several hundreds or thousands of cows. When the gift is accomplished, a model cow, made of pure gold, is erected and made sacred by the performance of some mystical ceremonies. The candidate must now crawl through her hollow body three times, and thus is transformed into a Brahman. The present Maharaja of Travankor, and even the great Raja of Benares, who died recently, were both Shudras who acquired their rights in this manner. We received all this information and a notion of the legendary Patar chronicle from our obliging host.

Having announced that we must now get ready for dinner, he disappeared in the company of all the gentlemen of our party. Being left to ourselves, Miss X—— and I decided to have a good look at the house whilst it was empty. The Babu, being a downright, modern Bengali, had no respect for the religious preparations for dinner, and chose to accompany us, proposing to explain to us all that we should otherwise fail to understand.

The Prabhu brothers always live together, but every married couple have separate rooms and servants of their own. The habitation of our host was very spacious. There were small several bungalows, occupied by his brothers, and a chief building containing rooms for visitors, the general dining-room, a lying-in ward, a small chapel with any number of idols, and so on. The ground floor, of course, was surrounded by a verandah pierced with arches leading to a huge hall. All round this hall were wooden pillars adorned with exquisite carving. For some reason or other, it struck me that these pillars once belonged to some palace of the "dead town." On close examination I only grew more convinced that I was right. Their style bore no traces of Hindu taste; no gods, no fabulous monster animals, only arabesques and elegant leaves and flowers of non-existent plants. The pillars stood very close to each other, but the carvings prevented them from forming an uninterrupted wall, so that the ventilation was a little too strong. All the time we spent at the dinner table miniature hurricanes whistled from behind every pillar, waking up all our old rheumatisms and tooth-aches, which had peacefully slumbered since our arrival in India.

The front of the house was thickly covered with iron horse-shoes—the best precaution against evil spirits and evil eyes.

At the foot of a broad, carved staircase we came across a couch or a cradle, hung from the ceiling by iron chains. I saw somebody lying on it, whom, at first sight, I mistook for a sleeping Hindu, and was going to retreat discreetly, but, recognizing my old friend Hanuman, I grew bold and endeavoured to examine him. Alas! the poor idol possessed only a head and neck, the rest of his body was a heap of old rags.

On the left side of the verandah there were many more lateral rooms, each with a special destination, some of which I have mentioned already. The largest of these rooms was called "vattan," and was used exclusively by the fair sex. Brahman women are not bound to spend their lives under veils, like Mussulman women, but still they have very little communication with men, and keep aloof. Women cook the men's food, but do not dine with them. The elder ladies of the family are often held in great respect, and husbands sometimes show a shy courteousness towards their wives, but still a woman has no right to speak to her husband before strangers, nor even before the nearest relations, such as her sisters and her mother.

As to the Hindu widows, they really are the most wretched creatures in the whole world. As soon as a woman's husband dies she must have her hair and her eyebrows shaven off. She must part with all her trinkets, her earrings, her nose jewels, her bangles and toe-rings. After this is done she is as good as dead. The lowest outcast would not marry her. A man is polluted by her slightest touch, and must immediately proceed to purify himself. The dirtiest work of the household is her duty, and she must not eat with the married women and the children. The "sati," the burning of the widows, is abolished, but Brahmans are clever managers, and the widows often long for the sati.

At last, having examined the family chapel, full of idols, flowers, rich vases with burning incense, lamps hanging from its ceiling, and aromatic herbs covering its floor, we decided to get ready for dinner. We carefully washed ourselves, but this was not enough, we were requested to take off our shoes. This was a somewhat disagreeable surprise, but a real Brahmanical supper was worth the trouble.

However, a truly amazing surprise was still in store for us.

On entering the dining-room we stopped short at the entrance—both our European companions were dressed, or rather undressed, exactly like Hindus! For the sake of decency they kept on a kind of sleeveless knitted vest, but they were barefooted, wore the snow-white Hindu *dhutis* (a piece of muslin wrapped round to the waist and forming a petticoat), and looked like something between white Hindus and Constantinople *garcons de bains.* Both were indescribably funny, I never saw anything funnier. To the great discomfiture of the men, and the scandal of the grave ladies of the house, I could not restrain myself, but burst out laughing. Miss X—— blushed violently and followed my example.

A quarter of an hour before the evening meal every Hindu, old or young, has to perform a "puja" before the gods. He does not change his clothes, as we do in Europe, but takes off the few things he wore during the day. He bathes by the family well and loosens his hair, of which, if he is a Mahratti or an inhabitant of the Dekkan, he has only one long lock at the top of his shaven head. To cover the body and the head whilst eating would be sinful. Wrapping his waist and legs in a white *silk* dhuti, he goes once more to salute the idols and then sits down to his meal.

But here I shall allow myself to digress. "Silk possesses the property of dismissing the evil spirits who inhabit the magnetic fluids of the atmosphere," says the Mantram, book v., verse 23. And I cannot help wondering whether this apparent superstition may not contain a deeper meaning. It is difficult, I own, to part with our favourite theories about all the customs of ancient heathendom being mere ignorant superstitions. But have not some vague notions of these customs being founded originally on a true knowledge of scientific principles found their way amongst European scientific circles? At first sight the idea seems untenable. But why may we not suppose that the ancients prescribed this observance in the full knowledge that the effect of electricity upon the organs of digestion is truly beneficial? People who have studied the ancient philosophy of India with a firm resolve to penetrate the hidden meaning of its aphorisms have for the most part grown convinced that electricity and its effects were known to a considerable extent to some philosophers, as, for instance, to Patanjali. Charaka and Sushruta had propounded the system of Hippocrates long before the time of him who in Europe is supposed to be the "father of medicine." The Bhadrinath temple of Vishnu possesses a stone bearing evident proof of the fact that Surya-Sidhanta knew and calculated the expansive force of steam many centuries ago. The ancient Hindus were the first to determine the velocity of light and the laws of its reflection; and the table of Pythagoras and his celebrated theorem of the square of hypothenuse are to be found in the ancient books of Jyotisha. All this leads us to suppose that ancient Aryans, when instituting the strange custom of wearing silk during meals, had something serious in view, more serious, at all events, than the "dismissing of demons."

Having entered the "refectory," we immediately noticed what were the Hindu precautions against their being polluted by our presence. The stone floor of the hall was divided into two equal parts. This division consisted of a line traced in chalk, with Kabalistic signs at either end. One part was destined for the host's party and the guests belonging to the same caste, the other for ourselves. On our side of the hall there was yet a third square to contain Hindus of a different caste. The furniture of the two bigger squares was exactly similar. Along the two opposite walls there were narrow carpets spread on the floor, covered with cushions and low stools. Before every occupant there was an oblong on the bare floor, traced also with chalk, and divided, like a chess board, into small quadrangles which were destined for dishes and plates. Both the latter articles were made of the thick strong leaves of the *butea frondosa:* larger dishes of several leaves pinned together with thorns, plates and saucers of one leaf with its borders turned up. All the courses of the supper were already arranged on each square; we counted forty-eight dishes, containing about a mouthful of forty-eight different dainties. The materials of which they were composed were mostly *terra incognita* to us, but some of them tasted very nice. All this was vegetarian food. Of meat, fowl, eggs and fish there appeared no traces. There were *chutneys,* fruit and vegetables preserved in vinegar and honey, *panchamrits,* a mixture of pampello-berries, tamarinds, cocoa milk, treacle and olive oil, and *kushmer,* made of radishes, honey and flour; there were also burning hot pickles and spices. All this was crowned with a mountain of exquisitely cooked rice and another mountain of *chapatis,* which are something like brown pancakes. The dishes stood in four rows, each row containing twelve dishes; and between the rows burned three aromatic sticks of the size of a small church taper. Our part of the hall was brightly lit with green and red candles. The chandeliers which held these candles were of a very queer shape. They each represented the trunk of a tree with a seven-headed cobra wound round it. From each of the seven mouths rose a red or a green wax candle of spiral form like a corkscrew. Draughts blowing from behind every pillar fluttered the yellow flames, filling the roomy refectory with fantastic moving shadows, and causing both our lightly-clad gentlemen to sneeze very frequently. Leaving the dark

silhouettes of the Hindus in comparative obscurity, this unsteady light made the two white figures still more conspicuous, as if making a masquerade of them and laughing at them.

The relatives and friends of our host came in one after the other. They were all naked down to the waist, all barefooted, all wore the triple Brahmanical thread and white silk dhutis, and their hair hung loose. Every sahib was followed by his own servant, who carried his cup, his silver, or even gold, jug filled with water, and his towel. All of them, having saluted the host, greeted us, the palms of their hands pressed together and touching their foreheads, their breasts, and then the floor. They all said to us: "Ram-Ram" and "Namaste" (salutation to thee), and then made straight for their respective seats in perfect silence. Their civilities reminded me that the custom of greeting each other with the twice pronounced name of some ancestor was usual in the remotest antiquity.

We all sat down, the Hindus calm and stately, as if preparing for some mystic celebration, we ourselves feeling awkward and uneasy, fearing to prove guilty of some unpardonable blunder. An invisible choir of women's voices chanted a monotonous hymn, celebrating the glory of the gods. These were half a dozen nautch-girls from a neighbouring pagoda. To this accompaniment we began satisfying our appetites. Thanks to the Babu's instructions, we took great care to eat only with our right hands. This was somewhat difficult, because we were hungry and hasty, but quite necessary. Had we only so much as touched the rice with our left hands whole hosts of Rakshasas (demons) would have been attracted to take part in the festivity that very moment; which, of course, would send all the Hindus out of the room. It is hardly necessary to say that there were no traces of forks, knives or spoons. That I might run no risk of breaking the rule I put my left hand in my pocket and held on to my pocket-handkerchief all the time the dinner lasted.

The singing lasted only a few minutes. During the rest of the time a dead silence reigned amongst us. It was Monday, a fast day, and so the usual absence of noise at meal times had to be observed still more strictly than on any other day. Usually a man who is compelled to break the silence by some emergency or other hastens to plunge into water the middle finger of his left hand, which till then had remained hidden behind his back, and to moisten both his eyelids with it. But a really pious man would not be content with this simple formula of purification; having spoken, he must leave the dining-room, wash thoroughly, and then abstain from food for the remainder of the day.

Thanks to this solemn silence, I was at liberty to notice everything that was going on with great attention. Now and again, whenever I caught sight of the colonel or Mr. Y——, I had all the difficulty in the world to preserve my gravity. Fits of foolish laughter would take possession of me when I observed them sitting erect with such comical solemnity and working so awkwardly with their elbows and hands. The long beard of the one was white with grains of rice, as if silvered with hoar-frost, the chin of the other was yellow with liquid saffron. But unsatisfied curiosity happily came to my rescue, and I went on watching the quaint proceedings of the Hindus.

Each of them, having sat down with his legs twisted under him, poured some water with his left hand out of the jug brought by the servant, first into his cup, then into the palm of his right hand. Then he slowly and carefully sprinkled the water round a dish with all kinds of dainties, which stood by itself, and was destined, as we learned afterwards, for the gods. During this procedure each Hindu repeated a Vedic mantram. Filling his right hand with rice, he pronounced a new series of couplets, then, having stored five pinches of rice on the right side of his own plate, he once more washed his hands to avert the evil eye, sprinkled more water, and pouring a few drops of it into his right palm, slowly drank it. After this he swallowed six pinches of rice, one after the other, murmuring prayers all the while, and wetted both his eyes with the middle finger of his left hand. All this done, he finally hid his left hand behind his back, and began eating with the right hand. All this took only a few minutes, but was performed very solemnly.

The Hindus ate with their bodies bent over the food, throwing it up and catching it in their mouths so dexterously that not a grain of rice was lost, not a drop of the various liquids spilt. Zealous to show his consideration for his host, the colonel tried to imitate all these movements. He contrived to bend over his food almost horizontally, but, alas! he could not remain long in this position. The natural weight of his powerful limbs overcame him, he lost his balance and nearly tumbled head foremost, dropping his spectacles into a dish of sour milk and garlic. After this unsuccessful experience the brave American gave up all further attempts to become "Hinduized," and sat very quietly.

The supper was concluded with rice mixed with sugar, powdered peas, olive oil, garlic and grains of pomegranate, as usual. This last dainty is consumed hurriedly. Everyone nervously glances askance at his neighbour, and is mortally afraid of being the last to finish, because this is considered a very bad sign. To conclude, they all take some water into their mouths, murmuring prayers the while, and this time they must swallow it in one gulp. Woe to the one who chokes! 'Tis a clear sign that a *bhuta* has taken possession of his throat. The unfortunate man must run for his life and get purified before the altar.

The poor Hindus are very much troubled by these wicked bhutas, the souls of the people who have died with ungratified desires and earthly passions. Hindu spirits, if I am to believe the unanimous assertions of one and all, are always swarming round the living, always ready to satisfy their hunger with other people's mouths and gratify their impure desires with the help of organs temporarily stolen from the living. They are feared and cursed all over India. No means to get rid of them are despised. The notions and conclusions of the Hindus on this point categorically contradict the aspirations and hopes of Western spiritualists.

"A good and pure spirit, they are confident, will not let his soul revisit the earth, if this soul is equally pure. He is glad to die and unite himself to Brahma, to live an eternal life in Svarga (heaven) and enjoy the society of the beautiful Gandharvas or singing angels. He is glad to slumber whole eternities, listening to their songs, whilst his soul is purified by a new incarnation in a body, which is more perfect than the one the soul abandoned previously."

The Hindus believe that the spirit or Atma, a particle of the GREAT ALL, which is Parabrahm, cannot be punished for sins in which it never participated. It is Manas, the animal intelligence, and the animal soul or Jiva, both half material illusions, that sin and suffer and transmigrate from one body into the other till they purify themselves. The spirit merely overshadows their earthly transmigrations. When the Ego has reached the final state of purity, it will be one with the Atma, and gradually will merge and disappear in Parabrahm. But this is not what awaits the wicked souls. The soul that does not succeed in getting rid of earthly cares and desires before the death of the body is weighed down by its sins, and, instead of reïncarnating in some new form, according to the laws of metempsychosis, it will remain bodiless, doomed to wander on earth. It will become a bhuta, and by its own sufferings will cause unutterable sufferings to its kinsmen. That is why the Hindu fears above all things to remain bodiless after his death.

"It is better for one to enter the body of a tiger, of a dog, even of a yellow-legged falcon, after death, than to become a bhuta!" an old Hindu said to me on one occasion. "Every animal possesses a body of his own and a right to make an honest use of it. Whereas the bhutas are doomed dakoits, brigands and thieves, they are ever watching for an opportunity to use what does not belong to them. This is a horrible state—a horror indescribable. This is the true hell. What is this spiritualism they talk so much of in the West? Is it possible the intelligent English and Americans are so mad as this?"

And all our remonstrances notwithstanding, he refused to believe that there are actually people who are fond of bhutas, who would do much to attract them into their homes.

After supper the men went again to the family well to wash, and then dressed themselves.

Usually at this hour of the night the Hindus put on clean *malmalas*, a kind of tight shirt, white turbans, and wooden sandals with knobs pressed between the toes. These curious shoes are left at the door whilst their owners return to the hall and sit down along the walls on carpets and cushions to chew betel, smoke hookahs and cheroots, to listen to sacred reading, and to witness the dances of the nautches. But this evening, probably in our honour, all the Hindus dressed magnificently. Some of them wore *darias* of rich striped satin, no end of gold bangles, necklaces mounted with diamonds and emeralds, gold watches and chains, and transparent Brahmanical scarfs with gold embroidery. The fat fingers and the right ear of our host were simply blazing with diamonds.

The women, who waited on us during the meal, disappeared afterwards for a considerable time. When they came back they also were luxuriously overdressed and were introduced to us formally as the ladies of the house. They were five: the wife of the host, a woman of twenty-six or twenty-seven years of age, then two others looking somewhat younger, one of whom carried a baby, and, to our great astonishment, was introduced as the married daughter of the hostess; then the old mother of the host and a little girl of seven, the wife of one of his brothers. So that our hostess turned out to be a grandmother, and her sister-in-law, who was to enter finally into matrimony in from two to three years, might have become a mother before she was twelve. They were all barefooted, with rings on each of their toes, and all, with the exception of the old woman, wore garlands of natural flowers round their necks and in their jet black hair. Their tight bodices, covered with embroidery, were so short that between them and the sari there was a good quarter of a yard of bare skin. The dark, bronze-coloured waists of these well-shaped women were boldly presented to any one's examination and reflected the lights of the room. Their beautiful arms and their ankles were covered with bracelets. At the least of their movements they all set up a tinkling silvery sound, and the little sister-in-law, who might easily be mistaken for an automaton doll, could hardly move under her load of ornaments. The young grandmother, our hostess, had a ring in her left nostril, which reached to the lower part of the chin. Her nose was considerably disfigured by the weight of the gold, and we noticed how unusually handsome she was only when she took it off to enable herself to drink her tea with some comfort.

The dances of the nautch girls began. Two of them were very pretty. Their dancing consisted chiefly in more or less expressive movements of their eyes, their heads, and even their ears, in fact, of the whole upper part of their bodies. As to their legs, they either did not move at all or moved with such a swiftness as to appear in a cloud of mist.

After this eventful day I slept the sleep of the just.

After many nights spent in a tent, it is more than agreeable to sleep in a regular bed, even if it is only a hanging one. The pleasure would, no doubt, have been considerably increased had I but known I was resting on the couch of a god. But this latter circumstance was revealed to me only in the morning, when descending the staircase I suddenly discovered the poor *général en chef*, Hanuman, deprived of his cradle and unceremoniously stowed away under the stairs. Decidedly, the Hindus of the nineteenth century are a degenerate and blaspheming race!

In the course of the morning we learned that this swinging throne of his, and an ancient sofa, were the only pieces of furniture in the whole house that could be transformed into beds.

Neither of our gentlemen had spent a comfortable night. They slept in an empty tower that was once the altar of a decayed pagoda and was situated behind the main building. In assigning to them this strange resting place, the host was guided by the praiseworthy intention of protecting them from the jackals, which freely penetrate into all the rooms of the ground floor, as they are pierced by numberless arches and have no door and no window frames. The jackals, however, did not trouble the gentlemen much that night, except by giving their nightly concert. But both Mr. Y—— and the colonel had to fight all the night long with a *vampire*, which, besides being a flying fox of an unusual size, happened to be a spirit, as we learned too late, to our great misfortune.

This is how it happened. Noiselessly hovering about the tower, the vampire from time to time alighted on the sleepers, making them shudder under the disgusting touch of his cold sticky wings. His intention clearly was to get a nice suck of European blood. They were wakened by his manipulations at least ten times, and each time frightened him away. But, as soon as they were dozing again, the wretched bat was sure to return and perch on their shoulders, heads, or legs. At last Mr. Y——, losing patience, had recourse to strong measures; he caught him and broke his neck.

Feeling perfectly innocent, the gentlemen mentioned the tragic end of the troublesome flying fox to their host, and instantly drew down on their heads all the thunder-clouds of heaven.

The yard was crowded with people. All the inhabitants of the house stood sorrowfully drooping their heads, at the entrance of the tower. Our host's old mother tore her hair in despair, and shrieked lamentations in all the languages of India. What was the matter with them all? We were at our wits' end. But when we learned the cause of all this, there was no limit to our confusion.

By certain mysterious signs, known only to the family Brahman, it had been decided ten years ago that the soul of our host's elder brother had incarnated in this bloodthirsty vampire-bat. This fact was stated as being beyond any doubt. For nine years the late Patarah Prabhu existed under this new shape, carrying out the laws of metempsychosis. He spent the hours between sunrise and the sunset in an old pipal-tree before the tower, hanging with his head downwards. But at night he visited the old tower and gave fierce chase to the insects that sought rest in this out-of-the-way corner. And so nine years were spent in this happy existence, divided between sleep, food, and the gradual redemption of old sins committed in the shape of a Patarah Prabhu. And now? Now his listless body lay in the dust at the entrance of his favourite tower, and his wings were half devoured by the rats. The poor old woman, his mother, was mad with sorrow, and cast, through her tears, reproachful, angry looks at Mr. Y——, who, in his new capacity of a heartless murderer, looked disgustingly composed.

But the affair was growing serious. The comical side of it disappeared before the sincerity and the intensity of her lamentations. Her descendants, grouped around her, were too polite to reproach us openly, but the expression of their faces was far from reassuring. The family priest and astrologer stood by the old lady, Shastras in hand, ready to begin the ceremony of purification. He solemnly covered the corpse with a piece of new linen, and so hid from our eyes the sad remains on which ants were literally swarming.

Mr. Y—— did his best to look unconcerned, but still, when the tactless Miss X—— came to him, expressing her loud indignation at all these superstitions of an inferior race, he at least seemed to remember that our host knew English perfectly, and he did not encourage her farther expressions of sympathy. He made no answer, but smiled contemptuously. Our host approached the colonel with respectful salaams and invited us to follow him.

"No doubt he is going tc ask us to leave his house immediately!" was my uncomfortable impression.

But my apprehension was not justified. At this epoch of my Indian pilgrimage I was far, as yet, from having fathomed the metaphysical depth of a Hindu heart.

Sham Rao began by delivering a very far-fetched, eloquent preface. He reminded us that he, personally, was an enlightened man, a man who possessed all the advantages of a Western education. He said that, owing to this, he was not quite sure that the body of the vampire was actually inhabited by his late brother. Darwin, of course, and some other great naturalists of the West, seemed to believe in the transmigration of souls, but, as far as he understood, they believed in it in an inverse sense; that is to say, if a baby had been born to his mother exactly at the moment of the vampire's death, this baby would indubitably have had a great likeness to a vampire, owing to the decaying atoms of the vampire being so close to her.

"Is not this an exact interpretation of the Darwinian school?" he asked.

We modestly answered that, having travelled almost incessantly during the last year, we could not help being a bit behindhand in the questions of modern science, and that we were not able to follow its latest conclusions.

"But I have followed them!" rejoined the good-natured Sham Rao, with a touch of pomposity. "And so I hope I may be allowed to say that I have understood and duly appreciated their most recent developments. I have just finished studying the magnificent *Anthropogenesis* of Hæckel, and have carefully discussed in my own mind his logical, scientific explanations of the origin of man from inferior animal forms through transformation. And what is this transformation, pray, if not the transmigration of the ancient and modern Hindus, and the metempsychosis of the Greeks?"

We had nothing to say against the identity, and even ventured to observe that, according to Hæckel, it *does* look like it.

"Exactly!" exclaimed he joyfully. "This shows that our conceptions are neither silly nor superstitious, as is maintained by some opponents of Manu. The great Manu anticipated Darwin and Hæckel. Judge for yourself; the latter derives the genesis of man from a group of plastides, from the jelly-like moneron; this moneron, through the amœba, the ascidian, the brainless and heartless amphioxus, and so on, transmigrates in the eighth remove into the lamprey, is transformed, at last, into a vertebrate amniote, into a premammalian, into a marsupial animal. . . . The vampire, in its turn, belongs to the species of vertebrates. You, being well read people all of you, cannot contradict this statement."

He was right in his supposition; we did not contradict it.

"In this case, do me the honour to follow my argument. . . ."

We did follow his argument with the greatest attention, but were at a loss to foresee whither it tended to lead us.

"Darwin," continued Sham Rao, "in his *Origin of Species*, reëstablished almost word for word the palingenetic teachings of our Manu. Of this I am perfectly convinced, and, if you like, I can prove it to you book in hand. Our ancient law-giver, amongst other sayings, speaks as follows: 'The great Parabrahm commanded man to appear in the universe, after traversing all the grades of the animal kingdom, and springing primarily from the worm of the deep sea mud.' The worm became a snake, the snake a fish, the fish a mammal, and so on. Is not this very idea at the bottom of Darwin's theory, when he maintains that the organic forms have their origin in more simple species, and says that the structureless protoplasm born in the mud of the Laurentian and Silurian periods—the Manu's 'mud of the seas,' I dare say—gradually transformed itself into the anthropoid ape, and then finally into the human being?"

We said it looked very like it.

"But, in spite of all my respect for Darwin and his eminent follower Hæckel, I cannot agree with their final conclusions, especially with the conclusions of the latter," continued Sham Rao. "This hasty and bilious German is perfectly accurate in copying the embryology of Manu and all the metamorphoses of our ancestors, but he forgets the evolution of the human soul, which, as it is stated by Manu, goes hand in hand with the evolution of matter. The son of Swayambhuva, the Self Becoming, speaks as follows: 'Everything created in a new cycle, in addition to the qualities of its preceding transmigrations, acquires new qualities, and the nearer it approaches to man, the highest type of the earth, the brighter becomes its divine spark; but, once it has become a Brahma, it will enter the cycle of conscious transmigrations.' Do you realize what that means? It means that from this moment, its transformations depend no longer on the blind laws of gradual evolution, but on the least of a man's actions, which brings either a reward or a punishment. Now you see that it depends on the man's will whether, on the one hand, he will start on the way to Moksha, the eternal bliss, passing from one Loka to another till he reaches Brahmaloka, or, on the other, owing to his sins, will be thrown back. You know that the average soul, once freed from earthly reïncarnations, has to ascend from one Loka to another, always in the human shape, though this shape will grow and perfect itself with every Loka. Some of our sects understood these Lokas to mean certain stars. These spirits, freed from earthly matter, are what we mean by Pitris and Devas, whom we worship. And did not your Kabalists of the middle ages designate these Pitris under the expression *Planetary Spirits?* But, in the case of a very sinful man, he will have to begin once more with the animal forms which he had already traversed unconsciously. Both Darwin and Hæckel lose sight of this, so to speak, second volume of their incomplete theory, but still neither of them advances any argument to prove it false. Is it not so?"

"Neither of them does anything of the sort, most assuredly."

"Why, in this case," exclaimed he, suddenly changing his colloquial tone for an aggressive one, "why am I, I who have studied the most modern ideas of Western science, I who believe in its representatives—why am I suspected, pray, by Miss X—— of belonging to the tribe of the ignorant and superstitious Hindus? Why does she think that our perfected scientific theories are superstitions, and we ourselves a fallen inferior race?"

Sham Rao stood before us with tears in his eyes. We were at a loss what to answer him, being confused to the last degree by this outburst.

"Mind you, I do not proclaim our popular beliefs to be infallible dogmas. I consider them as mere theories, and try to the best of my ability to reconcile the ancient and the modern science. I formulate hypotheses just like Darwin and Hæckel. Besides, if I understood rightly, Miss X—— is a spiritualist, so she believes in bhutas. And, believing that a bhuta is capable of penetrating the body of a medium, how can she deny that a bhuta, and more so a less sinful soul, may enter the body of a vampire-bat?"

I own, this logic was a little too condensed for us, and so, avoiding a direct answer to a metaphysical question of such delicacy, we tried to apologize and excuse Miss X——'s rudeness as well as we could.

"She did not mean to offend you," we said, "she only repeated a calumny, familiar to every European. Besides, if she had taken the trouble to think it over, she probably would not have said it. . . ."

Little by little we succeeded in pacifying our host. He recovered his usual cheerfulness, but could not resist the temptation of adding a few words to his long argumentation. He had just begun to reveal to us certain peculiarities of his late brother's character, which induced him to be prepared, judging by the laws of atavism, to see their repetition in the propensities of a vampire bat, when Mr. Y—— suddenly dashed in on our small group and spoiled all the results of our conciliatory words by screaming at the top of his voice: "The old woman has gone demented! She keeps on cursing us and says that the murder of this wretched bat is only the forerunner of a whole series of misfortunes brought on her house by you, Sham Rao," said he, hastily addressing the bewildered follower of Hæckel. "She says you have polluted your Brahmanical holiness by inviting us. . . Colonel, you had better send for the elephants. In another moment all this crowd will be on us. . . ."

"For goodness' sake!" exclaimed poor Sham Rao, "have some consideration for my feelings. She is an old woman, she has some superstitions, but she is my mother. You are educated people, learned people. . . Advise me, show me a way out of all these difficulties. What should you do in my place?"

"What should I do, sir?" exclaimed Mr. Y——, completely put out of temper by the utter ludicrousness of our awkward predicament. "What should I do? Were I a man in your position and a believer in all you are brought up to believe, I should take my revolver, and in the first place, shoot all the vampire bats in the neighbourhood, if only to rid all your late relations from the abject bodies of these creatures, and, in the second place, I should endeavour to smash the head of the conceited fraud in the shape of a Brahman who invented all this stupid story. That is what I should do, sir!"

But this advice did not content the miserable descendant of Rama. No doubt he would have remained a long time undecided as to what course of action to adopt, torn as he was between the sacred feelings of hospitality, the innate fear of the Brahman-priest, and his own superstitions, if our ingenious Babu had not come to our rescue. Learning that we all felt more or less indignant at all this row, and that we were preparing to leave the house as quickly as possible, he persuaded us to stay, if only for an hour, saying that our hasty departure would be a terrible outrage upon our host, whom, in any case, we could not find fault with. As to the stupid old woman, the Babu promised us to pacify her speedily enough: he had his own plans and views. In the meantime, he said, we had better go and examine the ruins of an old fortress close by.

We obeyed very reluctantly, feeling an acute interest in his "plans." We proceeded slowly. Our gentlemen were visibly out of temper, Miss X—— tried to calm herself by talking more than usual, and Narayan, as phlegmatic as usual, indolently and good-naturedly chaffed her about her beloved "spirits." Glancing back we saw the Babu accompanied by the family priest. Judging by their gestures they were engaged in some warm discussion. The shaven head of the Brahman nodded right and left, his yellow garment flapped in the wind, and his arms rose towards the sky, as if in an appeal to the gods to come down and testify to the truth of his words.

"I'll bet you a thousand dollars, no plans of our Babu's will be of any avail with this fanatic!" confidently remarked the colonel as he lit his pipe.

But we had hardly walked a hundred steps after this remark when we saw the Babu running after us and signalling us to stop.

"Everything ended first-rate!" screamed he, as soon as we could hear. "You are to be thanked . . . You happen to be the true saviours and benefactors of the deceased bhuta . . . You . . ."

Our Babu sank on the ground holding his narrow, panting breast with both his hands, and laughed, laughed till we all burst into laughter too, before learning anything at all.

"Think of it," began the Babu, and stopped short, prevented from going on by his exuberant hilarity. "Just think of it! The whole transaction is to cost me only ten rupees. . . I offered five at first . . . but he would not. . . He said this was a sacred matter. . . But ten he could not resist! Ho, ho, ho. . ."

At last we learned the story. All the metempsychoses depend on the imagination of the family *Gurus*, who receive for their kind offices from one hundred to one hundred and fifty rupees a year. Every rite is accompanied by a more or less considerable addition to the purse of the insatiable family Brahman, but the happy events pay better than the sad ones. Knowing all this, the Babu asked the Brahman point-blank to perform a false *samadhi*, that is to say, to feign an inspiration and to announce to the sorrowing mother that her late son's will had acted consciously in all the circumstances; that he brought about his end in the body of the flying fox, that he was tired of that grade of transmigration, that he longed for death in order to attain a higher position in the animal kingdom, that he is happy, and that he is deeply indebted to the sahib who broke his neck and so freed him from his abject embodiment.

Besides, the observant eye of our all-knowing Babu had not failed to remark that a she-buffalo of the Guru's was expecting a calf, and that the Guru was yearning to sell it to Sham Rao. This circumstance was a trump card in the Babu's hand. Let the Guru announce, under the influence of samadhi, that the freed spirit intends to inhabit the body of the future baby-buffalo and the old lady will buy the new incarnation of her first-born as sure as the sun is bright. This announcement will be followed by rejoicings and by new rites. And who will profit by all this if not the family priest?

At first the Guru had some misgivings, and swore by everything sacred that the vampire bat was veritably inhabited by the brother of Sham Rao. But the Babu knew better than to give in. The Guru ended by understanding that his skilful opponent saw through his tricks, and that he was well aware that the Shastras exclude the possibility of such a transmigration. Growing alarmed, the Guru also grew meek, and asked only ten rupees and a promise of silence for the performance of a samadhi.

On our way back we were met at the gate by Sham Rao, who was simply radiant. Whether he was afraid of our laughing at him, or was at loss to find an explanation of this new metamorphosis in the positive sciences in general, and Hæckel in particular, he did not attempt to explain why the affair had taken such an unexpectedly good turn. He merely mentioned awkwardly enough that his mother, owing to some new mysterious conjectures of hers, had dismissed all sad apprehensions as to the destiny of her elder son, and he then dropped the subject completely.

In order to wipe away the traces of the morning's perplexities from our minds, Sham Rao invited us to sit on the verandah, by the wide entrance of his idol room, whilst the family prayers were going on. Nothing could suit us better. It was nine o'clock, the usual time of the morning prayers. Sham Rao went to the well to get ready, and dress himself, as he said, though the process was more like undressing. In a few moments he came back wearing only a dhuti, as during dinner time, and with his head uncovered. He went straight to his idol room. The moment he entered we heard the loud stroke of a bell that hung under the ceiling, and that continued tolling all the time the prayers lasted.

The Babu explained to us that a little boy was pulling the bell rope from the roof.

Sham Rao stepped in with his right foot and very slowly. Then he approached the altar and sat on a little stool with his legs crossed. At the opposite side of the room, on the red velvet shelves of an altar that resembled an *étagère* in the drawing-room of some fashionable lady, stood many idols. They were made of gold, of silver, of brass and of marble, according to their importance and merits. Maha-Deva or Shiva was of gold, Gunpati or Ganesha of silver, Vishnu in the form of a round black stone from the river Gandaki in Nepal. In this form Vishnu is called Lakshmi-Narayan. There were also many other gods unknown to us, who were worshipped in the shapes of big sea-shells, called Chakra. Surya, the god of the sun, and the kula-devas, the domestic gods, were placed in the second rank. The altar was sheltered by a cupola of carved sandal-wood. During the night the gods and the offerings were covered by a huge bell glass. On the walls there were many sacred images representing the chief episodes in the biographies of the higher gods.

Sham Rao filled his left hand with ashes, murmuring prayers all the while, covered it for a second with the right one, then put some matter to the ashes, and mixing the two by rubbing his hands together, he traced a line on his face with this mixture by moving the thumb of his right hand from his nose upwards, then from the middle of the forehead to the right temple, then back again to the left temple. Having done with his face he proceeded to cover with wet ashes his throat, arms, shoulders, his back, head and ears. In one corner of the room stood a huge bronze font filled with water. Sham Rao made straight to it and plunged into it three times, dhuti, head, and all, after which he came out looking exactly like a well-favoured dripping wet Triton. He twisted the only lock of hair on the top of his shaved head and sprinkled it with water. This operation concluded the first act.

The second act began with religious meditations and with mantrams, which, by really pious people, must be repeated three times a day—at sunrise, at noon and at sunset. Sham Rao loudly pronounced the names of twenty-four gods, and each name was accompanied by a stroke of the bell. Having finished he first shut his eyes and stuffed his ears with cotton, then pressed his left nostril with two fingers of his left hand, and having filled his lungs with air through the right nostril, pressed the latter also. Then he tightly closed his lips, so that breathing became impossible. In this position every pious Hindu must mentally repeat a certain verse, which is called the Gayatri. These are sacred words which no Hindu will dare to pronounce aloud. Even in repeating them mentally he must take every precaution not to inhale anything impure.

I am bound by my word of honour never to repeat the whole of this prayer, but I may quote a few unconnected sentences:

"Om. . . . Earth. . . . Heaven . . . . Let the adored light of . . . . [here follows a name which must not be pronounced] shelter me. Let thy Sun, O thou only One, shelter me, the unworthy. . . . I shut my eyes, I shut my ears, I do not breathe . . . . . in order to see, hear and breathe thee alone. Throw light upon our thoughts [again the secret name]. . ."

It is curious to compare this Hindu prayer with the celebrated prayer of Descartes' "Méditation III" in his

L'Existence de Dieu. It runs as follows, if I remember rightly:

"Now I shut my eyes, cover my ears, and dismiss all my five senses, I will dwell on the thought of God alone, I will meditate on His quality and look on the beauty of this wondrous radiancy."

After this prayer Sham Rao read many other prayers, holding with two fingers his sacred Brahmanical thread.

After a while began the ceremony of "the washing of the gods." Taking them down from the altar, one after the other, according to their rank, Sham Rao first plunged them in the big font, in which he had just bathed himself, and then bathed them in milk in a smaller bronze font by the altar. The milk was mixed up with curds, butter, honey, and sugar, and so it cannot be said that this cleansing served its purpose. No wonder we were glad to see that the gods underwent a second bathing in the first font and then were dried with a clean towel.

When the gods were arranged in their respective places, the Hindu traced on them the sectarian signs with a ring from his left hand. He used white sandal paint for the lingam and red for Gunpati and Surya. Then he sprinkled them with aromatic oils and covered them with fresh flowers. The long ceremony was finished by "the awakening of the gods." A small bell was repeatedly rung under the noses of the idols, who, as the Brahman probably supposed, all went to sleep during this tedious ceremony.

Having noticed, or fancied, which often amounts to the same thing, that they were wide awake, he began offering them his daily sacrifices, lighting the incense and the lamps, and, to our great astonishment, snapping his fingers from time to time, as if warning the idols to "look out." Having filled the room with clouds of incense and fumes of burning camphor, he scattered some more flowers over the altar and sat on the small stool for a while, murmuring the last prayers. He repeatedly held the palms of his hands over the flame of the tapers and rubbed his face with them. Then he walked round the altar three times, and, having knelt three times, retreated backwards to the door.

A little while before our host had finished his morning prayers the ladies of the house came into the room. They brought each a small stool and sat in a row murmuring prayers and telling the beads of their rosaries.

The part played by the rosaries in India is as important as in all Buddhist countries. Every god has his favourite flower and his favourite material for a rosary. The fakirs are simply covered with rosaries. The rosary is called *mala* and consists of one hundred and eight beads. Very pious Hindus are not content to tell the beads when praying; they must hide their hands during this ceremony in a bag called *gomukha*, which means the cow's mouth.

We left the women to their prayers and followed our host to the cow house. The cow symbolizes the "fostering earth," or Nature, and is worshipped accordingly. Sham Rao sat down by the cow and washed her feet, first with her own milk, then with water. He gave her some sugar and rice, covered her forehead with powdered sandal, and adorned her horns and four legs with chains of flowers. He burned some incense under her nostrils and brandished a burning lamp over her head. Then he walked three times round her and sat down to rest. Some Hindus walk round the cow one hundred and eight times, rosary in hand. But our Sham Rao had a slight tendency to freethinking, as we knew, and besides, he was too much of an admirer of Hæckel. Having rested himself, he filled a cup with water, put in it the cow's tail for a moment, and then drank it!

After this he performed the rite of worshipping the sun and the sacred plant *tulsi*. Unable to bring the god Surya from his heavenly altar and wash him in the sacred font, Sham Rao contented himself by filling his own mouth with water, standing on one leg, and spirting this water towards the sun. Needless to say it never reached the orb of day, but, very unexpectedly, sprinkled us instead.

It is still a mystery to us why the plant tulsi, Royal Basilicum, is worshipped. However, towards the end of September we yearly witnessed the strange ceremony of the wedding of this plant with the god Vishnu, notwithstanding that tulsi bears the title of *Krishna's* bride, probably because of the latter being an incarnation of Vishnu. On these occasions pots of this plant are painted and adorned with tinsel. A magical circle is traced in the garden and the plant is put in the middle of it. A Brahman brings an idol of Vishnu and begins the marriage ceremony, standing before the plant. A married couple hold a shawl between the plant and the god, as if screening them from each other, the Brahman utters prayers, and young women, and especially unmarried girls, who are the most ardent worshippers of tulsi, throw rice and saffron over the idol and the plant. When the ceremony is concluded, the Brahman is presented with the shawl, the idol is put in the shade of his wife, the Hindus clap their hands, rend everyone's ears with the noise of tom-toms, let off fire-works, offer each other pieces of sugar-cane, and rejoice in every conceivable way till the dawn of the next day.

A WITCH'S DEN.

Our kind host Sham Rao was very gay during the remaining hours of our visit. He did his best to entertain us, and would not hear of our leaving the neighbourhood without having seen its greatest celebrity, its most interesting sight. A *jadu wâlâ*—sorceress—well known in the district, was just at this time under the influence of seven sister-goddesses, who took possession of her by turns, and spoke their oracles through her lips. Sham Rao said we must not fail to see her, be it only in the interests of science.

The evening closes in, and we once more get ready for an excursion. It is only five miles to the cavern of the Pythia of Hindostan; the road runs through a jungle, but it is level and smooth. Besides, the jungle and its ferocious inhabitants have ceased to frighten us. The timid elephants we had in the "dead city" are sent home, and we are to mount new behemoths belonging to a neighbouring Râjâ. The pair, that stand before the verandah like two dark hillocks, are steady and trustworthy. Many a time these two have hunted the royal tiger, and no wild shrieking or thunderous roaring can frighten them. And so, let us start! The ruddy flames of the torches dazzle our eyes and increase the forest gloom. Our surroundings seem so dark, so mysterious. There is something indescribably fascinating, almost solemn, in these night-journeys in the out-of-the-way corners of India. Everything is silent and deserted around you, everything is dozing on the earth and overhead. Only the heavy, regular tread of the elephants breaks the stillness of the night, like the sound of falling hammers in the underground smithy of Vulcan. From time to time uncanny voices and murmurs are heard in the black forest.

"The wind sings its strange song amongst the ruins," says one of us, "what a wonderful acoustic phenomenon!"

"Bhûta, bhûta!" whisper the awestruck torch-bearers. They brandish their torches and swiftly spin on one leg, and snap their fingers to chase away the aggressive spirits.

The plaintive murmur is lost in the distance. The forest is once more filled with the cadences of its invisible nocturnal life—the metallic whirr of the crickets, the feeble, monotonous croak of the tree-frog, the rustle of the leaves. From time to time all this suddenly stops short and then begins again, gradually increasing and increasing.

Heavens! What teeming life, what stores of vital energy are hidden under the smallest leaf, the most imperceptible blades of grass, in this tropical forest! Myriads of stars shine in the dark blue of the sky, and myriads of fireflies twinkle at us from every bush, moving sparks, like a pale reflection of the far-away stars.

We left the thick forest behind us, and reached a deep glen, on three sides bordered with the thick forest, where even by day the shadows are as dark as by night. We were about two thousand feet above the foot of the Vindhya ridge, judging by the ruined wall of Mandu, straight above our heads.

Suddenly a very chilly wind rose that nearly blew our torches out. Caught in the labyrinth of bushes and rocks, the wind angrily shook the branches of the blossoming syringas, then, shaking itself free, it turned back along the glen and flew down the valley, howling, whistling and shrieking, as if all the fiends of the forest together were joining in a funeral song.

"Here we are," said Sham Rao, dismounting. "Here is the village; the elephants cannot go any further."

"The village? Surely you are mistaken. I don't see anything but trees."

"It is too dark to see the village. Besides, the huts are so small, and so hidden by the bushes, that even by daytime you could hardly find them. And there is no light in the houses, for fear of the spirits."

"And where is your witch? Do you mean we are to watch her performance in complete darkness?"

Sham Rao cast a furtive, timid look round him; and his voice, when he answered our questions, was somewhat tremulous.

"I implore you not to call her a witch! She may hear you. . . . It is not far off, it is not more than half a mile. Do not allow this short distance to shake your decision. No elephant, and even no horse, could make its way there. We must walk. . . . But we shall find plenty of light there. . . ."

This was unexpected, and far from agreeable. To walk in this gloomy Indian night; to scramble through thickets of cactuses; to venture in a dark forest, full of wild animals—this was too much for Miss X——. She declared that she would go no further. She would wait for us in the howdah, on the elephant's back, and perhaps would go to sleep.

Narayan was against this *parti de plaisir* from the very beginning, and now, without explaining his reasons, he said she was the only sensible one among us.

"You won't lose anything," he remarked, "by staying

where you are. And I only wish everyone would follow your example."

"What ground have you for saying so, I wonder?" remonstrated Sham Rao, and a slight note of disappointment rang in his voice, when he saw that the excursion, proposed and organized by himself, threatened to come to nothing. "What harm could be done by it? I won't insist any more that the 'incarnation of gods' is a rare sight, and that the Europeans hardly ever have an opportunity of witnessing it; but, besides, the Kangalim in question is no ordinary woman. She leads a holy life; she is a prophetess, and her blessing could not prove harmful to any one. I insisted on this excursion out of pure patriotism."

"Sahib, if your patriotism consists in displaying before foreigners the worst of our plagues, then why did you not order all the lepers of your district to assemble and parade before the eyes of our guests? You are a *patèl*, you have the power to do it."

How bitterly Narayan's voice sounded to our unaccustomed ears. Usually he was so even-tempered, so indifferent to everything belonging to the exterior world.

Fearing a quarrel between the Hindus, the colonel remarked, in a conciliatory tone, that it was too late for us to reconsider our expedition. Besides, without being a believer in the "incarnation of gods," he was personally firmly convinced that demoniacs existed even in the West. He was eager to study every psychological phenomenon, wherever he met with it, and whatever shape it might assume.

It would have been a striking sight for our European and American friends if they had beheld our procession on that dark night. Our way lay along a narrow winding path up the mountain. Not more than two people could walk together—and we were thirty, including the torch-bearers. Surely some reminiscence of night sallies against the confederate Southerners had revived in the colonel's breast, judging by the readiness with which he took upon himself the leadership of our small expedition. He ordered all the rifles and revolvers to be loaded, despatched three torch-bearers to march ahead of us, and arranged us in pairs. Under such a skilled chieftain we had nothing to fear from tigers; and so our procession started, and slowly crawled up the winding path.

It cannot be said that the inquisitive travellers, who appeared later on, in the den of the prophetess of Mandu, shone through the freshness and elegance of their costumes. My gown, as well as the travelling suits of the colonel and of Mr. Y—— were nearly torn to pieces. The cactuses gathered from us whatever tribute they could, and the Babu's dishevelled hair swarmed with a whole colony of grasshoppers and fireflies, which, probably, were attracted thither by the smell of cocoa-nut oil. The stout Sham Rao panted like a steam engine. Narayan alone was like his usual self; that is to say, like a bronze Hercules, armed with a club. At the last abrupt turn of the path, after having surmounted the difficulty of climbing over huge, scattered stones, we suddenly found ourselves on a perfectly smooth place; our eyes, in spite of our many torches, were dazzled with light; and our ears were struck by a medley of unusual sounds.

A new glen opened before us, the entrance of which, from the valley, was well masked by thick trees. We understood how easily we might have wandered round it, without ever suspecting its existence. At the bottom of the glen we discovered the abode of the celebrated Kangalim.

The den, as it turned out, was situated in the ruin of an old Hindu temple in tolerably good preservation. In all probability it was built long before the "dead city," because during the epoch of the latter, the heathen were not allowed to have their own places of worship; and the temple stood quite close to the wall of the town, in fact, right under it. The cupolas of the two smaller lateral pagodas had fallen long ago, and huge bushes grew out of their altars. This evening, their branches were hidden under a mass of bright coloured rags, bits of ribbon, little pots, and various other talismans; because, even in them, popular superstition sees something sacred.

"And are not these poor people right? Did not these bushes grow on sacred ground? Is not their sap impregnated with the incense of offerings, and the exhalations of holy anchorites, who once lived and breathed here?"

The learned, but superstitious Sham Rao would only answer our questions by new questions.

But the central temple, built of red granite, stood unharmed by time, and, as we learned afterwards, a deep tunnel opened just behind its closely-shut door. What was beyond it no one knew. Sham Rao assured us that no man of the last three generations had ever stepped over the threshold of this thick iron door; no one had seen the subterranean passage for many years. Kangalim lived there in perfect isolation, and, according to the oldest people in the neighbourhood, she had always lived there. Some people said she was three hundred years old; others alleged that a certain old man on his death-bed had revealed to his son that this old woman was no one else than *his own uncle.* This fabulous uncle had settled in the cave in the times when the "dead city" still counted several hundreds of inhabitants. The hermit, busy paving his road to Moksha, had no intercourse with the rest of the world, and nobody knew how he lived and what he ate. But a good while ago, in the days when the Bellati (foreigners) had not yet taken possession of this mountain, the old hermit suddenly was transformed into a hermitess. She continues his pursuits and speaks with his voice, and often in his name; but she receives worshippers, which was not the practice of her predecessor.

We had come too early, and the Pythia did not at first appear. But the square before the temple was full of people, and a wild, though picturesque, scene it was. An enormous bonfire blazed in the centre, and round it crowded the naked savages like so many black gnomes, adding whole branches of trees sacred to the seven sister-goddesses. Slowly and evenly they all jumped from one leg to another to a tune of a single monotonous musical phrase, which they repeated in chorus, accompanied by several local drums and tambourines. The hushed trill of the latter mingled with the forest echoes and the hysterical moans of two little girls, who lay under a heap of leaves by the fire. The poor children were brought here by their mothers, in the hope that the goddesses would take pity upon them and banish the two evil spirits under whose obsession they were. Both mothers were quite young, and sat on their heels blankly and sadly staring at the flames. No one paid us the slightest attention when we appeared, and afterwards during all our stay these people acted as if we were invisible. Had we worn a cap of darkness they could not have behaved more strangely.

"They feel the approach of the gods! The atmosphere is full of their sacred emanations!" mysteriously explained Sham Rao, contemplating with reverence the natives, whom his beloved Hæckel might have easily mistaken for his "missing link," the brood of his "Bathybius Hæckelii."

"They are simply under the influence of toddy and opium!" retorted the irreverent Babu.

The lookers-on moved as in a dream, as if they all were only half-awakened somnambulists; but the actors were simply victims of St. Vitus's dance. One of them, a tall old man, a mere skeleton with a long white beard, left the ring and begun whirling vertiginously, with his arms spread like wings, and loudly grinding his long, wolf-like teeth. He was painful and disgusting to look at. He soon fell down, and was carelessly, almost mechanically, pushed aside by the feet of the others still engaged in their demoniac performance.

All this was frightful enough, but many more horrors were in store for us.

Waiting for the appearance of the *prima donna* of this forest opera company, we sat down on the trunk of a fallen tree, ready to ask innumerable questions of our condescending host. But I was hardly seated, when a feeling of indescribable astonishment and horror made me shrink back.

I beheld the skull of a monstrous animal, the like of which I could not find in my zoological reminiscences. This head was much larger than the head of an elephant skeleton. And still it could not be anything but an elephant, judging by the skilfully restored trunk, which wound down to my feet like a gigantic black leech. But an elephant has no horns, whereas this one had four of them! The front pair stuck from the flat forehead slightly bending forward and then spreading out; and the others had a wide base, like the root of a deer's horn, that gradually decreased almost up to the middle, and bore long branches enough to decorate a dozen ordinary elks. Pieces of the transparent amber-yellow rhinoceros skin were strained over the empty eye-holes of the skull, and small lamps burning behind them only added to the horror, the devilish appearance of this head.

"What can this be?" was our unanimous question. None of us had ever met anything like it, and even the colonel looked aghast.

"It is a Sivatherium," said Narayan. "Is it possible you never came across these fossils in European museums? Their remains are common enough in the Himalayas, though, of course, in fragments. They were called after Shiva."

"If the collector of this district ever hears that this antediluvian relic adorns the den of your—ahem!—witch," remarked the Babu, "it won't adorn it many days longer."

All round the skull, and on the floor of the portico there were heaps of white flowers, which, though not quite antediluvian, were totally unknown to us. They were as large as a big rose; and their white petals were covered with a red powder, the inevitable concomitant of every Indian religious ceremony. Further on, there were groups of cocoa-nuts, and large brass dishes filled with rice; and each adorned with a red or green taper. In the centre of the portico there stood a queer-shaped censer, surrounded with chandeliers. A little boy, dressed from head to foot in white, threw into it handfuls of aromatic powders.

"These people, who assemble here to worship Kangalim," said Sham Rao, "do not actually belong either to her sect or to any other. They are devil-worshippers. They do not believe in Hindu gods, but live in small communities; they belong to one of the many Indian races, which usually are called the hill-tribes. Unlike the Shanars of Southern Travancore, they do not use the blood of sacrificial animals; they do not build separate temples to their bhutas. But they are possessed by the strange fancy that the goddess Kâlî, the wife of Shiva, from time immemorial has had a grudge against them, and sends her favourite evil spirits to torture them. Save this little difference, they have the same beliefs as the Shanars. God does not exist for them; and even Shiva is considered by them as an ordinary spirit. Their chief worship is offered to the souls of the dead. These souls, however righteous and kind they may be in their lifetime, become after death as wicked as can be; they are happy only when they are torturing living men and cattle. As the opportunities of doing so are the only reward for the virtues they possessed when incarnated, a very wicked man is punished by becoming after his death a very soft-hearted ghost; he loathes his loss of daring, and is altogether miserable. The results of this strange logic are not bad, nevertheless. These savages and devil-worshippers are the kindest and the most truth-loving of all the hill-tribes. They do whatever they can to be worthy of their ultimate reward; because, don't you see, they all long to become the wickedest of devils! . . ."

And put in good humour by his own wittiness, Sham Rao laughed till his hilarity became offensive, considering the sacredness of the place.

"A year ago some business matters sent me to Tinevelli," continued he. "Staying with a friend of mine, who is a Shanar, I was allowed to be present at one of the ceremonies in the honour of devils. No European has as yet witnessed this worship—whatever the missionaries may say; but there are many converts amongst the Shanars, who willingly describe them to the *padres*. My friend is a wealthy man, which is probably the reason why the devils are especially vicious to him. They poison his cattle, spoil his crops and his coffee plants, and persecute his numerous relations, sending them sunstrokes, madness and epilepsy, over which illnesses they especially preside. These wicked demons have settled in every corner of his spacious landed property—in the woods, the ruins, and even in his stables. To avert all this, my friend covered his land with stucco pyramids, and prayed humbly, asking the demons to draw their portraits on each of them, so that he may recognize them and worship each of them separately, as the rightful owner of this, or that, particular pyramid. And what do you think? . . . Next morning all the pyramids were found covered with drawings. Each of them bore an incredibly good likeness of the dead of the neighbourhood. My friend had known personally almost all of them. He found also a portrait of his own late father amongst the lot. . . ."

"Well? And was he satisfied?"

"Oh, he was very glad, very satisfied. It enabled him to choose the right thing to gratify the personal tastes of each demon, don't you see? He was not vexed at finding his father's portrait. His father was somewhat irascible; once he nearly broke both his son's legs, administering to him fatherly punishment with an iron bar, so that he could not possibly be very dangerous after his death. But another portrait, found on the best and the prettiest of the pyramids, amazed my friend a good deal, and put him in a blue funk. The whole district recognized an English officer, a certain Captain Pole, who in his lifetime was as kind a gentleman as ever lived."

"Indeed? But do you mean to say that this strange people worshipped Captain Pole also?"

"Of course they did! Captain Pole was such a worthy man, such an honest officer, that, after his death, he could not help being promoted to the highest rank of Shanar devils. The Pe-Kovil, demon's house, sacred to his memory, stands side by side with the Pe-Kovil Bhadrakâlî, which was recently conferred on the wife of a certain German missionary, who also was a most charitable lady and so is very dangerous now."

"But what are their ceremonies? Tell us something about their rites."

"Their rites consist chiefly of dancing, singing, and killing sacrificial animals. The Shanars have no castes, and eat all kinds of meat. The crowd assembles about the Pe-Kovil, previously designated by the priest; there is a general beating of drums, and slaughtering of fowls, sheep and goats. When Captain Pole's turn came an ox was killed, as a thoughtful attention to the peculiar tastes of his nation. The priest appeared, covered with bangles, and holding a wand on which tinkled numberless little bells, and wearing garlands of red and white flowers round his neck, and a black mantle, on which were embroidered the ugliest fiends you can imagine. Horns were blown and drums rolled incessantly. And oh, I forgot to tell you there was also a kind of fiddle, the secret of which is known only to the Shanar priesthood. Its bow is ordinary enough, made of bamboo; but it is whispered that the strings are human veins. . . . . When Captain Pole took possession of the priest's body, the priest leapt high in the air, and then rushed on the ox and killed him. He drank off the hot blood, and then began his dance. But what a fright he was when dancing! You know, I am not superstitious. . . . . Am I? . . ."

Sham Rao looked at us inquiringly, and I, for one, was glad, at this moment, that Miss X—— was half a mile off, asleep in the howdah.

"He turned, and turned, as if possessed by all the demons of Nâraka. The enraged crowd hooted and howled when the priest begun to inflict deep wounds all over his body with the bloody sacrificial knife. To see him, with his hair waving in the wind and his mouth covered with foam; to see him bathing in the blood of the sacrificed animal, mixing it with his own, was more than I could bear. I felt as if hallucinated, I fancied I also was spinning round. . . ."

Sham Rao stopped abruptly, struck dumb. Kangalim stood before us!

Her appearance was so unexpected that we all felt embarrassed. Carried away by Sham Rao's description, we had noticed neither how nor whence she came. Had she appeared from beneath the earth we could not have been more astonished. Narayan stared at her, opening wide his big jet-black eyes; the Babu clicked his tongue in utter confusion.

Imagine a skeleton seven feet high, covered with brown leather, with a dead child's tiny head stuck on its bony shoulders; the eyes set so deep and at the same time flashing such fiendish flames all through your body that you begin to feel your brain stop working, your thoughts become entangled and your blood freeze in your veins.

I describe my personal impressions, and no words of mine can do them justice. My description is too weak.

Mr. Y—— and the colonel both grew pale under her stare, and Mr. Y—— made a movement as if about to rise.

Needless to say that such an impression could not last. As soon as the witch had turned her gleaming eyes to the kneeling crowd, it vanished as swiftly as it had come. But still all our attention was fixed on this remarkable creature.

Three hundred years old! Who can tell? Judging by her appearance, we might as well conjecture her to be a thousand. We beheld a genuine living mummy, or rather a mummy endowed with motion. She seemed to have been withering since the creation. Neither time, nor the ills of life, nor the elements could ever affect this living statue of death. The all-destroying hand of time had touched her and stopped short. Time could do no more, and so had left her. And with all this, not a single grey hair. Her long black locks shone with a greenish sheen, and fell in heavy masses down to her knees.

To my great shame, I must confess that a disgusting reminiscence flashed into my memory. I thought about the hair and the nails of corpses growing in the graves, and tried to examine the nails of the old woman.

Meanwhile, she stood motionless as if suddenly transformed into an ugly idol. In one hand she held a dish with a piece of burning camphor, in the other a handful of rice, and she never removed her burning eyes from the crowd. The pale yellow flame of the camphor flickered in the wind, and lit up her death-like head, almost touching her chin; but she paid no heed to it. Her neck, as wrinkled as a mushroom, as thin as a stick, was surrounded by three rows of golden medallions. Her head was adorned with a golden snake. Her grotesque, hardly human body was covered by a piece of saffron-yellow muslin.

The demoniac little girls raised their heads from beneath the leaves, and set up a prolonged animal-like howl. Their example was followed by the old man, who lay exhausted by his frantic dance.

The witch tossed her head convulsively, and began her invocations, rising on tiptoe, as if moved by some external force.

"The goddess, one of the seven sisters, begins to take possession of her," whispered Sham Rao, not even thinking of wiping away the big drops of sweat that streamed from his brow. "Look, look at her!"

This advice was quite superfluous. We *were* looking at her, and at nothing else.

At first, the movements of the witch were slow, unequal, somewhat convulsive; then, gradually, they became less angular; at last, as if catching the cadence of the drums, leaning all her long body forward, and writhing like an eel, she rushed round and round the blazing bonfire. A dry leaf caught in a hurricane could not fly swifter. Her bare bony feet trod noiselessly on the rocky ground. The long locks of her hair flew round her like snakes, lashing the spectators, who knelt, stretching their trembling arms towards her, and writhing as if they were alive. Whoever was touched by one of this Fury's black curls, fell down on the ground, overcome with happiness, shouting thanks to the goddess, and considering himself blessed for ever. It was not human hair that touched the happy elect, it was the goddess herself, one of the seven.

Swifter and swifter fly her decrepit legs; the young, vigorous hands of the drummer can hardly follow her. But she does not think of catching the measure of his music; she rushes, she flies forward. Staring with her expressionless, motionless orbs at something before her, at something that is not visible to our mortal eyes, she hardly glances at her worshippers; then her look becomes full of fire; and whoever she looks at feels burned through to the marrow of his bones. At every glance she throws a few grains of rice. The small handful seems inexhaustible, as if the wrinkled palm contained the bottomless bag of Prince Fortunatus.

Suddenly she stops as if thunderstruck.

The mad race round the bonfire had lasted twelve minutes, but we looked in vain for a trace of fatigue on the death-like face of the witch. She stopped only for a moment, just the necessary time for the goddess to release her. As soon as she felt free, by a single effort she jumped over the fire and plunged into the deep tank by the portico. This time, she plunged only once; and whilst she stayed under the water, the second sister-goddess entered her body. The little boy in white produced another dish, with a new piece of burning camphor, just in time for the witch to take it up, and to rush again on her headlong way.

The colonel sat with his watch in his hand. During the second obsession the witch ran, leaped, and raced for exactly fourteen minutes. After this, she plunged twice in the tank, in honour of the second sister; and with every new obsession the number of her plunges increased, till it became six.

It was already an hour and a half since the race began. All this time the witch never rested, stopping only for a few seconds, to disappear under the water.

"She is a fiend, she cannot be a woman!" exclaimed the colonel, seeing the head of the witch immersed for the sixth time in the water.

"Hang me if I know!" grumbled Mr. Y——, nervously pulling his beard. "The only thing I know is that a grain of her cursed rice entered my throat, and I can't get it out!"

"Hush, hush! Please, do be quiet!" implored Sham Rao. "By talking you will spoil the whole business!"

I glanced at Narayan and lost myself in conjectures.

His features, which usually were so calm and serene, were quite altered at this moment, by a deep shadow of suffering. His lips trembled, and the pupils of his eyes were dilated, as if by a dose of *belladonna*. His eyes were lifted over the heads of the crowd, as if in his disgust he tried not to see what was before him, and at the same time could not see it, engaged in a deep reverie, which carried him away from us, and from the whole performance.

"What is the matter with him?" was my thought, but I had no time to ask him, because the witch was again in full swing, chasing her own shadow.

But with the seventh goddess the programme was slightly changed. The running of the old woman changed to leaping. Sometimes bending down to the ground, like a black panther, she leaped up to some worshipper, and halting before him touched his forehead with her finger, while her long, thin body shook with inaudible laughter. Then, again, as if shrinking back playfully from her shadow, and chased by it, in some uncanny game, the witch appeared to us like a horrid caricature of Dinorah, dancing her mad dance. Suddenly she straightened herself to her full height, darted to the portico and crouched before the smoking censer, beating her forehead against the granite steps. Another jump, and she was quite close to us, before the head of the monstrous Sivatherium. She knelt down again and bowed her head to the ground several times, with the sound of an empty barrel knocked against something hard.

We had hardly the time to spring to our feet and shrink back when she appeared on the top of the Sivatherium's head, standing there amongst the horns.

Narayan alone did not stir, and fearlessly looked straight in the eyes of the frightful sorceress.

But what was this? Who spoke in those deep manly tones? Her lips were moving, from her breast were issuing those quick, abrupt phrases, but the voice sounded hollow as if coming from beneath the ground.

"Hush, hush!" whispered Sham Rao, his whole body trembling. "She is going to prophesy! . . ."

"She?" incredulously inquired Mr. Y——. "This a woman's voice? I don't believe it for a moment. Someone's uncle must be stowed away somewhere about the place. Not the fabulous uncle she inherited from, but a real live one! . . ."

Sham Rao winced under the irony of this supposition, and cast an imploring look at the speaker.

"Woe to you! woe to you!" echoed the voice. "Woe to you, children of the impure Jaya and Vijaya! of the mocking, unbelieving lingerers round great Shiva's door! Ye, who are cursed by eighty thousand sages! Woe to you who believe not in the goddess Kâlî, and you who deny us, her Seven divine Sisters! Flesh-eating, yellow-legged vultures! friends of the oppressors of our land! dogs who are not ashamed to eat from the same trough with the Bellati!" (foreigners).

"It seems to me that your prophetess only foretells the past," said Mr. Y——, philosophically putting his hands in his pockets. "I should say that she is hinting at you, my dear Sham Rao."

"Yes! and at us also," murmured the colonel, who was evidently beginning to feel uneasy.

As to the unlucky Sham Rao, he broke out in a cold sweat, and tried to assure us that we were mistaken, that we did not fully understand her language.

"It is not about you, it is not about you! It is of me she speaks, because I am in Government service. Oh, she is inexorable!"

"Râkshasas! Asuras!" thundered the voice. "How dare you appear before us? how dare you to stand on this holy ground in boots made of a cow's sacred skin? Be cursed for etern——"

But her curse was not destined to be finished. In an instant the Hercules-like Narayan had fallen on the Sivatherium, and upset the whole pile, the skull, the horns and the demoniac Pythia included. A second more, and we thought we saw the witch flying in the air towards the portico. A confused vision of a stout, shaven Brahman, suddenly emerging from under the Sivatherium and instantly disappearing in the hollow beneath it, flashed before my dilated eyes.

But, alas! after the third second had passed, we all came to the embarrassing conclusion that, judging from the loud clang of the door of the cave, the representative of the Seven Sisters had ignominiously fled. The moment she had disappeared from our inquisitive eyes to her subterranean domain, we all realized that the unearthly hollow voice we had heard had nothing supernatural about it and belonged to the Brahman hidden under the Sivatherium—to someone's live uncle, as Mr. Y—— had rightly supposed.

. . . .

Oh, Narayan! how carelessly, how disorderly the worlds rotate around us. . . . I begin to seriously doubt their reality. From this moment I shall earnestly believe that all things in the universe are nothing but illusion, a mere Mâyâ. I am becoming a Vedantin. . . . I doubt that in the whole universe there may be found anything more objective than a Hindu witch flying up the spout.

. . . .

Miss X—— woke up, and asked what was the meaning of all this noise. The noise of many voices and the sounds of the many retreating footsteps, the general rush of the crowd, had frightened her. She listened to us with a condescending smile, and a few yawns, and went to sleep again.

Next morning, at daybreak, we very reluctantly, it must be owned, bade good-bye to the kind-hearted, good-natured Sham Rao. The confoundingly easy victory of Narayan hung heavily on his mind. His faith in the holy hermitess and the seven goddesses was a good deal shaken by the shameful capitulation of the Sisters, who had surrendered at the first blow from a mere mortal. But during the dark hours of the night he had had time to think it over, and to shake off the uneasy feeling of having unwillingly misled and disappointed his European friends.

Sham Rao still looked confused when he shook hands with us at parting, and expressed to us the best wishes of his family and himself.

As to the heroes of this truthful narrative, they mounted their elephants once more, and directed their heavy steps towards the high road and Jubbulpore.

GOD'S WARRIOR.

THE direction of our pilgrimage of self-improvement lay towards the north-west, as was previously decided. We were very impatient to see these *statûs in statu* of Anglo-India, but . . . Do what you may, there always will be a *but*.

We left the Jubbulpore line several miles from Nassik; and, to return to it, we had to go back to Akbarpur, then travel by doubtful Local-Board roads to the station Vanevad and take the train of Holkar's line, which joins the Great Indian Peninsular Railway.

Meanwhile, the Bagh caves were quite close to us, not more than fifty miles off, to the east from Mandu. We were undecided whether to leave them alone or go back to the Nerbudda. In the country situated on the other side of Kandesh, our Babu had some "chums," as everywhere else in India; the omnipresent Bengali Babus, who are always glad to be of some service to you, are scattered all over Hindostan, like the Jews in Russia. Besides, our party was joined by a new member.

The day before we had received a letter from Swâmi Dayânand, carried to us by a travelling Sannyâsi. Dayânand informed us that the cholera was increasing every day in Hardwar, and that we must postpone making his acquaintance personally till the end of May, either in Dehra-Dun, at the foot of Himalaya, or in Saharanpur, which attracts every tourist by its charming situation.

The Sannyâsi brought us also a nosegay from the Swâmi, a nosegay of the most extraordinary flowers, which are totally unknown in Europe. They grow only in certain Himalayan valleys; they possess the wonderful capacity of changing their colour after midday, and do not look dead even when faded. The Latin name of this charming plant is *Hibiscus mutabilis*. At night they are nothing but a large knot of pressed green leaves, but from dawn till ten o'clock the flowers open and look like large snow-white roses; then, towards twelve o'clock, they begin to redden, and later in the afternoon they look as crimson as a peony. These flowers are sacred to the Asuras, a kind of fallen angels in Hindu mythology, and to the sun-god Surya. The latter deity fell in love with an Asurâ at the beginning of creation, and since then is constantly caught whispering words of fiery love to the flower that shelters her. But the Asurâ is a virgin; she gives herself entirely to the service of the goddess Chastity, who is the patroness of all the ascetic brotherhoods. The love of Surya is vain, Asurâ will not listen to him. But under the flaming arrows of the enamoured god she blushes and in appearance loses her purity. The natives call this plant *lajjâlu*, the modest one.

We were spending the night by a brook, under a shadowy fig-tree. The Sannyâsi, who had made a wide circuit to fulfil Dayânand's request, made friends with us; and we sat up late in the night, listening whilst he talked about his travels, the wonders of his native country, once so great, and about the heroic deeds of old Runjit-Sing, the Lion of the Punjab.

Strange, mysterious beings are found sometimes amongst these travelling monks. Some of them are very learned; read and talk Sanskrit; know all about modern science and politics; and, nevertheless, remain faithful to their ancient philosophical conceptions. Generally they do not wear any clothes, except a piece of muslin round the loins, which is insisted upon by the police of the towns inhabited by Europeans. They wander from the age of fifteen, all their lives, and die generally very aged. They live never giving a thought to the morrow, like the birds of heaven, and the lilies of the field. They never touch money, and are contented with a handful of rice. All their worldly possessions consist of a small dry pumpkin to carry water, a rosary, a brass cup and a walking stick. The Sannyâsis and the Swâmis are usually Sikhs from the Punjab, and monotheists. They despise idol-worshippers, and have nothing to do with them, though the latter very often call themselves by their names.

Our new friend was a native of Amritsar, in the Punjab, and had been brought up in the "Golden Temple," on the banks of Amrita-Saras, the "Lake of Immortality." The head Guru, or instructor, of Sikhs resides there. He never crosses the boundaries of the temple. His chief occupation is the study of the book called *Adigrantha*, which belongs to the sacred literature of this strange bellicose sect. The Sikhs respect him as much as the Tibetans respect their Dalai-Lama. The Lamas in general consider the latter to be the incarnation of Buddha, the Sikhs think that the Mahâ-Guru of Amritsar is the incarnation of Nânak, the founder of their sect. Nevertheless, no true Sikh will ever say that Nânak was a deity; they look on him as a prophet, inspired by the spirit of the only God.

This shows that our Sannyâsi was not one of the naked travelling monks, but a true Akali; one of the six hundred warrior-priests attached to the Golden Temple, for the purpose of serving God and protecting the temple from the destructive Mussulmans. His name was Ram-Runjit-Das; and his personal appearance was in perfect accordance with his title of "God's warrior." His exterior was very remarkable and typical; and he looked like a muscular centurion of ancient Roman legions, rather than a peaceable servant of the altar.

Ram-Runjit-Das appeared to us mounted on a magnificent horse, and accompanied by another Sikh, who respectfully walked some distance behind him, and was evidently passing through his noviciate. Our Hindu companions had discerned that he was an Akali, when he was still in the distance. He wore a bright blue tunic without sleeves, exactly like that we see on the statues of Roman warriors. Broad steel bracelets protected his strong arms, and a shield protruded from behind his back. A blue, conical turban covered his head, and round his waist were many steel circlets. The enemies of the Sikhs assert that these sacred sectarian belts become more dangerous in the hand of an experienced "God's warrior," than any other weapon.

The Sikhs are the bravest and the most warlike sect of the whole Punjab. The word *sikh* means disciple. Founded in the fifteenth century by the wealthy and noble Brahman Nânak, the new teaching spread so successfully amongst the northern soldiers, that in 1539 A.D., when the founder died, it counted one hundred thousand followers. At the present time, this sect, harmonizing closely with the fiery natural mysticism, and the warlike tendencies of the natives, is the reigning creed of the whole Punjab. It is based on the principles of theocratic rule; but its dogmas are almost totally unknown to Europeans; the teachings, the religious conceptions, and the rites of the Sikhs, are kept secret. The following details are known generally: the Sikhs are ardent monotheists, they refuse to recognize caste; have no restrictions in diet, like Europeans; and bury their dead, which, except among Mussulmans, is a rare exception in India. The second volume of the *Adi-grantha* teaches them "to adore the only true God; to avoid superstitions; *to help the dead, that they may lead a righteous life;* and to earn one's living, sword in hand." Govinda, one of the great Gurus of the Sikhs, ordered them never to shave their beards and moustaches, and not to cut their hair—in order that they may not be mistaken for Mussulmans or any other native of India.

Many a desperate battle the Sikhs fought and won, against the Mussulmans, and against the Hindus. Their leader, the celebrated Runjit-Sing, after having been acknowledged the autocrat of the Upper Punjab, concluded a treaty with Lord Auckland, at the beginning of this century, in which his country was proclaimed an independent state. But after the death of the "old lion," his throne became the cause of the most dreadful civil wars and disorders. His son, Maharaja Dhulip-Sing, proved quite unfit for the high post he inherited from his father, and, under him, the Sikhs became an ill-disciplined restless mob. Their attempt to conquer the whole of Hindostan proved disastrous. Persecuted by his own soldiers, Dhulip-Sing sought the help of Englishmen, and was sent away to Scotland. And some time after this, the Sikhs took their place amongst the rest of Britain's Indian subjects.

But still there remains a strong body of the great Sikh sect of old. The Kuks represent the most dangerous underground current of the popular hatred. This new sect was founded about thirty years ago [written in 1879] by Bâlaka-Râma, and, at first, formed a bulk of people near Attok, in the Punjab, on the east bank of the Indus, exactly on the spot where the latter becomes navigable. Bâlaka-Râma had a double aim; to restore the religion of the Sikhs to its pristine purity, and to organize a secret political body, which must be ready for everything, at a moment's notice. This brotherhood consists of sixty thousand members, who pledged themselves never to reveal their secrets, and never to disobey any order of their leaders. In Attok they are few, for the town is small. But we were assured that the Kuks live everywhere in India. Their community is so perfectly organized that it is impossible to find them out, or to learn the names of their leaders.

In the course of the evening our Akali presented us with a little crystal bottle, filled with water from the "Lake of Immortality." He said that a drop of it would cure all diseases of the eye. There are numbers of fresh springs at the bottom of this lake, and so its water is wonderfully pure and transparent, in spite of hundreds of people daily bathing in it. When, later on, we visited it, we had the opportunity to verify the fact that the smallest stone at the bottom is seen perfectly distinctly, all over the one hundred and fifty square yards of the lake. Amrita-Saras is the most charming of all the sights of Northern India. The reflection of the Golden Temple in its crystal waters makes a picture that is simply *féerique.*

We had still seven weeks at our disposal. We were undecided between exploring the Bombay Presidency, the North-West Provinces and the Rajistan. Which were we to choose? Where were we to go? How best to employ our time? Before such a variety of interesting places we became irresolute. Hyderabad, which is said to transport the tourists into the scenery of the *Arabian Nights*, seemed so attractive that we seriously thought of turning our elephants back to the territory of the Nizam. We grew fond of the idea of visiting this

"City of the Lion," which was built in 1589 by the magnificent Mohamed-Kuli-Kutb-Shah, who was so used to luxuries of every kind as to grow weary even of Golkonda, with all its fairyland castles and bright gardens. Some buildings of Hyderabad, mere remnants of the past glory, are still known to renown. Mir-Abu-Talib, the keeper of the Royal Treasury, states that Mohamed-Kuli-Shah spent the fabulous sum of £2,800,000 sterling on the embellishment of the town, at the beginning of his reign; though the labour of the workmen did not cost him anything at all. Save these few memorials of greatness, the town looks like a heap of rubbish nowadays. But all tourists are unanimous on one point, namely, that the British Residency of Hyderabad still deserves its title of the Versailles of India.

The title the British Residency bears, and everything it may contain at the present time, are mere trifles compared with the past. I remember reading a chapter of the *History of Hyderabad*, by an English author, which contained something to the following effect: Whilst the Resident entertained the gentlemen, his wife was similarly employed receiving the ladies a few yards off, in a separate palace, which was as sumptuous, and bore the name of Rang-Mahal. Both palaces were built by Colonel Kirkpatrick, the late minister at the Nizam's court. Having married a native princess, be constructed this charming abode for her personal use. Its garden is surrounded by a high wall, as is customary in the Orient, and the centre of the garden is adorned with a large marble fountain, covered with scenes from the *Râmâyana*, and mosaics. Pavilions, galleries and terraces—everything in this garden is loaded with adornments of the most costly Oriental style, that is to say, with abundance of inlaid designs, paintings, gilding, ivory and marble. The great attraction of Mrs. Kirkpatrick's receptions were the nautches, magnificently dressed, thanks to the generosity of the Resident. Some of them wore a cargo of jewels worth £30,000, and literally shone from head to foot with diamonds and other precious stones.

The glorious times of the East India Company are beyond recall, and no Residents, and even no native princes, could now afford to be so "generous." India, this "most precious diamond of the British crown," is utterly exhausted, like a pile of gold in the hands of an alchemist, who thriftlessly spent it in the hope of finding the philosopher's stone. Besides ruining themselves and the country, the Anglo-Indians commit the greatest blunders, at least in two points of their present Government system. These two points are: first, the Western education they give to the higher classes; and, secondly, the protection and maintenance of the rights of idol-worship. Neither of these systems is wise. By means of the first they successfully replace the religious feelings of old India, which, however false, had the great advantage of being sincere, by a positive atheism amongst the young generation of the Brahmans; and by the means of the second they flatter only the ignorant masses, from whom nothing is to be feared under any circumstances. If the patriotic feelings of the bulk of the population could possibly be roused, the English would have been slaughtered long ago. The rural populace is unarmed, it is true, but a crowd seeking revenge could use the brass and stone idols, sent to India by thousands from Birmingham, with as great success as if they were so many swords. But, as it is, the masses of India are indifferent and harmless; so that the only existing danger comes from the side of the educated classes. And the

English fail to see that the better the education they give them, the more careful they must be to avoid reopening the old wounds, always alive to new injury, in the heart of every true Hindu. The Hindus are proud of the past of their country, dreams of past glories are their only compensation for the bitter present. The English education they receive only enables them to learn that Europe was plunged in the darkness of the Stone Age, when India was in the full growth of her splendid civilization. And so the comparison of their past with their present is only the more sad. This consideration never hinders the Anglo-Indians from hurting the feelings of the Hindus. For instance, in the unanimous opinion of travellers and antiquarians, the most interesting building of Hyderabad is Chahar-Minar, a college that was built by Mohamed-Kuli-Khan on the ruins of a still more ancient college. It is built at the crossing of four streets, on four arches, which are so high that loaded camels and elephants with their turrets pass through freely. Over these arches rise the several stories of the college. Each story once was destined for a separate branch of learning. Alas! the times when India studied philosophy and astronomy at the feet of her great sages are gone, and the English have transformed the college itself into a warehouse. The hall, which served for the study of astronomy, and was filled with quaint, mediæval apparatus, is now used for a depôt of opium; and the hall of philosophy contains huge boxes of liqueurs, rum and champagne, which are prohibited by the Koran, as well as by the Brahmans.

We were so enchanted by what we heard about Hyderabad, that we resolved to start thither the very next morning, when our *ciceroni* and companions destroyed all our plans by a single word. This word was: heat. During the hot season in Hyderabad the thermometer reaches ninety-eight degrees Fahrenheit in the shade, and the temperature of the water in the Indus is the temperature of the blood. As to Upper Sindh, where the dryness of the air, and the extreme aridity of the sandy soil reproduce the Sahara in miniature, the usual shade temperature is one hundred and thirty degrees Fahrenheit. No wonder the missionaries have no chance there. The most eloquent of Dante's descriptions of hell could hardly produce anything but a cooling effect on a populace who live perfectly contented under these circumstances.

Calculating that there was no obstacle to our going to the Bagh caves, and that going to Sindh was a perfect impossibility, we recovered our equanimity. Then the general council decided that we had better abandon all ideas of a predetermined plan, and travel as fancy led us.

We dismissed our elephants, and next day, a little before sunset, arrived at the spot where the Vagrey and Girna join. These are two little rivers, quite famous in the annals of the Indian mythology, and which are generally conspicuous by their absence, especially in summer. At the opposite side of the river, there lay the illustrious Bagh caves, with their four openings blinking in the thick evening mist.

We thought of crossing to them immediately, by the help of a ferry boat, but our Hindu friends and the boatmen interposed. The former said that visiting these caves is dangerous even by daytime; because all the neighbourhood is full of beasts of prey and of tigers, who, I concluded, are like the Bengali Babus, to be met with everywhere in India. Before venturing into these caves, you must send a reconnoitring party of torch-bearers and armed shikaris. As to the boatmen, they protested on different grounds, but protested strongly. They said that no Hindu would dare to approach these caves after the sun set. No one but a Bellati would fancy that Vagrey and Girna are ordinary rivers, for every Hindu knows they are divine spouses, the god Shiva and his wife Pârvatî. This, in the first instance; and in the second, the Bagh tigers are no ordinary tigers either. The sahibs are totally mistaken. These tigers are the servants of the Sadhus, of the holy miracle-workers, who have haunted the caves now for many centuries, and who deign sometimes to take the shape of a tiger. And neither the gods, nor the Sadhus, nor the glamour, nor the true tigers are fond of being disturbed in their nightly rest.

What could we say against all this? We cast one more sorrowful look at the caves, and returned to our antediluvian carriages. The Babu and Narayan said we must spend the night at the house of a certain "chum" of the Babu, who resided in a small town, three miles further on, and bearing the same name as the caves; and we unwillingly acquiesced.

Many things in India are wonderful and unintelligible, but one of the most wonderful and the most unintelligible, is the geographical and the topographical disposition of the numberless territories of this country. Political conjunctures in India seem to be everlastingly playing the French game *casse-tête*, changing the pattern, diminishing one part and adding to another. The land that only yesterday belonged to this Raja or that Takur, is sure to be found to-day in the hands of quite a different set of people. For instance, we were in the Raj of Amjir in Malva, and we were going to the little city of Bagh, which also belongs to Malva and is included in the Amjir Raj. In the documents, Malva is included in the independent possessions of Holkar; and nevertheless the Amjir Raj does not belong to Tukuji-Rao-Holkar, but to the son of the independent Raja of Amjir, who was hanged, "by inadvertence" as we were assured, in 1857. The city, and the caves of Bagh, very oddly belong to the Maharaja Sindya of Gwalior, who, besides, does not own them personally, having made a kind of present of them, and their nine thousand rupees of revenue, to some poor relation. This poor relation, in his turn, does not enjoy the property in the least, because a certain Rajput Takur stole it from him, and will not consent to give it back. Bagh is situated on the road from Gujerat to Malva, in the defile of Oodeypur, which is owned accordingly by the Maharana of Oodeypur. Bagh itself is built on the top of a woody hillock, and being disputed property does not belong to any one in particular, properly speaking; but a small fortress, and a bazaar in the centre of it are the private possessions of a certain *dhani;* who, besides being the chieftain of the Bhimalah tribe, was the personal "chum" of our Babu, and a "great thief and highway robber," according to the assertions of the said Babu.

"But why do you intend taking us to the place of a man whom you consider as a thief and a robber?" objected one of us timidly.

"He *is* a thief and a brigand," coolly answered the Bengali, "but only in the political sense. Otherwise he is an excellent man, and the truest of friends. Besides, if he does not help us, we shall starve; the bazaar and everything in the shops belong to him."

These explanations of the Babu notwithstanding, we were glad to learn that the "chum" in question was absent, and we were received by a relation of his. The garden was put at our disposal, and before our tents were pitched, we saw people coming from every side of the garden, bringing us provisions. Having deposited what he had brought, each of them, on leaving the tent, threw over his shoulder a pinch of betel and soft sugar, an offering to the "foreign bhutas," which were supposed to accompany us wherever we went. The Hindus of our party asked us, very seriously, not to laugh at this performance, saying it would be dangerous in this out-of-the-way place.

No doubt they were right. We were in Central India, the very nest of all kinds of superstitions, and were surrounded by Bhils. All along the Vindya ridge, from Yama, on the west of the "dead city," the country is thickly populated by this most daring, restless and superstitious of all the half-savage tribes of India.

The Orientalists think that the name Bhils comes from the Sanskrit root *bhid*, which means to separate. Sir J. Malcolm supposes accordingly that the Bhils are sectarians, who separated from the Brahmanical creed, and were excommunicated. All this looks very probable, but their tribal traditions say something different. Of course, in this case, as in every other, their history is strongly entangled with mythology; and one has to go through a thick shrubbery of fancy before reaching the tribe's genealogical tree.

The relation of the absent *dhani*, who spent the evening with us, told us the following: The Bhils are the descendants of one of the sons of Mahâdeva, or Shiva, and of a fair woman, with blue eyes and a white face, whom he met in some forest on the other side of the Kâlapâni, "black waters," or ocean. This pair had several sons, one of whom, as handsome as he was vicious, killed the favourite ox of his grandfather Mahâdeva, and was banished by his father to the Jodpur desert. Banished to its remotest southern corner, he married; and soon his descendants filled the whole country. They scattered along the Vindya ridge, on the western frontier of Malva and Kandesh; and, later, in the woody wilderness, on the shores of the rivers Mahâ, Narmadâ and Tapti. And all of them, inheriting the beauty of their forefather, his blue eyes and fair complexion, inherited also his turbulent disposition and his vice.

"We are thieves and robbers," naïvely explained the relative of the Babu's "chum," "but we can't help it, because this is the decree of our mighty forefather, the great Mahâ-deva-Shiva. Sending his grandson to repent his sins in the desert, he said to him: 'Go, wretched murderer of my son and your brother, the ox Nardi; go and live the life of an exile and a brigand, to be an everlasting warning to your brethren! . .' These are the very words of the great god. Now, do you think we could disobey his orders? The least of our actions is always regulated by our *Bhamyas*—chieftains—who are the direct descendants of Nadir-Sing, the first Bhil, the child of our exiled ancestor, and being this, it is only natural that the great god speaks to us through him."

Is not it strange that Apis, the sacred ox of the Egyptians, is honoured by the followers of Zoroaster, as well as by the Hindus? The ox Nardi, the emblem of life in nature, is the son of the creating father, or rather his life-giving breath. Ammianus Marcellinus mentions, in one of his works, that there exists a book which gives the *exact age* of Apis, the clue to the mystery of creation and the cyclic calculations. The Brahmans also explain the allegory of the ox Nardi by the continuation of life on our globe.

The "mediators" between Shiva and the Bhils possess such unrestricted authority that the most awful crimes are accomplished at their lightest word. The tribe have thought it necessary to decrease their power to a certain extent by instituting a kind of council in every village. This council is called *tarvi,* and tries to cool down the hot-headed fancies of the *dhanis,* their brigand lords. However, the word of the Bhils is sacred, and their hospitality is boundless.

The history ana the annals of the princes of Jodpur and Oodeypur confirm the legend of the Bhil emigration from their primitive desert, but how they happened to be there nobody knows. Colonel Tod is positive that the Bhils, together with the Merases and the Goands, are the aborigines of India, as well as the tribes who inhabit the Nerbuda forests. But why the Bhils should be almost fair and blue-eyed, whereas the rest of the hill-tribes are almost African in type, is a question that is not answered by this statement. The fact that all these aborigines call themselves *Bhûmaputra* and *Vanaputra,* sons of the earth and sons of the forest, when the Rajputs, their first conquerors, call themselves Sûrya-vansa and the Brahmans Indu-putras, descendants of the sun and the moon, does not prove everything. It seems to me, that in the present case, their appearance, which confirms their legends, is of much greater value than philology. Dr. Clark, the author of *Travels in Scandinavia,* is very logical in saying that, "by directing our attention on the traces of the ancient superstitions of a tribe, we shall find out who were its primitive forefathers much more easily than by scientific examination of their tongue; the superstitions are grafted on the very root, whereas the tongue is subjected to all kinds of changes."

But, unfortunately, everything we know about the history of the Bhils is reduced to the above-mentioned tradition, and to a few ancient songs of their bards. These bards or *bhattas* live in Rajistan, but visit the Bhils yearly, in order not to lose the leading thread of the achievements of their countrymen. Their songs are history, because the bhattas have existed from time immemorial, composing their lays for future generations, for this is their hereditary duty. And the songs of the remotest antiquity point to the lands over the Kâla-pâni as the place whence the Bhils came; that is to say, some place in Europe. Some Orientalists, especially Colonel Tod, seek to prove that the Rajputs, who conquered the Bhils, were newcomers of Scythian origin, and that the Bhils are the true aborigines. To prove this, they put forward some features common to both peoples, Rajput and Scythian, for instance (1) the worship of the sword, the lance, the shield and the horse; (2) the worship of, and the sacrifice to, the sun (which, as far as I know, never was worshipped by the Scythians); (3) the passion of gambling (which again is as strong amongst the Chinese and the Japanese); (4) the custom of drinking blood out of the skull of an enemy (which is also practised by some aborigines of America), etc., etc.

I do not intend entering here on a scientific ethnological discussion; and, besides, I am sure no one fails to see that the reasoning of scientists sometimes takes a very strange turn when they set to prove some favourite theory of theirs. It is enough to remember how entangled and obscure is the history of the ancient Scythians to abstain from drawing any positive conclusions whatsoever from it. The tribes that go under one general denomination of Scythians were many, and still it is impossible to deny that there is a good deal of similitude between the customs of the old Scandinavians, worshippers of Odin, whose land indeed was occupied by the Scythians more than five hundred years B.C. and the customs of the Rajputs. But this similitude gives as much right to the Rajputs to say that we are a colony of Sûrya-vansas settled in the West as to us to maintain that the Rajputs are the descendants of Scythians who emigrated to the East. The Scythians of Herodotus and the Scythians of Ptolemy, and some other classical writers, are two perfectly distinct nationalities. Under Scythia, Herodotus means the extension of land from the mouth of Danube to the Sea of Azoff, according to Niebuhr; and to the mouth of Don, according to Rawlinson; whereas the Scythia of Ptolemy is a country strictly Asiatic, including the whole space between the river Volga and Serika, or China. Besides this, Scythia was divided by the western Himalayas, which the Roman writers call *Imaus*, into Scythia *intra* Imaum, and Scythia *extra* Imaum. Given this lack of precision, the Rajputs may be called the Scythians of Asia, and the Scythians the Rajputs of Europe, with the same degree of likelihood. Pinkerton's opinion is that European contempt for the Tartars would not be half so strong if the European public learned how closely we are related to them; that our forefathers came from northern Asia, and that our primitive customs, laws and mode of living were the same as theirs; in a word, that we are nothing but a Tartar colony . . . Cimbri, Kelts and Gauls, who conquered the northern part of Europe, are different names of the same tribe, whose origin is Tartary. Who were the Goths, the Swedes, the Vandals, the Huns and the Franks, if not separate swarms of the same beehive? The annals of Sweden point to Kashgar as the fatherland of the Swedes. The likeness between the languages of the Saxons and the Kipchak-Tartars is striking; and the Keltic, which still exists in Brittany and in Wales, is the best proof that their inhabitants are descendants of the Tartar nation.

Whatever Pinkerton and others may say, the modern Rajput warriors do not answer in the least the description Hippocrates gives us of the Scythians. The "father of medicine" says: "The bodily structure of these men is thick, coarse and stunted; their joints are weak and flabby; they have almost no hair, and each of them resembles the other." No man, who has seen the handsome, gigantic warriors of Rajistan, with their abundant hair and beards, will ever recognize this portrait drawn by Hippocrates as theirs. Besides, the Scythians, whoever they may be, buried their dead, which the Rajputs never did, judging by the records of their most ancient MSS. The Scythians were a wandering nation, and are described by Hesiod as "living in covered carts and feeding on mare's milk." And the Rajputs have been a sedentary people from time immemorial, inhabiting towns, and having their history at least several hundred years before Christ—that is to say, earlier than the epoch of Herodotus. They do celebrate the Ashvamedha, the horse sacrifice; but will not touch mare's milk, and despise all Mongolians. Herodotus says that the Scythians, who called themselves Skoloti, hated foreigners, and never let any stranger in their country; and the Rajputs are one of the most hospitable peoples of the world. In the epoch of the wars of Darius, 516 B.C., the Scythians were still in their own district, about the mouth of the Danube. And at the same epoch the Rajputs were already known in India and had their own kingdom. As to the Ashvamedha, which Colonel Tod thinks to be the chief illustration of his theory, the custom of killing horses in honour of the sun is mentioned in the *Rig-Veda*, as well as in the *Aitareya-Brâhmana*. Martin Haug states that the latter has probably been in existence since 2000-2400 B.C.

But it strikes me that the digression from the Babu's chum to the Scythians and the Rajputs of the antediluvian epoch threatens to become too long, so I beg the reader's pardon and resume the thread of my narrative.

THE BANNS OF MARRIAGE.

Next day, early in the morning, the local shikaris went under the leadership of the warlike Akali, to hunt glamoured and real tigers in the caves. It took them longer than we expected. The old Bhil, who represented to us the absent *dhani*, proposed that in the meanwhile we should witness a Brahmanical wedding ceremony. Needless to say, we jumped at this. The ceremonies of betrothal and marriage have not changed in India during the last two millenniums at least. They are performed according to the directions of Manu, and the old theme has no new variations. India's religious rites have crystallized long ago. Whoever has seen a Hindu wedding in 1879, saw it as it was celebrated in ancient Âryâvarta many centuries ago.

A few days before we left Bombay we read in a small local newspaper two announcements of marriages: the first the marriage of a Brahman heiress, the second of a daughter of the fire-worshippers. The first announcement was something to the following effect: "The family of Bimbay Mavlankar, etc., etc., are preparing for a happy event. This respectable member of our community, unlike the rest of the less fortunate Brahmans of his caste, has found a husband for his granddaughter in a rich Gujerat family of the same caste. The little Rama-bai is already five, her future husband is seven. The wedding is to take place in two months and promises to be brilliant."

The second announcement referred to an accomplished fact. It appeared in a Parsi paper, which strongly insists on the necessity of giving up "disgusting superannuated customs," and especially the early marriage. It justly ridiculed a certain Gujerati newspaper, which had just described in very pompous expressions a recent wedding ceremony in Poona. The bridegroom, who had just entered his sixth year "pressed to his heart a blushing bride of two and a half!" The usual answers of this couple entering into matrimony proved so indistinct that the Mobed had to address the questions to their parents: "Are you willing to have him for your lawful husband, O daughter of Zaratushta?" and "Are you willing to be her husband, O son of Zoroaster?" "Everything went as well as it could be expected," continued the newspaper; "the bridegroom was led out of the room by the hand, and the bride, who was carried away in arms, greeted the guests, not with smiles, but with a tremendous howl, which made her forget the existence of such a thing as a pocket-handkerchief, and remember only her feeding-bottle; for the latter article she asked repeatedly, half choked with sobs, and throttled with the weight of the family diamonds. Taking it all in all, it was a Parsi marriage, which shows the progress of our speedily developing nation with the exactitude of a weather glass," added the satirical newspaper.

Having read this we laughed heartily, though we did not give full credit to this description, and thought it a good deal exaggerated. We knew Parsi and Brahman families in which were husbands of ten years of age; but had never heard as yet of a bride who was a baby in arms.

It is not without reason that the Brahmans are fervent upholders of the ancient law which prohibits to everyone, except the officiating Brahmans, the study of Sanskrit and the reading of the *Vedas*. The Shûdras and even the high-born Vaishyas were in olden times to be executed for such an offence. The secret of this rigour lies in the fact that the *Vedas* do not permit matrimony for women under fifteen to twenty years of age, and for men under twenty-five, or even thirty. Eager above all that every religious ceremony should fill their pockets, the Brahmans never stopped at disfiguring their ancient sacred literature; and not to be caught, they pronounced its study accursed. Amongst other "criminal inventions," to use the expression of Swâmi Dayânand, there is a text in the Brahmanical books, which contradicts everything that is to be found in the *Vedas* on this particular matter: I speak of the Kudva Kunbis, the wedding season of all the agricultural classes of Central Asia. This season is to be celebrated once in every twelve years, but it appears to be a field from which *Messieurs les* Brahmans gathered the most abundant harvest. At this epoch, all the mothers have to seek audiences from the goddess Mâtâ, the great mother—of course through her rightful oracles the Brahmans. Mâtâ is the special patroness of all the four kinds of marriages practised in India: the marriages of adults, of children, of babies, and of specimens of humanity that are as yet to be born.

The latter is the queerest of all, because the feelings it excites are so very like gambling. In this case, the marriage ceremony is celebrated between the mothers of the future children. Many a curious incident is the result of these matrimonial parodies. But a true Brahman will never allow the derision of fate to shake his dignity, and the docile population never will doubt the infallibility of these "elect of the gods." An open antagonism to the Brahmanical institutions is more than rare; the feelings of reverence and dread the masses show to the Brahmans are so blind and so sincere, that an outsider cannot help smiling at them and respecting them at the same time.

If both the mothers have children of the same sex, it will not upset the Brahman in the least; he will say this was the will of the goddess Mâtâ, it shows that she desires the new-born babies to be two loving brothers, or two loving sisters, as the case may be, in future. And if the children grow up, they will be acknowledged heirs to the properties of both mothers. In this case, the Brahman breaks the bonds of the marriage by the order of the goddess, is paid for doing so, and the whole affair is dropped altogether. But if the children are of different sexes these bonds cannot be broken, even if they are born cripples or idiots.

While I am dealing with the family life of India, I had better mention some other features, not to return to them any more. No Hindu has the right to remain single. The only exceptions are, in case the child is destined to monastic life from the first days of his existence, and in case the child is consecrated to the service of one of the gods of the Trimûrti even before he is born. Religion insists on matrimony for the sake of having a son, whose duty it will be to perform every prescribed rite, in order that his departed father may enter *Swarga*, or paradise. Even the caste of Brahmachâryas, who take vows of chastity, but take a part and interest in worldly life—and so are the unique lay-celibates of India—are bound to adopt sons. The rest of the Hindus must remain in matrimony till the age of forty; after which they earn the right to leave the world, and to seek salvation, leading an ascetic life in some jungle. If a member of some Hindu family happens to be afflicted from birth with some organic defect, this will not be an impediment to his marrying, on the condition that his wife should be also a cripple, if she belongs to the same caste. The defects of husband and wife must be different: if he is blind, she must be hump-backed or lame, and *vice versâ*. But if the young man in question is prejudiced, and wants a healthy wife, he must condescend to make a *mésalliance;* he must stoop to choose a wife in a caste that is exactly one degree lower than his own. But in this case his kinsmen and associates will not acknowledge her; the *parvenue* will not be received on any conditions whatever. Besides, all these exceptional instances depend entirely on the family Guru—on the priest who is inspired by the gods.

All the above holds good as far as the men are concerned; but with the women it is quite different.

Only the nautches—dancing girls consecrated to gods, and living in temples—can be said to be free and happy. Their occupation is hereditary, but they are vestals and daughters of vestals, however strange this may sound to a European ear. But the notions of the Hindus, especially on questions of morality, are quite independent, and even anti-Western, if I may use this expression. No one is more severe and exacting in the questions of feminine honour and chastity; but the Brahmans proved to be more cunning than even the Roman augurs. Rhea Sylvia, for instance, the mother of Romulus and Remus, was buried alive by the ancient Romans, in spite of the god Mars taking an active part in her *faux pas*. Numa and Tiberius took exceedingly good care that the good morals of their priestesses should not become merely nominal. But the vestals on the banks of the Ganges and the Indus understand the question differently from those on the banks of the Tiber. The intimacy of the nautch-girls with the gods, which is generally accepted, cleanses them from every sin and makes them in every one's eyes irreproachable and infallible. A nautcha cannot sin, in spite of the crowd of the "celestial musicians" who swarm in every pagoda, in the form of baby-vestals and their little brothers. No virtuous Roman matron was ever so respected as the pretty little nautcha. This great reverence for the happy "brides of the gods" is especially striking in the purely native towns of Central India, where the population has preserved intact their blind faith in the Brahmans.

Every nautcha can read, and receives the highest Hindu education. They all read and write in Sanskrit, and study the best literature of ancient India, and her six chief philosophies, but especially music, singing and dancing. Besides these "godborn" priestesses of the pagodas, there are also public nautches, who, like the Egyptian almeas, are within the reach of ordinary mortals, not only of gods; they also are in most cases women of a certain culture.

But the fate of an honest woman of Hindostan is quite different; and a bitter and incredibly unjust fate it is. The life of a thoroughly good woman, especially if she happens to possess warm faith and unshaken piety, is simply a long chain of fatal misfortunes. And the higher her family and social position, the more wretched is her life. Married women are so afraid of resembling the professional dancing girls, that they cannot be persuaded to learn anything the latter are taught. If a Brahman woman is rich her life is spent in demoralizing idleness; if she is poor, so much the worse, her earthly existence is concentrated in monotonous performances of mechanical rites. There is no past, and no future for her; only a tedious present, from which there is no possible escape. And this only if everything be well, if her family be not visited by sad losses. Needless to say that, amongst Brahman women, marriage is not a question of free choice, and still less of affection. Her choice of a husband is restricted by the caste to which her father and mother happen to belong; and so, to find a suitable match for a girl is a matter of great difficulty, as well as of great expense. In India, the high-caste woman is not bought, but she has to buy the right to get married. Accordingly, the birth of a girl is not a joy, but a sorrow, especially if her parents are not rich. She *must* be married not later than when she is seven or eight; a little girl of ten is an old maid in India, she is a discredit to her parents and is the miserable butt of all her more fortunate contemporaries.

One of the few noble achievements of Englishmen in India which have succeeded is the decrease of infanticide, which some time ago was a daily practice, and still is not quite got rid of. Little girls were killed by their parents everywhere in India; but this dreadful custom was especially common amongst the tribes of Jadej, once so powerful in Sindh, and now reduced to petty brigandage. Probably these tribes were the first to spread this heartless practice. Obligatory marriage for little girls is a comparatively recent invention, and it alone is responsible for the parents' decision rather to see them dead than unmarried. The ancient Âryans knew nothing of it. Even the ancient Brahmanical literature shows that, amongst the pure Âryans, woman enjoyed the same privileges as man. Her voice was listened to by the statesmen; she was free either to choose a husband, or to remain single. Many a woman's name plays an important part in the chronicles of the ancient Âryan land; many women have come down to posterity as eminent poets, astronomers, philosophers, and even sages and lawyers.

But with the invasion of the Persians, in the seventh century, and later on of the fanatical, all-destroying Mussulmans, all this changed. Woman became enslaved, and the Brahmans did everything to humiliate her. In towns, the position of the Hindu woman is still worse than amongst agricultural classes.

The wedding ceremonies are very complicated and numerous. They are divided into three groups: the rites before the wedding; the rites during the ceremony; and the rites after the celebration has taken place. The first group consists of eleven ceremonies: the asking in marriage; the comparison of the two horoscopes; the sacrifice of a goat; the fixing of a propitious day; the building of the altar; the purchase of the sacred pots for household use; the invitation of guests; the sacrifices to the household gods; mutual presents and so on. All this must be accomplished as a religious duty, and is full of entangled rites. As soon as a little girl in some Hindu family is four years old, her father and mother send for the family Guru, give him her horoscope, drawn up previously by the astrologer of their caste (a very important post), and send the Guru to this or that inhabitant of the place who is known to have a son of appropriate age. The father of the little boy has to put the horoscope on the altar before the family gods and to answer: "I am well disposed towards the Pânigrhana; let Rudra help us." The Guru must ask when the union is to take place, after which he is bowed out. A few days later the father of the little boy takes the horoscope of his son as well as of the little girl to the chief astrologer. If the latter finds them propitious to the intended marriage, it will take place; if not, his decision is immediately sent to the father of the little girl, and the whole affair is dropped. If the astrologer's opinion is favourable, however, the bargain is concluded on the spot. The astrologer offers a cocoa-nut and a handful of sugar to the father, after which nothing can be altered; otherwise a Hindu *vendetta* will be handed down from generation to generation. After the obligatory goat-sacrifice, the couple are irrevocably betrothed, and the astrologer fixes the day of the wedding.

The sacrifice of the goat is very interesting, so I am going to describe it in detail.

A child of the male sex is sent to invite several married ladies, old women of twenty or twenty-five, to witness the worship of the Lares and Penates. Each family has a household goddess of its own—which is not impossible, since the Hindu gods number thirty-three crores. On the eve of the sacrificial day, a kid is brought into the house, and all the family sleep round him. Next morning, the reception hall in the lower story is made ready for the ceremony. The floor is thickly covered with cow-dung, and, right in the middle of the room a square is traced with white chalk, in which is placed a high pedestal, with the statue of the goddess. The patriarch of the family brings the goat, and, holding him by the horns, lowers his head to salute the goddess. After this, the "old" and young women sing marriage hymns, tie the legs of the goat, cover his head with red powder, and make a lamp smoke under his nose, to banish the evil spirits from round him. When all this is done, the female element puts itself out of the way, and the patriarch comes again upon the stage. He treacherously puts a ration of rice before the goat, and as soon as the victim becomes innocently absorbed in gratifying his appetite, the old man chops his head off with a single stroke of his sword, and bathes the goddess in the smoking blood coming from the head of the animal, which he holds in his right arm, over the idol. The women sing in chorus, and the ceremony of betrothal is over.

The ceremonies with the astrologers, and the exchange of presents, are too long to be described. I shall mention only, that in all these ceremonies the astrologer plays the double part of an augur and a family lawyer. After a general invocation to the elephant-headed god Ganesha, the marriage contract is written on the reverse of the horoscopes and sealed, and a general blessing is pronounced over the assembly.

Needless to say that all these ceremonies had been accomplished long ago in the family to whose marriage party we were invited in Bagh. All these rites are sacred, and most probably we, being mere strangers, would not have been allowed to witness them. We saw them all later on in Benares—thanks to the intercession of our Babu.

When we arrived on the spot, where the Bagh ceremony was celebrated, the festivity was at its height.

The bridegroom was not more than fourteen years old, while the bride was only ten. Her small nose was adorned with a huge golden ring with some very brilliant stone, which dragged her nostril down. Her face looked comically piteous, and sometimes she cast furtive glances at us. The bridegroom, a stout, healthy-looking boy, attired in cloth of gold and wearing the many storied Indra hat, was on horseback, surrounded by a whole crowd of male relations.

The altar, especially erected for this occasion, presented a queer sight. Its regulation height is three times the length of the bride's arm from the shoulder down to the middle finger. Its materials are bricks and whitewashed clay. Forty-six earthen pots painted with red, yellow and green stripes—the colours of the Trimûrti—rose in two pyramids on both sides of the "god of marriages" on the altar; and all round it a crowd of little married girls were busy grinding ginger. When it was reduced to powder the whole crowd rushed on the bridegroom, dragged him from his horse, and, having undressed him, began rubbing him with wet ginger. As soon as the sun dried him he was dressed again by some of the little ladies, whilst one part of them sang and the other sprinkled his head with water from lotus leaves twisted into tubes. We understood that this was a delicate attention to the water gods.

We were also told that the whole of the previous night had been given up to the worship of various spirits. The last rites, begun weeks ago, were hurriedly brought to an end during this last night. Invocations to Ganesha, to the god of marriages; to the gods of the elements, water, fire, air and earth; to the goddess of the small-pox and other illnesses; to the spirits of ancestors and planetary spirits, to the evil spirits, good spirits, family spirits, and so on, and so on. Suddenly our ears were struck by strains of music. . . . Good heavens! what a dreadful symphony it was! The ear-splitting sounds of Indian tom-toms, Tibetan drums, Singalese pipes, Chinese trumpets, and Burmese gongs deafened us on all sides, awakening in our souls hatred for humanity and humanity's inventions.

"De tous les bruits du monde celui de la musique est le plus désagréable!" was my ever-recurring thought.

Happily, this agony did not last long, and was replaced by the choral singing of Brahmans and nautches, which was very original, but perfectly bearable. The wedding was a rich one, and so the "vestals" appeared in state. A moment of silence, of restrained whispering, and one of them, a tall, handsome girl with eyes literally filling half her forehead, began approaching one guest after the other in perfect silence, and rubbing their faces with her hand, leaving traces of sandal and saffron powders. She glided towards us also, noiselessly moving over the dusty road with her bare feet; and before we realized what she was doing she had daubed me as well as the colonel and Miss X——, which made the latter sneeze and wipe her face for at least ten minutes, with loud but vain utterances of indignation.

The Babu and Mulji offered their faces to the little hand, full of saffron, with smiles of condescending generosity. But the indomitable Narayan shrank from the vestal so unexpectedly at the precise moment when, with fiery glances at him, she stood on tiptoe to reach his face, that she quite lost countenance and sent a full dose of powder over his shoulder, whilst he turned away from her with knitted brow. Her forehead also showed several threatening lines, but in a moment she overcame her anger and glided towards Ram-Runjit-Das, sparkling with engaging smiles. But here she met with still less luck; offended at once in his monotheism and his chastity, the "God's warrior" pushed the vestal so unceremoniously that she nearly upset the elaborate pot-decoration of the altar. A dissatisfied murmur ran through the crowd, and we were preparing to be condemned to shameful banishment for the sins of the warlike Sikh, when the drums sounded again and the procession moved on. In front of everyone drove the trumpeters and the drummers in a car gilded from top to bottom, and dragged by bullocks loaded with garlands of flowers; next after them walked a whole detachment of pipers, and then a third body of musicians on horseback, who frantically hammered huge gongs. After them proceeded the *cortége* of the bridegroom's and the bride's relations on horses adorned with rich harness, feathers and flowers; they went in pairs. They were followed by a regiment of Bhils in full . . . disarmour—because no weapons but bows and arrows had been left to them by the English Government. All these Bhils looked as if they had tooth-ache, because of the odd way they have of arranging the ends of their white *pagris*. After them walked clerical Brahmans, with aromatic tapers in their hands and surrounded by the flitting battalion of nautches, who amused themselves all the way by graceful *glissades* and *pas*. They were followed by the lay Brahmans—the "twice born." The bridegroom rode on a handsome horse; on both sides walked two couples of warriors, armed with yaks' tails to wave the flies away. They were accompanied by two more men on each side with silver fans. The bridegroom's group was wound up by a naked Brahman, perched on a donkey and holding over the head of the boy a huge red silk umbrella. After him a car loaded with a thousand cocoa-nuts and a hundred bamboo-baskets, tied together by a red rope. The god who looks after marriages drove in melancholy isolation on the vast back of an elephant, whose mahout led him by a chain of flowers. Our humble party modestly advanced just behind the elephant's tail.

The performance of rites on the way seemed endless.

We had to stop before every tree, every pagoda, every sacred tank and bush, and at last before a sacred cow. When we came back to the house of the bride it was four in the afternoon, and we had started a little after six in the morning. We all were utterly exhausted, and Miss X—— literally threatened to fall asleep on her feet. The indignant Sikh had left us long ago, and had persuaded Mr. Y—— and Mulji—whom the colonel had nicknamed the "mute general"—to keep him company. Our respected president was bathed in his own perspiration, and even Narayan the unchangeable yawned and sought consolation in a fan. But the Babu was simply astonishing. After a nine hours' walk under the sun, with his head unprotected, he looked fresher than ever, without a drop of sweat on his dark satin-like forehead. He showed his white teeth in an eternal smile, and chaffed us all, reciting the "Diamond Wedding" of Steadman.

We struggled against our fatigue in our desire to witness the last ceremony, after which the woman is for ever cut off from the external world. It was just going to begin; and we kept our eyes and ears wide open.

The bridegroom and the bride were placed before the altar. The officiating Brahman tied their hands with some kus-kus grass, and led them three times round the altar. Then their hands were untied, and the Brahman mumbled a mantram. When he had finished, the boy husband lifted his diminutive bride and carried her three times round the altar in his arms, then again three turns round the altar, but the boy preceding the girl, and she following him like an obedient slave. When this was over, the bridegroom was placed on a high chair by the entrance door, and the bride brought a basin of water, took off his shoes, and, having washed his feet, wiped them with her long hair. We learned that this was a very ancient custom. On the right side of the bridegroom sat his mother. The bride knelt before her also, and, having performed the same operation over her feet, she retired to the house. Then her mother came out of the crowd and repeated the same ceremony, but without using her hair as a towel. The young couple were married. The drums and the tom-toms rolled once more; and half-deaf we started for home.

In the tent we found the Akali in the middle of a sermon, delivered for the edification of the "mute general" and Mr. Y——. He was explaining to them the advantages of the Sikh religion, and comparing it with the faith of the "devil-worshippers," as he called the Brahmans.

It was too late to go to the caves, and, besides, we had had enough sights for one day. So we sat down to rest, and to listen to the words of wisdom falling from the lips of the "God's warrior." In my humble opinion, he was right in more than one thing; in his most imaginative moments Satan himself could not have invented anything more unjust and more refinedly cruel than what was invented by these "twice-born" egotists in their relation to the weaker sex. An unconditioned civil death awaits her in case of widowhood—even if this sad fate befalls her when she is two or three years old. It is of no importance for the Brahmans if the marriage never actually took place; the goat sacrifice, at which the personal presence of the little girl is not even required—she being represented by the wretched victim—is considered binding for her. As for the man, not only is he permitted to have several lawful wives at a time, but he is even required by the law to marry again if his wife dies. Not to be unjust, I must mention that, with the exception of some vicious and depraved Rajas, we never heard of a Hindu availing himself of this privilege, and having more than one wife.

At the present time, the whole of orthodox India is shaken by the struggle in favour of the re-marriage of widows. This agitation was begun in Bombay, by a few reformers, and opponents of Brahmans. It is already ten years since Mulji-Taker-Sing and others raised this question; but we know only of three or four men who have dared as yet to marry widows. This struggle is carried on in silence and secrecy, but nevertheless it is fierce and obstinate.

In the meanwhile, the fate of the widow is what the Brahmans wish it to be. As soon as the corpse of her husband is burned the widow must shave her head, and never let it grow again as long as she lives. Her bangles, necklaces and rings are broken to pieces and burned, together with her hair and her husband's remains. During the rest of her life she must wear nothing but white if she was less than twenty-five at her husband's death, and red if she was older. Temples, religious ceremonies, society, are closed to her for ever. She has no right to speak to any of her relations, and no right to eat with them. She sleeps, eats and works separately; her touch is considered impure for seven years. If a man, going out on business, meets a widow, he goes home again, abandoning every pursuit, because to see a widow is accounted an evil omen.

In the past all this was seldom practised, and concerned only the rich widows, who refused to be burned; but now, since the Brahmans have been caught in the false interpretation of the *Vedas*, with the criminal intention of appropriating the widows' wealth, they insist on the fulfilment of this cruel precept, and make what once was the exception the rule. They are powerless against British law, and so they revenge themselves on the innocent and helpless women, whom fate has deprived of their natural protectors. Professor Wilson's demonstration of the means by which the Brahmans distorted the sense of the *Vedas*, in order to justify the practice of widow-burning, is well worth mentioning. During the many centuries that this terrible practice prevailed, the Brahmans had appealed to a certain Vedic text for their justification, and had claimed to be rigidly fulfilling the institutes of Manu, which contain for them the interpretation of Vedic law. When the East India Company's Government first turned its attention to the suppression of *suttee*, the whole country, from Cape Comorin to the Himalayas, rose in protest, under the influence of the Brahmans. "The English promised not to interfere in our religious affairs, and they must keep their word!" was the general outcry. Never was India so near revolution as in those days. The English saw the danger and gave up the task. But Professor Wilson, the best Sanskritist of the time, did not consider the battle lost. He applied himself to the study of the most ancient MSS., and gradually became convinced that the alleged precept did not exist in the *Vedas;* though in the *Laws of Manu* it was quite distinct, and had been translated accordingly by T. Colebrooke and other Orientalists. An attempt to prove to the fanatic population that Manu's interpretation was wrong would have been equivalent to an attempt to reduce water to powder. So Wilson set himself to study Manu, and to compare the text of the *Vedas* with the text of this law-giver. This was the result of his labours: the *Rig-Veda* orders the Brahman to place the widow side by side with the corpse, and then, after the performance of certain rites, to lead her down from the funeral pyre and to sing the following verse from Grhya Sutra:

> Arise, O woman! return to the world of the living!
> Having gone to sleep by the dead, awake again!
> Long enough thou hast been a faithful wife
> To the one who made thee mother of his children.

Then those present at the burning were to rub their eyes with collyrium, and the Brahman to address to them the following verse:

> Approach, you married women, not widows,
> With your husbands bring ghi and butter.
> *Let the mothers go up to the womb first,*
> Dressed in festive garments and costly adornments.

The line before the last was misinterpreted by the Brahmans in the most skilful way. In Sanskrit it reads as follows:

> Arohantu janayo yonim agre .

Yonim agre literally means to the *womb first*. Having changed only one letter of the last word agre, "first," in Sanskrit अग्रे, the Brahmans wrote instead agneh, "fire's," in Sanskrit अग्ने, and so acquired the right to send the wretched widows *yonim agneh*—to the womb of fire. It is difficult to find on the face of the world another such fiendish deception.

The *Vedas* never permitted the burning of the widows, and there is a place in Taittirîya-Aranyaka, of the *Yajur Veda*, where the brother of the deceased, or his disciple, or even a trusted friend, is recommended to say to the widow, whilst the pyre is set on fire: "Arise, O woman! do not lie down any more beside the lifeless corpse; return to the world of the living, and become the wife of the one who holds you by the hand, and is willing to be your husband." This verse shows that during the Vedic period the re-marriage of widows was allowed. Besides, in several places in the ancient books, pointed out to us by Swâmi Dayânand, we found orders to the widows "to keep the ashes of the husband for several months after his death and to perform over them certain final rituals."

However, in spite of the scandal created by Professor Wilson's discovery, and of the fact that the Brahmans were put to shame before the double authority of the *Vedas* and of Manu, the custom of centuries proved so strong that some pious Hindu women still burn themselves whenever they can. Not more than two years ago the four widows of Yung-Bahadur, the chief minister of Nepal, insisted upon being burned. Nepal is not under the British rule, and so the Anglo-Indian Government had no right to interfere.

THE CAVES OF BAGH.

AT four o'clock in the morning we crossed the Vagrey and Girna, or rather, *comme coloris local*, Shiva and Pârvatî. Probably, following the bad example of the average mortal husband and wife, this divine couple were engaged in a quarrel, even at this early hour of the day. They were frightfully rough, and our ferry, striking on something at the bottom, nearly upset us into the cold embrace of the god and his irate better half.

Like all the cave temples of India, the Bagh caverns are dug out in the middle of a vertical rock—with the intention, as it seems to me, of testing the limits of human patience. Taking into consideration that such a height does not prevent either glamour or tigers reaching the caves, I cannot help thinking that the sole aim of the ascetic builders was to tempt weak mortals into the sin of irritation by the inaccessibility of their airy abodes. Seventy-two steps, cut out in the rock, and covered with thorny weeds and moss, are the beginning of the ascent to the Bagh caves. Foot-marks worn in the stone through centuries spoke of the numberless pilgrims who had come here before us. The roughness of the steps, with deep holes here and there, and thorns, added attractions to this ascent; join to this a number of mountain springs exuding through the pores of the stone, and no one will be astonished if I say that we simply felt faint under the weight of life and our archæological difficulties. The Babu, who, taking off his slippers, scampered over the thorns as unconcernedly as if he had hoofs instead of vulnerable human heels, laughed at the "helplessness of Europeans," and only made us feel worse.

But on reaching the top of the mountain we stopped grumbling, realizing at the first glance that we should receive our reward. We saw a whole enfilade of dark caves, through regular square openings, six feet wide. We felt awestruck with the gloomy majesty of this deserted temple. There was a curious ceiling over the square platform that once served as a verandah; there was also a portico with broken pillars hanging over our heads; and two rooms on each side, one with a broken image of some flat-nosed goddess, the other containing a Ganesha; but we did not stop to examine all this in detail. Ordering the torches to be lit, we stepped into the first hall.

A damp breath as of the tomb met us. At our first word we all shivered: a hollow, prolonged echoing howl, dying away in the distance, shook the ancient vaults and made us all lower our voices to a whisper. The torch-bearers shrieked "Devi! . . Devi! . ." and, kneeling in the dust, performed a fervent *pujâ* in honour of the voice of the invisible goddess of the caves, in spite of the angry protestations of Narayan and of the "God's warrior."

The only light of the temple came from the entrance, and so two-thirds of it looked still gloomier by contrast. This hall, or the central temple, is very spacious, eighty-four feet square, and sixteen feet high. Twenty-four massive pillars form a square, six pillars at each side, including the corner ones, and four in the middle to prop up the centre of the ceiling; otherwise it could not be kept from falling, as the mass of the mountain which presses on it from the top is much greater than in Karli or Elephanta.

There are at least three different styles in the architecture of these pillars. Some of them are grooved in spirals, gradually and imperceptibly changing from round to sixteen sided, then octagonal and square. Others, plain for the first third of their height, gradually finished under the ceiling by a most elaborate display of ornamentation, which reminds one of the Corinthian style. The third with a square plinth and semi-circular friezes. Taking it all in all, they made a most original and graceful picture. Mr. Y——, an architect by profession, assured us that he never saw anything more striking. He said he could not imagine by the aid of what instruments the ancient builders could accomplish such wonders.

The construction of the Bagh caves, as well as of all the cave temples of India, whose history is lost in the darkness of time, is ascribed by the European archæologists to the Buddhists, and by the native tradition to the Pându brothers. Indian paleography protests in every one of its new discoveries against the hasty conclusions of the Orientalists. And much may be said against the intervention of Buddhists in this particular case. But I shall indicate only one particular. The theory which declares that all the cave temples of India are of Buddhist origin is wrong. The Orientalists may insist as much as they choose on the hypothesis that the Buddhists became again idol-worshippers; it will explain nothing, and contradicts the history of both Buddhists and Brahmans. The Brahmans began persecuting and banishing the Buddhists precisely because they had begun a crusade against idol-worship. The few Buddhist communities who remained in India and deserted the pure, though, maybe—for a shallow observer—somewhat atheistic teachings of Gautama Siddhârtha, never joined Brahmanism, but coalesced with the Jainas, and gradually became absorbed in them. Then why not suppose that if, amongst hundreds of Brahmanical gods, we find one statue of Buddha, it only shows that the masses of half-converts to Buddhism added this new god to the ancient Brahmanical temple. This would be much more sensible than to think that the Buddhists of the two centuries before and after the beginning of the Christian era dared to fill their temples with idols, in defiance of the spirit of the reformer Gautama. The figures of Buddha are easily discerned in the swarm of heathen gods; their position is always the same, and the palm of its right hand is always turned upwards, blessing the worshippers with two fingers. We examined almost every remarkable vihâra of the so-called Buddhist temples, and never met with one statue of Buddha which could not have been added in a later epoch than the construction of the temple; it does not matter whether it was a year or a thousand years later. Not being perfectly self-confident in this matter, we always took the opinion of Mr. Y——, who, as I said before, was an experienced architect; and he invariably came to the conclusion that the Brahmanical idols formed a harmonic and genuine part of the whole, pillars, decorations, and the general style of the temple; whereas the statue of Buddha was an additional and discordant patch. Out of thirty or forty caves of Ellora, all filled with idols, there is only one, the one called the Temple of the Tri-Lokas, which contains nothing but statues of Buddha, and of Ananda, his favourite disciple. Of course, in this case it would be perfectly right to think it is a Buddhist vihâra.

Most probably, some of the Russian archæologists will protest against the opinions I maintain, that is to say, the opinions of the Hindu archæologists, and will treat me as an ignoramus, outraging science. In self-defence, and in order to show how unstable a ground to base one's opinions upon are the conclusions even of such a great authority as Mr. Fergusson, I must mention the following instance. This great architect, but very mediocre archæologist, proclaimed at the very beginning of his scientific career that "all the cave temples of Kanara, without exception, were built between the fifth and the tenth centuries." This theory became generally accepted, when suddenly Dr. Bird found a brass plate in a certain Kanara monument, called a *tope*. The plate announced in pure and distinct Sanskrit that this tope was erected as a homage to the *old temple*, at the beginning of 245 of the Hindu astronomical (Samvat) era. According to Prinsep and Dr. Stevenson, this date coincides with 189 A.D., and so it clearly settles the question of when the tope was built. But the question of the antiquity of the temple itself still remains open, though the inscription states that it was an old temple in 189 A.D., and contradicts the above-quoted opinion of Fergusson. However, this important discovery failed to shake Fergusson's equanimity. For him, ancient inscriptions are of no importance, because, as he says, "the antiquity of ruins must not be fixed on the basis of inscriptions, but on the basis of certain architectural canons and rules," discovered by Mr. Fergusson in person. *Fiat hypothesis, ruat cœlum!*

And now I shall return to my narrative.

Straight before the entrance a door leads to another hall, which is oblong, with hexagonal pillars and niches, containing statues in a tolerable state of preservation; goddesses ten feet and gods nine feet high. After this hall there is a room with an altar, which is a regular hexagon, having sides each three feet long, and protected by a cupola cut in the rock. Nobody was admitted here, except the initiates of the mysteries of the adytum. All round this room there are about twenty priests' cells. Absorbed in the examination of the altar, we did not notice the absence of the colonel, till we heard his loud voice in the distance calling to us:

"I have found a secret passage. . . . Come along, let us find where it leads to!"

Torch in hand, the colonel was far ahead of us, and very eager to proceed; but each of us had a little plan of his own, and so we were reluctant to obey his summons. The Babu took upon himself to answer for the whole party:

"Take care, colonel. This passage leads to the den of the glamour. . . . Mind the tigers!"

But once fairly started on the way to discoveries, our president was not to be stopped. *Nolens volens* we followed him.

He was right; he had made a discovery; and on entering the cell we saw a most unexpected tableau. By the opposite wall stood two torch-bearers with their flaming torches, as motionless as if they were transformed into stone caryatides; and from the wall, about five feet above the ground, protruded two legs clad in white trousers. There was no body to them; the body had disappeared, and but that the legs were shaken by a convulsive effort to move on, we might have thought that the wicked goddess of this place had cut the colonel into two halves, and having caused the upper half instantly to evaporate, had stuck the lower half to the wall, as a kind of trophy.

"What is become of you, Mr. President? Where are you?" were our alarmed questions.

Instead of an answer, the legs were convulsed still

more violently, and soon disappeared completely, after which we heard the voice of the colonel, as if coming through a long tube:

"A room . . . a secret cell. . . . Be quick! I see a whole row of rooms. . . . Confound it! my torch is out! Bring some matches and another torch!"

But this was easier said than done. The torch-bearers refused to go on; as it was, they were already frightened out of their wits. Miss X—— glanced with apprehension at the wall thickly covered with soot and then at her pretty gown. Mr. Y—— sat down on a broken pillar and said he would go no farther, preferring to have a quiet smoke in the company of the timid torch-bearers.

There were several vertical steps cut in the wall; and on the floor we saw a large stone of such a curiously irregular shape that it struck me that it could not be natural. The quick-eyed Babu was not long in discovering its peculiarities, and said he was sure "it was the *stopper* of the secret passage." We all hurried to examine the stone most minutely, and discovered that, though it imitated as closely as possible the irregularity of the rock, its under surface bore evident traces of workmanship and had a kind of hinge to be easily moved. The hole was about three feet high, but not more than two feet wide.

The muscular "God's warrior" was the first to follow the colonel. He was so tall that when he stood on a broken pillar the opening came down to the middle of his breast, and so he had no difficulty in transporting himself to the upper story. The slender Babu joined him with a single monkey-like jump. Then, with the Akali pulling from above and Narayan pushing from below, I safely made the passage, though the narrowness of the hole proved most disagreeable, and the roughness of the rock left considerable traces on my hands. However trying archæological explorations may be for a person afflicted by an unusually fine presence, I felt perfectly confident that with two such Hercules-like helpers as Narayan and Ram-Runjit-Das the ascent of the Himalayas would be perfectly possible for me. Miss X—— came next, under the escort of Mulji, but Mr. Y—— stayed behind.

The secret cell was a room of twelve feet square. Straight above the black hole in the floor there was another in the ceiling, but this time we did not discover any "stopper." The cell was perfectly empty with the exception of black spiders as big as crabs. Our apparition, and especially the bright light of the torches, maddened them; panic-stricken they ran in hundreds over the walls, rushed down, and tumbled on our heads, tearing their thin ropes in their inconsiderate haste. The first movement of Miss X—— was to kill as many as she could. But the four Hindus protested strongly and unanimously. The old lady remonstrated in an offended voice:

"I thought that at least you, Mulji, were a reformer, but you are as superstitious as any idol-worshipper."

"Above everything I am a Hindu," answered the "mute general." "And the Hindus, as you know, consider it sinful before nature and before their own consciences to kill an animal put to flight by the strength of man, be it even poisonous. As to the spiders, in spite of their ugliness, they are perfectly harmless."

"I am sure all this is because you think you will transmigrate into a black spider!" she replied, her nostrils trembling with anger.

"I cannot say I do," retorted Mulji; "but if all the

English ladies are as unkind as you I should rather be a spider than an Englishman."

This lively answer coming from the usually taciturn Mulji was so unexpected that we could not help laughing. But to our great discomfiture Miss X—— was seriously angry, and, under pretext of giddiness, said she would rejoin Mr. Y—— below.

Her constant bad spirits were becoming trying for our cosmopolitan little party, and so we did not press her to stay.

As to us we climbed through the second opening, but this time under the leadership of Narayan. He disclosed to us that this place was not new to him; he had been here before, and confided to us that similar rooms, one on the top of the other, go up to the summit of the mountain. Then, he said, they take a sudden turn, and descend gradually to a whole underground palace, which is sometimes temporarily inhabited. Wishing to leave the world for a while and to spend a few days in isolation, the Râj-Yogis find perfect solitude in this underground abode. Our president looked askance at Narayan through his spectacles, but did not find anything to say. The Hindus also received this information in perfect silence.

The second cell was exactly like the first one; we easily discovered the hole in its ceiling, and reached the third cell. There we sat down for a while. I felt that breathing was becoming difficult to me, but I thought I was simply out of breath and tired, and so did not mention to my companions that anything was wrong. The passage to the fourth cell was almost stopped by earth mixed with little stones, and the gentlemen of the party were busy clearing it out for about twenty minutes. Then we reached the fourth cell.

Narayan was right, the cells were one straight over the other, and the floor of the one formed the ceiling of the other. The fourth cell was in ruins. Two broken pillars lying one on the other presented a very convenient stepping-stone to the fifth story. But the colonel stopped our zeal by saying that now was the time to smoke "the pipe of deliberation" after the fashion of red Indians.

"If Narayan is not mistaken," he said, "this going up and up may continue till to-morrow morning."

"I am not mistaken," said Narayan almost solemnly. "But since my visit here I have heard that some of these passages were filled with earth, so that every communication is stopped; and, if I remember rightly, we cannot go further than the next story."

"In that case there is no use trying to go any further. If the ruins are so shaky as to stop the passages, it would be dangerous for us."

"I never said the passages were stopped by the hand of time. . . *They* did it on purpose. . ."

"Who *they?* Do you mean glamour? . . ."

"Colonel!" said the Hindu with an effort. "Don't laugh at what I say. . . . I speak seriously."

"My dear fellow, I assure you my intention is neither to offend you nor to ridicule a serious matter. I simply do not realize whom you mean when you say *they*."

"I mean the brotherhood. . . . The Râj-Yogis. Some of them live quite close to here."

By the dim light of the half-extinguished torches we saw that Narayan's lips trembled and that his face grew pale as he spoke. The colonel coughed, rearranged his spectacles and remained silent for a while.

"My dear Narayan," at last said the colonel, "I do not want to believe that your intention is to make fun of our credulity. But I can't believe either, that you seriously mean to assure us that any living creature, be it an animal or an ascetic, could exist in a place where there is no air. I paid special attention to the fact, and so I am perfectly sure I am not mistaken: there is not a single bat in these cells, which shows that there is a lack of air. And just look at our torches! you see how dim they are growing. I am sure, that on climbing two or three more rooms like this, we should be suffocated!"

"And in spite of all these facts, I speak the truth," repeated Narayan. "The caves further on are inhabited by *them.* And I have seen them with my own eyes."

The colonel grew thoughtful, and stood glancing at the ceiling in a perplexed and undecided way. We all kept silent, breathing heavily.

"Let us go back!" suddenly shouted the Akali. "My nose is bleeding."

At this very moment I felt a strange and unexpected sensation, and I sank heavily on the ground. In a second I felt an indescribably delicious, heavenly sense of rest, in spite of a dull pain beating in my temples. I vaguely realized that I had really fainted, and that I should die if not taken out into the open air. I could not lift my finger; I could not utter a sound; and, in spite of it, there was no fear in my soul—nothing but an apathetic, but indescribably sweet feeling of rest, and a complete inactivity of all the senses except hearing. A moment came when even this sense forsook me, because I remember that I listened with imbecile intentness to the dead silence around me. Is this death? was my indistinct wondering thought. Then I felt as if mighty wings were fanning me. "Kind wings, caressing, kind wings!" were the recurring words in my brain, like the regular movements of a pendulum, and interiorily under an unreasoning impulse, I laughed at these words. Then I experienced a new sensation: I rather *knew* than *felt* that I was lifted from the floor, and fell down and down some unknown precipice, amongst the hollow rollings of a distant thunder-storm. Suddenly a loud voice resounded near me. And this time I think I did not hear, but felt it. There was something palpable in this voice, something that instantly stopped my helpless descent, and kept me from falling any further. This was a voice I knew well, but whose voice it was I could not in my weakness remember. . . . . .

In what way I was dragged through all these narrow holes will remain an eternal mystery for me. I came to myself on the verandah below, fanned by fresh breezes, and as suddenly as I had fainted above in the impure air of the cell. When I recovered completely the first thing I saw was a powerful figure clad in white, with a raven black Rajput beard, anxiously leaning over me. As soon as I recognized the owner of this beard, I could not abstain from expressing my feelings by a joyful exclamation: "Where do *you* come, from?" It was our friend Takur Gulab-Lal-Sing, who, having promised to join us in the North-West Provinces, now appeared to us in Bagh, as if falling from the sky or coming out of the ground.

But my unfortunate accident, and the pitiable state of the rest of the daring explorers, were enough to stop any further questions and expressions of astonishment. On one side of me the frightened Miss X——, using my nose as a cork for her sal-volatile bottle; on the other the "God's warrior" covered with blood as if returning from a battle with the Afghans; further on, poor Mulji with a dreadful headache. Narayan and the colonel, happily for our party, did not experience anything worse than a slight vertigo. As to the Babu, no carbonic acid gas could inconvenience his wonderful Bengali nature. He said he was safe and comfortable enough, but awfully hungry.

At last the outpour of entangled exclamations and unintelligible explanations stopped, and I collected my thoughts and tried to understand what had happened to me in the cave. Narayan was the first to notice that I had fainted, and hastened to drag me back to the passage. And this very moment they all heard the voice of Gulab-Sing coming from the upper cell: "*Tumhare iha aneka kya kam tha?*" "What on earth brought you here?" Even before they recovered from their astonishment he ran quickly past them, and descending to the cell beneath called to them to "pass him down the bai" (sister). This "passing down" of such a solid object as my body, and the picture of the proceeding, vividly imagined, made me laugh heartily, and I felt sorry I had not been able to witness it. Handing him over their half-dead load, they hastened to join the Takur; but he contrived to do without their help, though how he did it they were at a loss to understand. By the time they succeeded in getting through one passage Gulab-Sing was already at the next one, in spite of the heavy burden he carried; and they never were in time to be of any assistance to him. The colonel, whose main feature is the tendency to go into the details of everything, could not conceive by what proceedings the Takur had managed to pass my almost lifeless body so rapidly through all these narrow holes.

"He could not have thrown her down the passage before going in himself, for every single bone of her body would have been broken," mused the colonel. "And it is still less possible to suppose that, descending first himself, he dragged her down afterwards. It is simply incomprehensible!"

These questions harassed him for a long time afterwards, until they became something like the puzzle: Which was created first, the egg or the bird?

As to the Takur, when closely questioned, he shrugged his shoulders, and answered that he really did not remember. He said that he simply did whatever he could to get me out into the open air; that all our travelling companions were there to watch his proceedings; he was under their eyes all the time, and that in circumstances when every second is precious people do not think, but act.

But all these questions arose only in the course of the day. As to the time directly after I was laid down on the verandah, there were other things to puzzle all our party; no one could understand how the Takur happened to be on the spot exactly when his help was most needed, nor where he came from—and everyone was anxious to know. On the verandah they found me lying on a carpet, with the Takur busy restoring me to my senses, and Miss X—— with her eyes wide open at the Takur, whom she decidedly believed to be a materialized ghost.

However, the explanations our friend gave us seemed perfectly satisfactory, and at first did not strike us as unnatural. He was in Hardwar when Swâmi Dayânand sent us the letter which postponed our going to him. On arriving at Kandua by the Indore railway, he had visited Holkar; and, learning that we were so near, he decided to join us sooner than he had expected. He had come to Bagh yesterday evening, but knowing that we were to start for the caves early in the morning he went there before us, and simply was waiting for us in the caves.

"There is the whole mystery for you," said he.

"The whole mystery?" exclaimed the colonel. "Did you know, then, beforehand that we would discover the cells, or what?"

"No, I did not. I simply went there myself because it is a long time since I saw them last. Examining them took me longer than I expected, and so I was too late to meet you at the entrance."

"Probably the Takur-Sahib was enjoying the freshness of the air in the cells," suggested the mischievous Babu, showing all his white teeth in a broad grin.

Our president uttered an energetic exclamation.

"Exactly! How on earth did I not think of that before? . . . You could not possibly have any breathing air in the cells above the one you found us in. . . . And, besides, . . . how did you reach the fifth cell, when the entrance of the fourth was nearly stopped and we had to dig it out?"

"There are other passages leading to them. I know all the turns and corridors of these caves, and everyone is free to choose his way," answered Gulab-Sing; and I thought I saw a look of intelligence pass between him and Narayan, who simply cowered under his fiery eyes. "However, let us go to the cave where breakfast is ready for us. Fresh air will do all of you good."

On our way we met with another cave, twenty or thirty steps south from the verandah, but the Takur did not let us go in, fearing new accidents for us. So we descended the stone steps I have already mentioned, and after descending about two hundred steps towards the foot of the mountain, made a short reäscent again and entered the "dining-room," as the Babu denominated it. In my *rôle* of "interesting invalid," I was carried to it, sitting in my folding chair, which never left me in all my travels.

This temple is much the less gloomy of the two, in spite of considerable signs of decay. The frescoes of the ceiling are better preserved than in the first temple. The walls, the tumbled down pillars, the ceiling, and even the interior rooms, which were lighted by ventilators cut through the rock, were once covered by a varnished stucco, the secret of which is now known only to the Madrasis, and which gives the rock the appearance of pure marble.

We were met by the Takur's four servants, whom we remembered since our stay in Karli, and who bowed down in the dust to greet us. The carpets were spread, and the breakfast ready. Every trace of carbonic acid had left our brains, and we sat down to our meal in the best of spirits. Our conversation soon turned to the Hardwar Mela, which our unexpectedly-recovered friend had left exactly five days ago. All the information we got from Gulab-Lal-Sing was so interesting that I wrote it down at the first opportunity.

After a few weeks we visited Hardwar ourselves, and since I saw it, my memory has never grown tired of recalling the charming picture of its lovely situation. It is as near a primitive picture of earthly Paradise as anything that can be imagined.

Every twelfth year, which the Hindus call *Kumbha*, the planet Jupiter enters the constellation of Aquarius, and this event is considered very propitious for the beginning of the religious fair; for which this day is accordingly fixed by the astrologers of the pagodas. This gathering attracts the representatives of all sects, as I said before, from princes and maharajas down to the last fakir. The former come for the sake of religious discussions, the latter, simply to plunge into the waters of Ganges at its very source, which must be done at a certain propitious hour, fixed also by the position of the stars.

Ganges is a name invented in Europe. The natives always say *Gangâ*, and consider this river to belong strictly to the feminine sex. Gangâ is sacred in the eyes of the Hindus, because she is the most important of all the fostering goddesses of the country, and a daughter of the old Himavat (Himalaya), from whose heart she springs for the salvation of the people. That is why she is worshipped, and why the city of Hardwar, built at her very source, is so sacred.

Hardwar is written *Hari-dvâra*, the doorway of the sun-god, or Krishna, and is also often called Gangâdvâra, the doorway of Gangâ; there is still a third name of the same town, which is the name of a certain ascetic *Kapela*, or rather *Kapila*, who once sought salvation on this spot, and left many miraculous traditions.

The town is situated in a charming flowery valley, at the foot of the southern slope of the Sivalik ridge, between two mountain chains. In this valley, raised 1,024 feet above the sea-level, the northern nature of the Himalayas struggles with the tropical growth of the plains; and, in their efforts to excel each other, they have created the most delightful of all the delightful corners of India. The town itself is a quaint collection of castle-like turrets of the most fantastical architecture; of ancient vihâras; of wooden fortresses, so gaily painted that they look like toys; of pagodas, with loopholes and overhanging curved little balconies; and all this overgrown by such abundance of roses, dahlias, aloes and blossoming cactuses, that it is hardly possible to tell a door from a window. The granite foundations of many houses are laid almost in the bed of the river, and so, during four months of the year, they are half covered with water. And behind this handful of scattered houses, higher up the mountain slope, crowd snow-white, stately temples. Some of them are low, with thick walls, wide wings and gilded cupolas; others rise in majestical many-storied towers; others again with shapely pointed roofs, which look like the spires of a bell tower. Strange and capricious is the architecture of these temples, the like of which is not to be seen anywhere else. They look as if they had suddenly dropped from the snowy abodes of the mountain spirits above, standing there in the shelter of the mother mountain, and timidly peeping over the head of the small town below at their own images reflected in the pure, untroubled waters of the sacred river.

Here the Ganges is not yet polluted by the dirt and the sins of her many million adorers. Releasing her worshippers, cleansed from her icy embrace, the pure maiden of the mountains carries her transparent waves through the burning plains of Hindostan; and only three hundred and forty-eight miles lower down, on passing through Cawnpore, do her waters begin to grow thicker and darker, while, on reaching Benares, they transform themselves into a kind of peppery pea soup.

Once, while talking to an old Hindu, who tried to convince us that his compatriots are the cleanest nation in the world, we asked him:

"Why is it then that, in the less populous places, the Ganges is pure and transparent, whilst in Benares, especially towards evening, it looks like a mass of liquid mud?"

"O sahibs!" answered he mournfully, "it is not the dirt of our bodies, as you think, it is not even the blackness of our sins, that the devi (goddess) washes away. . . . Her waves are black with the sorrow and shame of her children. Her feelings are sad and sorrowful; hidden suffering, burning pain and humiliation, despair and shame at her own helplessness, have been her lot for many past centuries. She has suffered all this till her waters have become waves of black bile. Her waters are poisoned and black, but not from physical causes. She is our mother, and how could she help resenting the degradation we have brought ourselves to in this dark age."

This sorrowful, poetical allegory made us feel very keenly for the poor old man; but, however great our sympathy, we could not but suppose that probably the woes of the maiden Gangâ do not affect her sources. In Hardwar the colour of Ganges is crystal *aqua marina*, and the waters run gaily murmuring to the shore-reeds about the wonders they saw on their way from the Himalayas.

The beautiful river is the greatest and the purest of goddesses, in the eyes of the Hindus; and many are the honours given to her in Hardwar. Besides the Mela celebrated once every twelve years, there is a month in every year when the pilgrims flock together to the Harika-Paira, stairs of Vishnu. Whosoever succeeds in throwing himself first into the river, at the appointed day, hour and moment, will not only expiate all his sins, but also have all bodily sufferings removed. This zeal to be first is so great that, owing to a badly-constructed and narrow stair leading to the water, it used to cost many lives yearly, until, in 1819, the East India Company, taking pity upon the pilgrims, ordered this ancient relic to be removed, and a new stairway, one hundred feet wide, and consisting of sixty steps, to be constructed.

The month when the waters of the Ganges are most salutary, falls, according to the Brahmanical computation, between March 12th and April 10th, and is called Chaitra. The worst of it is that the waters are at their best only at the first moment of a certain propitious hour, indicated by the Brahmans, and which sometimes happens to be midnight. You can fancy what it must be when this moment comes, in the midst of a crowd which exceeds two millions. In 1819 more than four hundred people were crushed to death. But even after the new stairs were constructed, the goddess Gangâ has carried away on her virgin bosom many a disfigured corpse of her worshippers. Nobody pitied the drowned, on the contrary, they were envied. Whoever happens to be killed during this purification by bathing, is sure to go straight to Swarga (heaven). In 1760, the two rival brotherhoods of Sannyâsis and Bairâgis had a regular battle amongst them on the sacred day of *Purbi*, the last day of the religious fair. The Bairâgis were conquered, and there were eighteen thousand people slaughtered.

"And in 1796," proudly narrated our warlike friend the Akali, "the pilgrims from Punjab, all of them Sikhs, desiring to punish the insolence of the Hossains, killed here about five hundred of these heathens. My own grandfather took part in the fight!"

Later on we verified this in the *Gazetteer of India*, and the "God's warrior" was cleared of every suspicion of exaggeration and boasting.

In 1879, however, no one was drowned, or crushed to death, but a dreadful epidemic of cholera broke out. We were disgusted at this impediment; but had to keep at a distance in spite of our impatience to see Hardwar. And unable to behold distant summits of old Himavat ourselves, we had in the meanwhile to be contented with what we could hear about him from other people.

So we talked long after our breakfast under the cave vault was finished. But our talk was not so gay as it might have been, because we had to part with Ram-Runjit-Das, who was going to Bombay. The worthy Sikh shook hands with us in the European way, and then raising his right hand gave us his blessing, after the fashion of all the followers of Nânaka. But when he approached the Takur to take leave of him, his countenance suddenly changed. This change was so evident that we all noted it. The Takur was sitting on the ground leaning on a saddle, which served him as a cushion. The Akali did not attempt either to give him his blessing or to shake hands with him. The proud expression of his face also changed, and showed confusion and anxious humility instead of the usual self-respect and self-sufficiency. The brave Sikh knelt down before the Takur, and instead of the ordinary "Namaste!"—"Salutation to you," whispered reverently, as if addressing the Guru of the Golden Lake: "I am your servant, Sadhu-Sahib! give me your blessing!"

Without any apparent reason or cause, we all felt self-conscious and ill at ease, as if guilty of some indiscretion. But the face of the mysterious Rajput remained as calm and as dispassionate as ever. He was looking at the river before this scene took place, and slowly moved his eyes to the Akali, who lay prostrated before him. Then he touched the head of the Sikh with his index finger, and rose with the remark that we also had better start at once, because it was getting late.

We drove in our carriage, moving very slowly because of the deep sand which covers all this locality, and the

Takur followed us on horseback all the way. He told us the epic legends of Hardwar and Rajistan, of the great deeds of the Hari-Kulas, the heroic princes of the solar race. *Hari* means sun, and *Kula* family. Some of the Rajput princes belong to this family, and the Maharanas of Oodeypur are especially proud of their astronomical origin.

The name of Hari-Kula gives to some Orientalists ground to suppose that a member of this family emigrated to Egypt in the remote epoch of the first Pharaonic dynasties, and that the ancient Greeks, borrowing the name as well as the traditions, thus formed their legends about the mythological Hercules. It is believed that the ancient Egyptians adored the sphinx under the name of *Hari-Mukh*, or the "sun on the horizon." On the mountain chain which fringes Kashmir on the north, thirteen thousand feet above the sea, there is a huge summit, which is exactly like a head, and which bears the name of Harimukh. This name is also met with in the most ancient of the *Purânas*. Besides, popular tradition considers this Himalayan stone head to be the image of the *setting sun*.

Is it possible, then, that all these coincidences are only accidental? And why is it that the Orientalists will not give it more serious attention? It seems to me that this is a rich soil for future research, and that it is no more to be explained by mere chance than the fact that both Egypt and India held the cow sacred, and that the ancient Egyptians had the same religious horror of killing certain animals, as the modern Hindus.

AN ISLE OF MYSTERY.

WHEN evening began to draw on, we were driving beneath the trees of a wild jungle; arriving soon after at a large lake, we left the carriages. The shores were overgrown with reeds—not the reeds that answer our European notions, but rather such as Gulliver was likely to meet with in his travels to Brobdingnag. The place was perfectly deserted, but we saw a boat fastened close to the land. We had still about an hour and a half of daylight before us, and so we quietly sat down on some ruins and enjoyed the splendid view, whilst the servants of the Takur transported our bags, boxes and bundles of rugs from the carriages to the ferry boat. Mr. Y—— was preparing to paint the picture before us, which indeed was charming.

"Don't be in a hurry to take down this view," said Gulab-Sing. "In half an hour we shall be on the islet, where the view is still lovelier. We may spend there the night and to-morrow morning as well."

"I am afraid it will be too dark in an hour," said Mr. Y——, opening his colour box. "And as for to-morrow, we shall probably have to start very early."

"Oh, no! there is not the slightest need to start early. We may even stay here part of the afternoon. From here to the railway station it is only three hours, and the train only leaves for Jubbulpore at eight in the evening. And do you know," added the Takur, smiling in his usual mysterious way, "I am going to treat you to a concert. To-night you shall be witness of a very interesting natural phenomenon connected with this island."

We all pricked up our ears with curiosity.

"Do you mean that island there? and do you really think we must go?" asked the colonel. "Why should not we spend the night here, where we are so deliciously cool, and where . . ."

"Where the forest swarms with playful leopards, and the reeds shelter snug family parties of the serpent race, were you going to say, colonel?" interrupted the Babu, with a broad grin. "Don't you admire this merry gathering, for instance? Look at them! There is the father and the mother, uncles, aunts, and children. . . . I am sure I could point out even a mother-in-law."

Miss X—— looked in the direction he indicated and shrieked, till all the echoes of the forest groaned in answer. Not farther than three steps from her there were at least forty grown up serpents and baby snakes. They amused themselves by practising somersaults, coiled up, then straightened again and interlaced their tails, presenting to our dilated eyes a picture of perfect innocence and primitive contentment. Miss X—— could not stand it any longer and fled to the carriage, whence she showed us a pale, horrified face. The Takur, who had arranged himself comfortably beside Mr. Y—— in order to watch the progress of his painting, left his seat and looked attentively at the dangerous group, quietly smoking his *gargari*—Rajput narghile—the while.

"If you do not stop screaming you will attract all the wild animals of the forest in another ten minutes," said he. "None of you have anything to fear. If you do not excite an animal he is almost sure to leave you alone, and most probably will run away from you."

With these words he lightly waved his pipe in the direction of the serpentine family-party. A thunderbolt falling in their midst could not have been more effectual. The whole living mass looked stunned for a moment, and then rapidly disappeared among the reeds with loud hissing and rustling.

"Now this is pure mesmerism, I declare," said the colonel, on whom not a gesture of the Takur was lost. "How did you do it, Gulab-Sing? Where did you learn this science?"

"They were simply frightened away by the sudden movement of my chibook, and there was no science and no mesmerism about it. Probably by this fashionable modern word you mean what we Hindus call *vashi-kârana vidyâ*—that is to say, the science of charming people and animals by the force of will. However, as I have already said, this has nothing to do with what I did."

"But you do not deny, do you, that you have studied this science and possess this gift?"

"Of course I don't. Every Hindu of my sect is bound to study the mysteries of physiology and psychology amongst other secrets left to us by our ancestors. But what of that? I am very much afraid, my dear colonel," said the Takur with a quiet smile, "that you are rather inclined to view the simplest of my acts through a mystical prism. Narayan has been telling you all kinds of things about me behind my back. . . . Now, is it not so?"

And he looked at Narayan, who sat at his feet, with an indescribable mixture of fondness and reproof. The Dekkan colossus dropped his eyes and remained silent.

"You have guessed rightly," absently answered Mr. Y——, busy over his drawing apparatus. "Narayan sees in you something like his late deity Shiva; something just a little less than Parabrahm. Would you believe it? He seriously assured us—in Nassik it was—that the Râj-Yogis, and amongst them yourself—though I must own I still fail to understand what a Râj-Yogi is, precisely—can force any one to see, not what is before his eyes at the given moment, but what is only in the imagination of the Râj-Yogi. If I remember rightly he called it Mâyâ. . . . Now, this seemed to me going a little too far!"

"Well! You did not believe, of course, and laughed at Narayan?" asked the Takur, fathoming with his eyes the dark green deeps of the lake.

"Not precisely. . . . Though, I dare say, I did just a little bit," went on Mr. Y——, absently, being fully engrossed by the view, and trying to fix his eyes on the most effective part of it. "I dare say I am too sceptical on this kind of question."

"And knowing Mr. Y—— as I do," said the colonel, "I can add, for my part, that even were any of these phenomena to happen to himself personally, he, like Dr. Carpenter, would doubt his own eyes rather than believe."

"What you say is a little bit exaggerated, but there is some truth in it. Maybe I would not trust myself in such an occurrence; and I tell you why. If I saw something that does not exist, or rather exists only for me, logic would interfere. However objective my vision may be, before believing in the materiality of a hallucination, I feel I am bound to doubt my own senses and sanity. . . . Besides, what bosh all this is! As if I ever will allow myself to believe in the reality of a thing that I alone saw; which belief implies also the admission of somebody else governing and dominating, for the time being, my optical nerves, as well as my brains."

"However, there are any number of people, who do not doubt, because they have had proof that this phenomenor really occurs," remarked the Takur, in a careless tone, which showed he had not the slightest desire to insist upon this topic.

However, this remark only increased Mr. Y——'s excitement.

"No doubt there are!" he exclaimed. "But what does that prove? Besides them, there are equal numbers of people who believe in the materialization of spirits. But do me the kindness of not including me among them!"

"Don't you believe in animal magnetism?"

"To a certain extent, I do. If a person suffering from some contagious illness can influence a person in good health, and make him ill, in his turn, I suppose somebody else's overflow of health can also affect the sick person, and, perhaps cure him. But between physiological contagion and mesmeric influence there is a great gulf, and I don't feel inclined to cross this gulf on the grounds of blind faith. It is perfectly possible that there are instances of thought-transference in cases of somnambulism, epilepsy, trance. I do not positively deny it, though I am very doubtful. Mediums and clairvoyants are a sickly lot, as a rule. But I bet you anything, a healthy man in perfectly normal conditions is not to be influenced by the tricks of mesmerists. I should like to see a magnetizer, or even a Râj-Yogi, inducing *me* to obey his will."

"Now, my dear fellow, you really ought not to speak so rashly," said the colonel, who, till then, had not taken any part in the discussion.

"Ought I not? Don't take it into your head that it is mere boastfulness on my part. I guarantee failure in my case, simply because every renowned European mesmerist has tried his luck with me, without any result; and that is why I defy the whole lot of them to try again, and feel perfectly safe about it. And why a Hindu Râj-Yogi should succeed where the strongest of European mesmerists failed, I do not quite see. . ."

Mr. Y—— was growing altogether too excited, and the Takur dropped the subject, and talked of something else.

For my part, I also feel inclined to deviate once more from my subject, and give some necessary explanations.

Miss X—— excepted, none of our party had ever been numbered amongst the spiritualists, least of all Mr. Y——. We Theosophists did not believe in the playfulness of departed souls, though we admitted the possibility of some mediumistic phenomena, while totally disagreeing with the spiritualists as to the cause and point of view. Refusing to believe in the interference, and even presence of the spirits, in the so-called spiritualistic phenomena, we nevertheless believe in the *living spirit of man;* we believe in the omnipotence of this spirit, and in its natural, though benumbed capacities. We also believe that, when incarnated, this spirit, this divine spark, may be apparently quenched, if it is not guarded, and if the life the man leads is unfavourable to its expansion, as it generally is; but, on the other hand, our conviction is that human beings can develop their potential spiritual powers; that, if they do, no phenomenon will be impossible for their liberated wills, and that they will perform what, in the eyes of the uninitiated, will be much more wondrous than the materialized forms of the spiritualists. If proper training can render the muscular strength ten times greater, as in the cases of renowned athletes, I do not see why proper training should fail in the case of moral capacities. We have also good grounds to believe that the secret of this proper training—though unknown to, and denied by, European physiologists and even psychologists—is known in some places in India, where its knowledge is hereditary, and entrusted to few.

Mr. Y—— was a novice in our Society and looked with distrust even on such phenomena as can be produced by mesmerism. He had been trained in the Royal Institute of British Architects, which he left with a gold medal, and with a fund of scepticism that caused him to distrust everything, *en dehors des mathématiques pures.* So that no wonder he lost his temper when people tried to convince him that there existed things which he was inclined to treat as "mere bosh and fables."

Now I return to my narrative.

The Babu and Mulji left us to help the servants to transport our luggage to the ferry boat. The remainder of the party had grown very quiet and silent. Miss X—— dozed peacefully in the carriage, forgetting her recent fright. The colonel, stretched on the sand, amused himself by throwing stones into the water. Narayan sat motionless, with his hands round his knees, plunged as usual in the mute contemplation of Gulab-Lal-Sing. Mr. Y—— sketched hurriedly and diligently, only raising his head from time to time to glance at the opposite shore, and knitting his brow in a preoccupied way. The Takur went on smoking, and as for me, I sat on my folding chair, looking lazily at everything round me, till my eyes rested on Gulab-Sing, and were fixed, as if by a spell.

"Who and what is this mysterious Hindu?" I wondered in my uncertain thoughts. "Who is this man, who unites in himself two such distinct personalities: the one exterior, kept up for strangers, for the world in general, the other interior, moral and spiritual, shown only to a few intimate friends? But even these intimate friends—do they know much beyond what is generally known? And what do they know? They see in him a Hindu who differs very little from the rest of educated natives, perhaps only in his perfect contempt for the social conventions of India and the demands of Western civilization. . . . And that is all—unless I add that he is known in Central India as a sufficiently wealthy man, and a Takur, a feudal chieftain of a Raj, one of the hundreds of similar Rajes. Besides, he is a true friend of ours, who offered us his protection in our travels and volunteered to play the mediator between us and the suspicious, uncommunicative Hindus. Beyond all this, we know absolutely nothing about him. It is true, though, that I know a little more than the others; but I have promised silence, and silent I shall be. But the little I know is so strange, so unusual, that it is more like a dream than a reality."

A good while ago, more than twenty-seven years, I met him in the house of a stranger in England, whither he came in the company of a certain dethroned Indian prince. Then our acquaintance was limited to two conversations; their unexpectedness, their gravity, and even severity, produced a strong impression on me then; but, in the course of time, like many other things, they sank into oblivion and Lethe. About seven years ago he wrote to me to America, reminding me of our conversation and of a certain promise I had made. Now we saw each other once more in India, his own country, and I failed to see any change wrought in his appearance by all these long years. I was, and looked, quite young, when I first saw him; but the passage of years had not failed to change me into an old woman. As to him, he appeared to me twenty-seven years ago a man of about thirty, and still looked no older, as if time were powerless against him. In England, his striking beauty, especially his extraordinary height and stature, together with his eccentric refusal to be presented to the Queen—an honour many a high-born Hindu has sought, coming over on purpose—excited the public notice and the attention of the newspapers. The newspaper-men of those days, when the influence of Byron was still great, discussed the "wild Rajput" with untiring pens, calling him "Raja-Misanthrope" and "Prince Jalma-Samson," and inventing fables about him all the time he stayed in England.

All this taken together was well calculated to fill me with consuming curiosity, and to absorb my thoughts till I forgot every exterior circumstance, sitting and staring at him in no wise less intensely than Narayan.

I gazed at the remarkable face of Gulab-Lal-Sing with a mixed feeling of indescribable fear and enthusiastic admiration; recalling the mysterious death of the Karli tiger, my own miraculous escape a few hours ago in Bagh, and many other incidents too many to relate. It was only a few hours since he appeared to us in the morning, and yet what a number of strange ideas, of puzzling occurrences, how many enigmas his presence stirred in our minds! The magic circle of my revolving thought grew too much for me. "What does all this mean!" I exclaimed to myself, trying to shake off my torpor, and struggling to find words for my meditation. "Who is this being whom I saw so many years ago, jubilant with manhood and life, and now see again, as young and as full of life, only still more austere, still more incomprehensible. After all, maybe it is his brother, or even his son?" thought I, trying to calm myself, but with no result. "No! there is no use doubting; it is he himself, it is the same face, the same little scar on the left temple. But, as a quarter of a century ago, so now: no wrinkles on those beautiful classic features; not a white hair in this thick jet-black mane; and, in moments of silence, the same expression of perfect rest on that face, calm as a statue of living bronze. What a strange expression, and what a wonderful Sphinx-like face!"

"Not a very brilliant comparison, my old friend!" suddenly spoke the Takur, and a good-natured laughing note rung in his voice, whilst I shuddered and grew red like a naughty schoolgirl. "This comparison is so inaccurate that it decidedly sins against history in two important points. *Primo*, the Sphinx is a lion; so am I, as indicates the word Sing in my name; but the Sphinx is winged, and I am not. *Secondo*, the Sphinx is a woman as well as a winged lion, but the Rajput Sinhas never had anything effeminate in their characters. Besides, the Sphinx is the daughter of Chimera, or Echidna, who were neither beautiful nor good; and so you might have chosen a more flattering and a less inaccurate comparison!"

I simply gasped in my utter confusion, and he gave vent to his merriment, which by no means relieved me.

"Shall I give you some good advice?" continued Gulab-Sing, changing his tone for a more serious one. "Don't trouble your head with such vain speculations. The day when this riddle yields its solution, the Rajput Sphinx will not seek destruction in the waves of the sea; but, believe me, it won't bring any profit to the Russian Œdipus either. You already know every detail you ever will learn. So leave the rest to our respective fates."

And he rose because the Babu and Mulji had informed

us that the ferry boat was ready to start, and were shouting and making signs to us to hasten.

"Just let me finish," said Mr. Y——, "I have nearly done. Just an additional touch or two."

"Let us see your work. Hand it round!" insisted the colonel and Miss X——, who had just left her haven of refuge in the carriage, and joined us still half asleep.

Mr. Y—— hurriedly added a few more touches to his drawing and rose to collect his brushes and pencils.

We glanced at his fresh wet picture and opened our eyes in astonishment. There was no lake on it, no woody shores, and no velvety evening mists that covered the distant island at this moment. Instead of all this we saw a charming sea view; thick clusters of shapely palm-trees scattered over the chalky cliffs of the littoral; a fortress-like bungalow with balconies and a flat roof, an elephant standing at its entrance, and a native boat on the crest of a foaming billow.

"Now what is this view, sir?" wondered the colonel. "As if it was worth your while to sit in the sun, and detain us all, to draw fancy pictures out of your own head!"

"What on earth are you talking about?" exclaimed Mr. Y——. "Do you mean to say you do not recognize the lake?"

"Listen to him—the lake! Where is the lake, if you please? Were you asleep, or what?"

By this time all our party gathered round the colonel, who held the drawing. Narayan uttered an exclamation, and stood still, the very image of bewilderment past description.

"I know the place!" said he, at last. "This is Dayri-Bol, the country house of the Takur-Sahib. I know it. Last year during the famine I lived there for two months."

I was the first to grasp the meaning of it all, but something prevented me from speaking at once.

At last Mr. Y—— finished arranging and packing his things, and approached us in his usual lazy, careless way, but his face showed traces of vexation. He was evidently bored by our persistency in seeing a sea, where there was nothing but the corner of a lake. But, at the first sight of his unlucky sketch, his countenance suddenly changed. He grew so pale, and the expression of his face became so piteously distraught that it was painful to see. He turned and re-turned the piece of Bristol board, then rushed like a madman to his drawing portfolio and turned the whole contents out, ransacking and scattering over the sand hundreds of sketches and of loose papers. Evidently failing to find what he was looking for, he glanced again at his sea-view, and suddenly covering his face with his hands totally collapsed.

We all remained silent, exchanging glances of wonder and pity, and heedless of the Takur, who stood on the ferry boat, vainly calling to us to join him.

"Look here, Y——!" timidly spoke the kind-hearted colonel, as if addressing a sick child. "Are you sure you remember drawing this view?"

Mr. Y—— did not give any answer, as if gathering strength and thinking it over. After a few moments he answered in hoarse and tremulous tones:

"Yes, I do remember. Of course I made this sketch, but I made it from nature. I painted only what I saw. And it is that very certainty that upsets me so."

"But why should you be upset, my dear fellow? Collect yourself! What happened to you is neither shameful nor dreadful. It is only the result of the temporary influence of one dominant will over another, less powerful. You simply acted under 'biological influence,' to use the expression of Dr. Carpenter."

"That is exactly what I am most afraid of. . . . I remember everything now. I have been busy over this view more than an hour. I saw it directly I chose the spot, and seeing it all the while on the opposite shore I could not suspect anything uncanny. I was perfectly conscious, . . . or, shall I say, I fancied I was conscious of putting down on paper what everyone of you had before your eyes. I had lost every notion of the place as I saw it before I began my sketch, and as I see it now. . . . But how do you account for it? Good gracious! am I to believe that these confounded Hindus really possess the mystery of this trick? I tell you, colonel, I shall go mad if I don't understand it all!"

"No fear of that, Mr. Y——," said Narayan, with a triumphant twinkle in his eyes. "You will simply lose the right to deny Yoga-Vidyâ, the great ancient science of my country."

Mr. Y—— did not answer him. He made an effort to calm his feelings, and bravely stepped on the ferry boat with firm foot. Then he sat down, apart from us all, obstinately looking at the large surface of water round us, and struggling to seem his usual self.

Miss X—— was the first to interrupt the silence.

"Ma chère!" said she to me in a subdued, but triumphant voice. "Ma chère, Monsieur Y—— devient vraiment un medium de première force!"

In moments of great excitement she always addressed me in French. But I also was too excited to control my feelings, and so I answered rather unkindly:

"Please stop this nonsense, Miss X——. You know I don't believe in spiritualism. Poor Mr. Y——, was not he upset?"

Receiving this rebuke and no sympathy from me, she could not think of anything better than drawing out the Babu, who, for a wonder, had managed to keep quiet till then.

"What do you say to all this? I for one am perfectly confident that no one but the disembodied soul of a great artist could have painted that lovely view. Who else is capable of such a wonderful achievement?"

"Why? The old gentleman in person. Confess that at the bottom of your soul you firmly believe that the Hindus worship devils. To be sure it is some deity of ours of this kind that had his august paw in the matter."

"Il est positivement malhonnête, ce Nègre-là!" angrily muttered Miss X——, hurriedly withdrawing from him.

The island was a tiny one, and so overgrown with tall reeds that, from a distance, it looked like a pyramidal basket of verdure. With the exception of a colony of monkeys, who bustled away to a few mango trees at our approach, the place seemed uninhabited. In this virgin forest of thick grass there was no trace of human life. Seeing the word *grass* the reader must not forget that it is not the grass of Europe I mean; the grass under which we stood, like insects under a rhubarb leaf, waved its feathery many-coloured plumes much above the head of Gulab-Sing (who stood six feet and a half in his stockings), and of Narayan, who measured hardly an inch less. From a distance it looked like a waving sea of black, yellow, blue, and especially of rose and green. On landing, we discovered that it consisted of separate thickets of bamboos, mixed up with the gigantic sirka reeds, which rose as high as the tops of the mangos.

It is impossible to imagine anything prettier and more graceful than the bamboos and sirka. The isolated tufts of bamboos show, in spite of their size, that they are nothing but grass, because the least gush of wind shakes them, and their green crests begin to nod like heads adorned with long ostrich plumes. There were some bamboos there fifty or sixty feet high. From time to time we heard a light metallic rustle in the reeds, but none of us paid much attention to it.

Whilst our coolies and servants were busy clearing a place for our tents, pitching them and preparing the supper, we went to pay our respects to the monkeys, the true hosts of the place. Without exaggeration there were at least two hundred. While preparing for their nightly rest, the monkeys behaved like decorous and well-behaved people; every family chose a separate branch and defended it from the intrusion of strangers lodging on the same tree, but this defence never passed the limits of good manners, and generally took the shape of threatening grimaces. There were many mothers with babies in arms amongst them; some of them treated the children tenderly, and lifted them cautiously, with a perfectly human care; others, less thoughtful, ran up and down, heedless of the child hanging at their breasts, preoccupied with something, discussing something, and stopping every moment to quarrel with other monkey ladies—a true picture of chatty old gossips on a market day, repeated in the animal kingdom. The bachelors kept apart, absorbed in their athletic exercises, performed for the most part with the ends of their tails. One of them, especially, attracted our attention by dividing his amusement between *sauts périlleux* and teasing a respectable looking grandfather, who sat under a tree hugging two little monkeys. Swinging backward and forward from the branch, the bachelor jumped at him, bit his ear playfully and made faces at him, chattering all the time. We cautiously passed from one tree to another, afraid of frightening them away; but evidently the years spent by them with the fakirs, who left the island only a year ago, had accustomed them to human society. They were sacred monkeys, as we learned, and so they had nothing to fear from men. They showed no signs of alarm at our approach, and, having received our greeting, and some of them a piece of sugar-cane, they calmly stayed on their branch-thrones, crossing their arms, and looking at us with a good deal of dignified contempt in their intelligent hazel eyes.

The sun had set, and we were told that the supper was ready. We all turned "homewards," except the Babu. The main feature of his character, in the eyes of orthodox Hindus, being a tendency to blasphemy, he could never resist the temptation to justify their opinion of him. Climbing up a high branch he crouched there, imitating every gesture of the monkeys and answering their threatening grimaces by still uglier ones, to the unconcealed disgust of our pious coolies.

As the last golden ray disappeared on the horizon, a gauze-like veil of pale lilac fell over the world. But as every moment decreased the transparency of this tropical twilight, the tint gradually lost its softness and became darker and darker. It looked as if an invisible painter, unceasingly moving his gigantic brush, swiftly laid one coat of paint over the other, ever changing the exquisite background of our islet. The phosphoric candles of the fireflies began to twinkle here and there, shining brightly against the black trunks of the trees, and lost again on the silvery background of opalescent evening sky. But in a few minutes more thousands of these living sparks, precursors of Queen Night, played round us, pouring like a golden cascade over the trees, and dancing in the air above the grass and the dark lake.

And behold! here is the queen in person. Noiselessly descending upon earth, she reassumes her rights. With her approach, rest and peace spread over us; her cool breath calms the activities of day. Like a fond mother, she sings a lullaby to nature, lovingly wrapping her in her soft black mantle; and, when everything is asleep, she watches over nature's dozing powers till the first streaks of dawn.

Nature sleeps; but man is awake, to be witness to the beauties of this solemn evening hour. Sitting round the fire we talked, lowering our voices as if afraid of awaking night. We were only six; the colonel, the four Hindus and myself, because Mr. Y—— and Miss X—— could not resist the fatigue of the day and had gone to sleep directly after supper.

Snugly sheltered by the high "grass," we had not the heart to spend this magnificent night in prosaic sleeping. Besides, we were waiting for the "concert" which the Takur had promised us.

"Be patient," said he, "the musicians will not appear before the moon rises."

The fickle goddess was late; she kept us waiting till after ten o'clock. Just before her arrival, when the horizon began to grow perceptibly brighter, and the opposite shore to assume a milky, silvery tint, a sudden wind rose. The waves, that had gone quietly to sleep at the feet of gigantic reeds, awoke and tossed uneasily, till the reeds swayed their feathery heads and murmured to each other as if taking counsel together about something that was going to happen. . . . Suddenly, in the general stillness and silence, we heard again the same musical notes, which we had passed unheeded, when we first reached the island, as if a whole orchestra were trying their musical instruments before playing some great composition. All round us, and over our heads, vibrated strings of violins, and thrilled the separate notes of a flute. In a few moments came another gust of wind tearing through the reeds, and the whole island resounded with the strains of hundreds of Æolian harps. And suddenly there began a wild unceasing symphony. It swelled in the surrounding woods, filling the air with an indescribable melody. Sad and solemn were its prolonged strains; they resounded like the *arpeggios* of some funeral march, then, changing into a trembling thrill, they shook the air like the song of a nightingale, and died away in a long sigh. They did not quite cease, but grew louder again, ringing like hundreds of silver bells, changing from the heartrending howl of a wolf, deprived of her young, to the precipitate rhythm of a gay tarantella, forgetful of every earthly sorrow; from the articulate song of a human voice, to the vague majestic accords of a violoncello, from merry child's laughter to angry sobbing. And all this was repeated in every direction by mocking echo, as if hundreds of fabulous forest maidens, disturbed in their green abodes, answered the appeal of the wild musical Saturnalia.

The colonel and I glanced at each other in our great astonishment.

"How delightful! What witchcraft is this?" we exclaimed at the same time.

The Hindus smiled, but did not answer us. The Takur smoked his gargari as peacefully as if he was deaf.

There was a short interval, after which the invisible orchestra started again with renewed energy. The sounds poured and rolled in unrestrainable, overwhelming waves. We had never heard anything like this inconceivable wonder. Listen! A storm in the open sea, the wind tearing through the rigging, the swish of the maddened waves rushing over each other, or the whirling snow wreaths on the silent steppes. Suddenly the vision is changed; now it is a stately cathedral and the thundering strains of an organ rising under its vaults. The powerful notes now rush together, now spread out through space, break off, intermingle, and become entangled, like the fantastic melody of a delirious fever, some musical phantasy born of the howling and whistling of the wind.

Alas! the charm of these sounds is soon exhausted, and you begin to feel that they cut like knives through your brain. A horrid fancy haunts our bewildered heads; we imagine that the invisible artists strain our own veins, and not the strings of imaginary violins; their cold breath freezes us, blowing their imaginary trumpets, shaking our nerves and impeding our breathing.

"For God's sake stop this, Takur! This is really too much," shouted the colonel, at the end of his patience, and covering his ears with his hands. "Gulab-Sing, I tell you you must stop this."

The three Hindus burst out laughing; and even the grave face of the Takur lit up with a merry smile.

"Upon my word," said he, "do you really take me for the great Parabrahm? Do you think it is in my power to stop the wind, as if I were Marut, the lord of the storms, in person. Ask for something easier than the instantaneous uprooting of all these bamboos."

"I beg your pardon; I thought these strange sounds also were some kind of psychologic influence."

"So sorry to disappoint you, my dear colonel; but you really must think less of psychology and electrobiology. This develops into a mania with you. Don't you see that this wild music is a natural acoustic phenomenon? Each of the reeds around us—and there are thousands on this island—contains a natural musical instrument; and the musician, Wind, comes here daily to try his art after nightfall—especially during the last quarter of the moon."

"The wind!" murmured the colonel. "Oh, yes! But this music begins to change into a dreadful roar. Is there no way out of it?"

"I at least cannot help it. But keep up your patience, you will soon get accustomed to it. Besides, there will be intervals when the wind falls."

We were told that there are many such natural orchestras in India. The Brahmans know well their wonderful properties, and calling this kind of reed *vînâ-devi*, the lute of the gods, keep up the popular superstition and say the sounds are divine oracles. The sirka grass and the bamboos always shelter a number of tiny beetles, which make considerable holes in the hollow reeds. The fakirs of the idol-worshipping sects add art to this natural beginning and work the plants into musical instruments. The islet we visited bore one of the most celebrated *vinâ-devis*, and so, of course, was proclaimed sacred.

"To-morrow morning," said the Takur, "you will see what deep knowledge of all the laws of acoustics was in the possession of the fakirs. They enlarged the holes made by the beetle according to the size of the reed, sometimes shaping it into a circle, sometimes into an oval. These reeds in their present state can be justly considered as the finest illustration of mechanism applied to acoustics. However, this is not to be wondered at, because some of the most ancient Sanskrit books about music minutely describe these laws, and mention many musical instruments which are not only forgotten, but totally incomprehensible in our days."

All this was very interesting, but still, disturbed by the din, we could not listen attentively.

"Don't worry yourselves," said the Takur, who soon understood our uneasiness, in spite of our attempts at composure. "After midnight the wind will fall, and you will sleep undisturbed. However, if the too close neighbourhood of this musical grass is too much for you, we may as well go nearer to the shore. There is a spot from which you can see the sacred bonfires on the opposite shore."

We followed him, but while walking through the thickets of reeds we did not leave off our conversation.

"How is it that the Brahmans manage to keep up such an evident cheat?" asked the colonel. "The stupidest man cannot fail to see in the long run who made the holes in the reeds, and how they come to give forth music."

"In America stupid men may be as clever as that; I don't know," answered the Takur, with a smile; "but not in India. If you took the trouble to show, to describe, and to explain how all this is done to any Hindu, be he even comparatively educated, he will still see nothing. He will tell you that he knows as well as yourself that the holes are made by the beetles and enlarged by the fakirs. But what of that? The beetle in his eyes is no ordinary beetle, but one of the gods incarnated in the insect for this special purpose; and the fakir is a holy ascetic, who has acted in this case by the order of the same god. That will be all you will ever get out of him. Fanaticism and superstition took centuries to develop in the masses, and now they are as strong as a necessary physiological function. Kill these two and the crowd will have its eyes opened, and will see truth, but not before. As to the Brahmans, India would have been very fortunate if everything they have done were as harmless. Let the crowds adore the muse and the spirit of harmony. This adoration is not so very wicked, after all."

The Babu told us that in Dehra-Dun this kind of reed is planted on both sides of the central street, which is more than a mile long. The buildings prevent the free action of the wind, and so the sounds are heard only in time of east wind, which is very rare. A year ago Swâmi Dayânand happened to camp off Dehra-Dun. Crowds of people gathered round him every evening. One day he delivered a very powerful sermon against superstition. Tired out by this long, energetic speech, and, besides, being a little unwell, the Swâmi sat down on his carpet and shut his eyes to rest as soon as the sermon was finished. But the crowd, seeing him so unusually quiet and silent, all at once imagined that his soul, abandoning him in this prostration, entered the reeds—that had just begun to sing their fantastical rhapsody—and was now conversing with the gods through the bamboos. Many a pious man in this gathering, anxious to show the teacher in what fulness they grasped his teaching and how deep was their respect for him personally, knelt down before the singing reeds and performed a most ardent pujâ.

"What did the Swâmi say to that?"

"He did not say anything. . . . Your question shows that you don't know our Swâmi yet," laughed the Babu. "He simply jumped to his feet, and, uprooting the first sacred reed on his way, gave such a lively *European bakshish* (thrashing) to the pious pujâ-makers, that they instantly took to their heels. The Swâmi ran after them for a whole mile, giving it hot to everyone in his way. He is wonderfully strong is our Swâmi, and no friend to useless talk, I can tell you."

"But it seems to me," said the colonel, "that that is not the right way to convert crowds. Dispersing and frightening is not converting."

"Not a bit of it. The masses of our nation require peculiar treatment. . . Let me tell you the end of this story. Disappointed with the effect of his teachings on the inhabitants of Dehra-Dun, Dayânand Saraswati went to Patna, some thirty-five or forty miles from there. And before he had even rested from the fatigues of his journey, he had to receive a deputation from Dehra-Dun, who on their knees entreated him to come back. The leaders of this deputation had their backs covered with bruises, made by the bamboo of the Swâmi! They brought him back with no end of pomp, mounting him on an elephant and spreading flowers all along the road. Once in Dehra-Dun, he immediately proceeded to found a Samâj, a society as you would say, and the Dehra-Dun Ârya-Samâj now counts at least two hundred members, who have renounced idol-worship and superstition for ever."

"I was present," said Mulji, "two years ago in Benares, when Dayânand broke to pieces about a hundred idols in the bazaar, and the same stick served him to beat a Brahman with. He caught the latter in the hollow idol of a huge Shiva. The Brahman was quietly sitting there talking to the devotees in the name, and so to speak, with the voice of Shiva, and asking money for a new suit of clothes the idol wanted."

"Is it possible the Swâmi had not to pay for this new achievement of his?"

"Oh, yes. The Brahman dragged him into a law court, but the judge had to pronounce the Swâmi in the right, because of the crowd of sympathizers and defenders who followed the Swâmi. But still he had to pay for all the idols he had broken. So far so good; but the Brahman died of cholera that very night, and of course, the opposers of the reform said his death was brought on by the sorcery of Dayânand Saraswati. This vexed us all a good deal."

"Now, Narayan, it is your turn," said I. "Have you no story to tell us about the Swâmi? And do you not look up to him as to your Guru?"

"I have only one Guru and only one God on earth, as in heaven," answered Narayan; and I saw that he was very unwilling to speak. "And while I live, I shall not desert them."

"I know who is his Guru and his God!" thoughtlessly exclaimed the quick-tongued Babu. "It is the Takur-Sahib. In his person both coincide in the eyes of Narayan."

"You ought to be ashamed to talk such nonsense, Babu," coldly remarked Gulab-Sing. "I do not think myself worthy of being anybody's Guru. As to my being a god, the mere words are a blasphemy, and I must ask you not to repeat them. . . . Here we are!" added he more cheerfully, pointing to the carpets spread by the servants on the shore, and evidently desirous of changing the topic. "Let us sit down!"

We arrived at a small glade some distance from the bamboo forest. The sounds of the magic orchestra reached us still, but considerably weakened, and only from time to time. We sat to the windward of the reeds, and so the harmonic rustle we heard was exactly like the low tones of an Æolian harp, and had nothing disagreeable in it. On the contrary, the distant murmur only added to the beauty of the whole scene around us.

We sat down, and only then I realized how tired and sleepy I was—and no wonder, after being on foot since four in the morning, and after all that had happened to me on this memorable day. The gentlemen went on talking, and I soon became so absorbed in my thoughts that their conversation reached me only in fragments.

"Wake up, wake up!" repeated the colonel, shaking me by the hand. "The Takur says that sleeping in the moonlight will do you harm."

I was not asleep; I was simply thinking, though exhausted and sleepy. But wholly under the charm of this enchanting night, I could not shake off my drowsiness, and did not answer the colonel.

"Wake up, for God's sake! Think of what you are risking!" continued the colonel. "Wake up and look at the landscape before us, at this wonderful moon. Have you ever seen anything to equal this magnificent panorama?"

I looked up, and the familiar lines of Pushkin about the golden moon of Spain flashed into my mind. And indeed this *was* a golden moon. At this moment she radiated rivers of golden light, poured forth liquid gold into the tossing lake at our feet, and sprinkled with golden dust every blade of grass, every pebble, as far as the eye could reach, all round us. Her disk of silvery yellow swiftly glided upward amongst the big stars, on their dark blue ground.

Many a moonlit night have I seen in India, but every time the impression was new and unexpected. It is no use trying to describe these *féerique* pictures, they cannot be represented either in words or in colours on canvas, they can only be felt—so fugitive is their grandeur and beauty! In Europe, even in the south, the full moon eclipses the largest and most brilliant of the stars, so that hardly any can be seen for a considerable distance round her. In India it is quite the contrary; she looks like a huge pearl surrounded by diamonds, rolling on a blue velvet ground. Her light is so intense that one can read a letter written in small handwriting; one even can perceive the different greens of the trees and bushes—a thing unheard of in Europe. The effect of the moon is especially charming on tall palm trees. From the first moment of her appearance her rays glide over the tree downwards, beginning with the feathery crests, then lighting up the scales of the trunk, and descending lower and lower till the whole palm is literally bathing in a sea of light. Without any metaphor the surface of the leaves seems to tremble in liquid silver all the night long, whereas their under surfaces seem blacker and softer than black velvet. But woe to the thoughtless novice, woe to the mortal who gazes at the Indian moon with his head uncovered. It is very dangerous not only to sleep under, but even to gaze at the chaste Indian Diana. Fits of epilepsy, madness and death are the punishments wrought by her treacherous arrows on the modern Acteon who dares to contemplate the cruel daughter of Latona in her full beauty. The Hindus never go out in the moonlight without their turbans or pagris. Even our invulnerable Babu always wore a kind of white cap during the night.

As soon as the reeds concert reaches its height and the inhabitants of the neighbourhood hear the distant "voices of the gods," whole villages flock together to the bank of the lake, light bonfires, and perform their pujâs. The fires lit up one after the other, and the black silhouettes of the worshippers moved about on the opposite shore. Their sacred songs and loud exclamations, "Hari, Hari, Mahâ-deva!" resounded with a strange loudness and a wild emphasis in the pure air of the night. And the reeds, shaken in the wind, answered them with tender musical phrases. The whole stirred a vague feeling of uneasiness in my soul, a strange intoxication crept gradually over me, and in this enchanting place the idol-worship of these passionate, poetical souls, sunk in dark ignorance, seemed more intelligible and less repulsive. A Hindu is a born mystic, and the luxuriant nature of his country has made of him a zealous pantheist.

Sounds of *alguja*, a kind of Pandean pipe with seven openings, struck our attention; their music was wafted by the wind quite distinctly from somewhere in the wood. They also startled a whole family of monkeys in the branches of a tree over our heads. Two or three monkeys carefully slipped down, and looked round as if waiting for something.

"What is this new Orpheus, to whose voice these monkeys answer?" asked I laughingly.

"Some fakir probably. The *alguja* is generally used to invite the sacred monkeys to their meals. The community of fakirs, who once inhabited this island, have removed to an old pagoda in the forest. Their new resting-place brings them more profit, because there are many passers by, whereas the island is perfectly isolated."

"Probably they were compelled to desert this dreadful place because they were threatened by chronic deafness," Miss X—— expressed her opinion. She could not help being out of temper at being prevented from enjoying her quiet slumber, our tents being right in the middle of the orchestra.

"*À propos* of Orpheus," asked the Takur, "do you

know that the lyre of this Greek demigod was not the first to cast spells over people, animals and even rivers? Kui, a certain Chinese musical artist, as they are called, expresses something to this effect: 'When I play my *kyng* the wild animals hasten to me, and range themselves into rows, spell-bound by my melody.' This Kui lived one thousand years before the supposed era of Orpheus."

"What a funny coincidence!" exclaimed I. "Kui is the name of one of our best artists in St. Petersburg. Where did you read this?"

"Oh, this is not a very rare piece of information. Some of your Western Orientalists have it in their books. But I personally found it in an ancient Sanskrit book, translated from the Chinese in the second century before your era. But the original is to be found in a very ancient work, named *The Preserver of the Five Chief Virtues*. It is a kind of chronicle or treatise on the development of music in China. It was written by the order of Emperor Hoang-Tee many hundred years before your era."

"Do you think, then, that the Chinese ever understood anything about music?" said the colonel, with an incredulous smile. "In California and other places I heard some travelling artists of the celestial empire. . . Well, I think, that kind of musical entertainment would drive any one mad."

"That is exactly the opinion of many of your Western musicians on the subject of our ancient Âryan, as well as of modern Hindu, music. But, in the first instance, the idea of melody is perfectly arbitrary; and, in the second, there is a good deal of difference between the technical knowledge of music, and the creation of melodies fit to please the educated, as well as the uneducated, ear. According to technical theory, a musical piece may be perfect, but the melody, nevertheless, may be above the understanding of an untrained taste, or simply unpleasant. Your most renowned operas sound for us like a wild chaos, like a rush of strident, entangled sounds, in which we do not see any meaning at all, and which give us headaches. I have visited the London and the Paris opera; I have heard Rossini and Meyerbeer; I was resolved to render myself an account of my impressions, and listened with the greatest attention. But I own I prefer the simplest of our native melodies to the productions of the best European composers. Our popular songs speak to me, whereas they fail to produce any emotion in you. But leaving the tunes and songs out of question, I can assure you that our ancestors, as well as the ancestors of the Chinese, were far from inferior to the modern Europeans, if not in technical instrumentation, at least in their abstract notions of music."

"The Âryan nations of antiquity, perhaps; but I hardly believe this in the case of the Turanian Chinese!" said our president doubtfully.

"But the music of nature has been everywhere the first step to the music of art. This is a universal rule. But there are different ways of following it. Our musical system is the greatest art, if—pardon me this seeming paradox—avoiding all artificiality is art. We do not allow in our melodies any sounds that cannot be classified amongst the living voices of nature; whereas the modern Chinese tendencies are quite different. The Chinese system comprises eight chief tones, which serve as a tuning-fork to all derivatives; which are accordingly classified under the names of their generators. These eight sounds are: the notes metal, stone, silk, bamboo, pumpkin, earthenware, leather and wood. So that they have metallic sounds, wooden sounds, silk sounds, and so on. Of course, under these conditions they cannot produce any melody; their music consists of an entangled series of separate notes. Their imperial hymn, for instance, is a series of endless unisons. But we Hindus owe our music only to living nature, and in nowise to inanimate objects. In a higher sense of the word, we are pantheists, and so our music is, so to speak, pantheistic; but, at the same time, it is highly scientific. Coming from the cradle of humanity, the Âryan races, who were the first to attain manhood, listened to the voice of nature, and concluded that melody as well as harmony are both contained in our great common mother. Nature has no false and no artificial notes; and man, the crown of creation, felt desirous of imitating her sounds. In their multiplicity, all these sounds—according to the opinion of some of your Western physicists—make only one tone, which we all can hear, if we know how to listen, in the eternal rustle of the foliage of big forests, in the murmur of water, in the roar of the storming ocean, and even in the distant roll of a great city. This tone is the middle F, the fundamental tone of nature. In our melodies it serves as the starting point, which we embody in the key-note, and around which are grouped all the other sounds. Having noticed that every musical note has its typical representative in the animal kingdom, our ancestors found out that the seven chief tones correspond to the cries of the goat, the peacock, the ox, the parrot, the frog, the tiger, and the elephant. So the octave was discovered and founded. As to its subdivisions and measure, they also found their basis in the complicated sounds of the same animals."

"I am no judge of your ancient music," said the colonel,

"nor do I know whether your ancestors did, or did not, work out any musical theories, so I cannot contradict you; but I must own that, listening to the songs of the modern Hindus, I could not give them any credit for musical knowledge."

"No doubt it is so, because you have never heard a professional singer. When you have visited Poona, and have listened to the Gayan Samâj, we shall resume our present conversation. The Gayan Samâj is a society whose aim is to restore the ancient national music."

Gulab-Lal-Sing spoke in his usual calm voice, but the Babu was evidently burning to break forth for his country's honour, and at the same time, he was afraid of offending his seniors by interrupting their conversation. At last he lost patience.

"You are unjust, colonel!" he exclaimed. "The music of the ancient Âryans is an antediluvian plant, no doubt, but nevertheless it is well worth studying, and deserves every consideration. This is perfectly proved now by a compatriot of mine, the Raja Surendronath Tagor. . . He is a *Mus. D.*, he has lots of decorations from all kinds of kings and emperors of Europe for his book about the music of Âryans. . . And, well, this man has proved, as clear as daylight, that ancient India has every right to be called the mother of music. Even the best musical critics of England say so! . . . Every school, whether Italian, German or Âryan, saw the light at a certain period, developed in a certain climate and in perfectly different circumstances. Every school has its characteristics, and its peculiar charm, at least for its followers; and our school is no exception. You Europeans are trained in the melodies of the West, and acquainted with Western schools of music; but our musical system, like many other things in India, is totally unknown to you. So you must forgive my boldness, colonel, when I say that you have no right to judge!"

"Don't get so excited, Babu," said the Takur. "Every one has the right, if not to discuss, then to ask questions about a new subject. Otherwise no one would ever get any information. If Hindu music belonged to an epoch as little distant from us as the European—which you seem to suggest, Babu, in your hot haste; and if, besides, it included all the virtues of all the previous musical systems, which the European music assimilates; then no doubt it would have been better understood, and better appreciated than it is. But our music belongs to pre-historic times. In one of the sarcophagi at Thebes, Bruce found a harp with twenty strings, and, judging by this instrument, we may safely say that the ancient inhabitants of Egypt were well acquainted with the mysteries of harmony. But, except the Egyptians, we were the only people possessing this art, in the remote epochs, when the rest of mankind were still struggling with the elements for bare existence. We possess hundreds of Sanskrit MSS. about music, which have never been translated, even into modern Indian dialects. Some of them are four thousand and eight thousand years old. Whatever your Orientalists may say to the contrary, we will persist in believing in their antiquity, because we have read and studied them, while the European scientists have never yet set their eyes on them. There are many of these musical treatises, and they have been written at different epochs; but they all, without exception, show that in India music was known and systematized in times when the modern civilized nations of Europe still lived like savages. However true, all this does not give us the right to grow indignant when Europeans say they do not like our music, as long as their ears are not accustomed to it, and their minds cannot understand its spirit. . . To a certain extent we can explain to you its technical character, and give you a right idea of it as a science. But nobody can create in you, in a moment, what the Âryans used to call *Rakti;* the capacity of the human soul to receive and be moved by the combinations of the various sounds of nature. This capacity is the alpha and omega of our musical system, but you do not possess it, as we do not possess the possibility to fall into raptures over Bellini."

"But why should it be so? What are these mysterious virtues of your music, that can be understood only by yourselves? Our skins are of different colours, but our organic mechanism is the same. In other words, the physiological combination of bones, blood, nerves, veins and muscles, which forms a Hindu, has as many parts, combined exactly after the same model as the living mechanism known under the name of an American, Englishman, or any other European. They come into the world from the same workshop of nature; they have the same beginning and the same end. From a physiological point of view we are duplicates of each other."

"Physiologically yes. And it would be as true psychologically, if education did not interfere, which, after all is said and done, could not but influence the mental and the moral direction taken by a human being. Sometimes it extinguishes the divine spark; at other times it only increases it, transforming it into a lighthouse which becomes man's lode-star for life."

"No doubt this is so. But the influence it has over the physiology of the ear cannot be so overpowering after all."

"Quite the contrary. Only remember what a strong influence climatic conditions, food and everyday surroundings have on the complexion, vitality, capacity for reproduction, and so on, and you will see that you are mistaken. Apply this same law of gradual modification to the purely psychic element in man, and the results will be the same. Change the education and you will change the capacities of a human being. . . . For instance, you believe in the powers of gymnastics, you believe that special exercise can almost transform the human body. We go one step higher. The experience of centuries shows that gymnastics exist for the soul as well as for the body. But what the soul's gymnastics are is our secret. What is it that gives to the sailor the sight of an eagle, that endows the acrobat with the skill of a monkey, and the wrestler with muscles of iron? Practice and habit. Then why should not we suppose the same possibilities in the soul of the man as well as in his body? Perhaps on the grounds of modern science —which either dispenses with the soul altogether, or does not acknowledge in it a life distinct from the life of the body. . ."

"Please do not speak in this way, Takur. You, at least, ought to know that I believe in the soul and in its immortality!"

"We believe in the immortality of spirit, not of soul, following the triple division of body, soul and spirit. However, this has nothing to do with the present discussion. . . And so you agree to the proposition that every dormant possibility of the soul may be led to perfected strength and activity by practice, and also that if not properly used it may grow numb and even disappear altogether. Nature is so zealous that all her gifts should be used properly, that it is in our power to develop or to kill in our descendants any physical or mental gift. A systematic training or a total disregard will accomplish both in the lifetime of a few generations."

"Perfectly true; but that does not explain to me the secret charm of your melodies. . . ."

"These are details and particulars. Why should I dwell on them when you must see for yourself that my reasoning gives you the clue, which will solve many similar problems? Centuries have accustomed the ear of a Hindu to be receptive only of certain combinations of atmospheric vibrations; whereas the ear of a European is used to perfectly different combinations. Hence the soul of the former will be enraptured where the soul of the latter will be perfectly indifferent. I hope my explanation has been simple and clear, and I might have ended it here were it not that I am anxious to give you something better than the feeling of satisfied curiosity. As yet I have solved only the physiological aspect of the secret, which is as easily admitted as the fact that we Hindus eat by the handful spices which would give you inflammation of the intestines if you happened to swallow a single grain. Our aural nerves, which, at the beginning, were identical with yours, have been changed through different training, and became as distinct from yours as our complexion and our stomachs. Add to this that the eyes of the Kashmir weavers, men and women, are able to distinguish three hundred shades more than the eye of a European. . . . The force of habit, the law of atavism, if you like. But things of this kind practically solve the apparent difficulty. You have come all the way from America to study the Hindus and their religion; but you will never understand the latter if you do not realize how closely all our sciences are related, not to the modern ignorant Brahmanism, of course, but to the philosophy of our primitive Vedic religion."

"I see. You mean that your music has something to do with the *Vedas?*"

"Exactly. It has a good deal—almost everything—to do with the *Vedas.* All the sounds of nature, and, in consequence, of music, are directly allied to astronomy and mathematics; that is to say, to the planets, the signs of the zodiac, the sun and moon, and to rotation and numbers. Above all, they depend on the *Âkâsha,* the ether of space, of the existence of which your scientists have not made perfectly sure as yet. This was the teaching of the ancient Chinese and Egyptians, as well as of ancient Aryans. The doctrine of the 'music of the spheres' first saw the light here in India, and not in Greece or Italy, whither it was brought by Pythagoras after he had studied under the Indian Gymnosophists. And most certainly this great philosopher—who revealed to the world the heliocentric system before Copernicus and Galileo—knew better than anyone else how dependent are the least sounds in nature on Âkâsha and its inter-relations. One of the four *Vedas,* namely, the *Sâma-Veda,* entirely consists of hymns. This is a collection of mantrams sung during the sacrifices to the gods, that is to say, to the elements. Our ancient priests were hardly acquainted with the modern methods of chemistry and physics; but, to make up for it, they knew a good deal which has not as yet been thought of by modern scientists. So it is not to be wondered at that, sometimes, our priests, so perfectly acquainted with natural sciences as they were, forced the elementary gods, or rather the blind forces of nature, to answer their prayers by various portents. Every sound of these mantrams has its meaning, its importance, and stands exactly where it ought to stand; and, having a *raison d'être,* it does not fail to produce its effect. Remember

Professor Leslie, who says that the science of sound is the most subtle, the most unseizable and the most complicated of all the series of physical sciences. And if ever this teaching was worked out to perfection it was in the times of the Rishis, our philosophers and saints, who left to us the *Vedas*."

"Now, I think I begin to understand the origin of all the mythological fables of the Greek antiquity," thoughtfully said the colonel; "the syrinx of Pan, his pipe of seven reeds, the fauns, the satyrs, and the lyre of Orpheus himself. The ancient Greeks knew little about harmony; and the rhythmical declamations of their dramas, which probably never reached the pathos of the simplest of modern recitals, could hardly suggest to them the idea of the magic lyre of Orpheus. I feel strongly inclined to believe what was written by some of our great philologists: Orpheus must be an emigrant from India; his very name ὀρφὸς, or ὀρφνὸς, shows that, even amongst the tawny Greeks, he was remarkably dark. This was the opinion of Lemprière and others."

"Some day this opinion may become a certainty. There is not the slightest doubt that the purest and the highest of all the musical forms of antiquity belongs to India. All our legends ascribe magic powers to music; it is a gift and a science coming straight from the gods. As a rule, we ascribe all our arts to divine revelation, but music stands at the head of everything else. The invention of the *vînâ*, a kind of lute, belongs to Nârada, the son of Brahmâ. You will probably laugh at me if I tell you that our ancient priests, whose duty it was to sing during the sacrifices, were able to produce phenomena that could not but be considered by the ignorant as signs from supernatural powers; and this, remember, without a shadow of trickery, but simply with the help of their perfect knowledge of nature and certain combinations well known to them. The phenomena produced by the priests and the Râj-Yogis are perfectly natural for the initiate—however miraculous they may seem to the masses."

"But do you really mean that you have no faith whatever in the spirits of the dead?" timidly asked Miss X——, who was always ill at ease in the presence of the Takur.

"With your permission, I have none."

"And . . . and have you no regard for mediums?"

"Still less than for the spirits, my dear lady. I do believe in the existence of many psychic diseases, and, amongst their number, in mediumism, for which we have got a queer sounding name from time immemorial. We call it *Bhûta-Dâk*, literally a bhuta-hostelry. I sincerely pity the real mediums, and do whatever is in my power to help them. As to the charlatans, I despise them, and never lose an opportunity of unmasking them."

The witch's den near the "dead city" suddenly flashed into my mind; the fat Brahman, who played the oracle in the head of the Sivatherium, caught and rolling down the hole; the witch herself suddenly taking to her heels. And with this recollection also occurred to me what I had never thought of before: Narayan had acted under the orders of the Takur—doing his best to expose the witch and her ally.

"The unknown power which possesses the mediums (which the spiritualists believe to be spirits of the dead, while the superstitious see in it the devil, and the sceptics deceit and infamous tricks), true men of science suspect to be a natural force, which has not as yet been discovered. It is, in reality, a terrible power. Those possessed by it are generally weak people, often women and children. Your beloved spiritualists, Miss X——, only help the growth of dreadful psychic diseases, but people who know better seek to save them from this force you know nothing whatever about, and it is no use discussing this matter now. I shall only add one word: the real living spirit of a human being is as free as Brahma; and even more than this for us, for, according to our religion and our philosophy, our spirit is Brahma himself, higher than whom there is only the unknowable, the all-pervading, the omnipotent essence of Parabrahm. The living spirit of man cannot be ordered about like the spirits of the spiritualists, it cannot be made a slave of. . . . However, it is getting so late that we had better go to bed. Let us say good-bye for to-night."

Gulab-Lal-Sing would not talk any more that night, but I have gathered from our previous conversations many a point without which the above conversation would remain obscure.

The Vedantins and the followers of Shankarâchârya's philosophy, in talking of themselves, often avoid using the pronoun *I*, and say, "this body went," "this hand took," and so on, in everything concerning the automatic actions of man. The personal pronouns are only used concerning mental and moral processes, such as, "I thought," "he desired." The body in their eyes is not the man, but only a covering to the real man.

The real interior man possesses many bodies; each of them more subtle and more pure than the preceding; and each of them bears a different name and is independent of the material body. After death, when the earthly vital principle disintegrates, together with the material body, all these interior bodies join together, and either advance on the way to Moksha, and are called *Deva* (divine), though it still has to pass many stadia before the final liberation, or is left on earth, to wander and to suffer in the invisible world, and, in this case, is called bhuta. But a Deva has no tangible intercourse with the living. Its only link with the earth is its posthumous affection for those it loved in its lifetime, and the power of protecting and influencing them. *Love* outlives every earthly feeling, and a Deva can appear to the beloved ones only in their dreams—unless it be as an illusion, which cannot last, because the body of a Deva undergoes a series of gradual changes from the moment it is freed from its earthly bonds; and, with every change, it grows more intangible, losing every time something of its objective nature. It is reborn; it lives and dies in new *Lokas* or spheres, which gradually become purer and more subjective. At last, having got rid of every shadow of earthly thoughts and desires, it becomes *nothing* from a material point of view. It is extinguished like a flame, and, having become one with Parabrahm, it lives the life of spirit, of which neither our material conception nor our language can give any idea. But the eternity of Parabrahm is not the eternity of the soul. The latter, according to a Vedânta expression, is an eternity in eternity. However holy, the life of a soul had its beginning and its end, and, consequently, no sins and no good actions can be punished or rewarded in the eternity of Parabrahm. This would be contrary to justice, *disproportionate,* to use an expression of Vedânta philosophy. Spirit alone lives in eternity, and has neither beginning nor end, neither limits nor central point. The Deva lives in Parabrahm, as a drop lives in the ocean, till the next regeneration of the universe from Pralaya; a periodical chaos, a disappearance of the worlds from the region of objectivity. With every new Mahâ-yuga (great cycle) the Deva separates from that which is eternal, attracted by existence in objective worlds, like a drop of water first drawn up by the sun, then starting again downwards, passing from one region to another, and returning at last to the dirt of our planet. Then, having dwelt there whilst a small cycle lasted, it proceeds again upwards on the other side of the circle. So it gravitates in the eternity of Parabrahm, passing from one minor eternity to another. Each of these "human," that is to say conceivable, eternities consists of 4,320,000,000 years of objective life and of as many years of subjective life in Parabrahm, altogether 8,640,000,000 years, which are enough, in the eyes of the Vedantins, to redeem any mortal sin, and also to reap the fruit of any good actions performed in such a short period as human life. The individuality of the soul, teaches the Vedânta, is not lost when plunged in Parabrahm, as is supposed by some of the European Orientalists.

Only the souls of bhutas—when the last spark of repentance and of tendency to improvement are extinguished in them—will evaporate for ever. Then their divine spirit, the undying part of them, separates from the soul and returns to its primitive source; the soul is reduced to its primordial atoms, and the monad plunges into the darkness of eternal unconsciousness. This is the only case of total destruction of personality.

Such is the Vedânta teaching concerning the spiritual man. And this is why no true Hindu believes in the disembodied souls voluntarily returning to earth, except in the case of bhutas.

JUBBLEPORE.

LEAVING Malva and Indore, the quasi-independent country of Holkar, we found ourselves once more on strictly British territory. We were going to Jubblepore by railway.

This town is situated in the district of Saugor and Nerbudda; once it belonged to the Mahrattis, but, in 1817, the English army took possession of it. We stopped in the town only for a short time, being anxious to see the celebrated Marble Rocks. As it would have been a pity to lose a whole day, we hired a boat and started at 2 A.M., which gave us the double advantage of avoiding the heat, and enjoying a splendid bit of the river ten miles from the town.

The neighbourhood of Jubblepore is charming; and besides, both a geologist and a mineralogist would find here the richest field for scientific researches. The geological formation of the rocks offers an infinite variety of granites; and the long chains of mountains might keep a hundred of Cuviers busy for life. The limestone caves of Jubblepore are a true ossuary of antediluvian India; they are full of skeletons of monstrous animals, now disappeared for ever.

At a considerable distance from the rest of the mountain ridges, and perfectly separate, stand the Marble Rocks, a most wonderful natural phenomenon, not very rare, though, in India. On the flattish banks of the Nerbudda, overgrown with thick bushes, you suddenly perceive a long row of strangely-shaped white cliffs.

They are there without any apparent reason, as if they were a wart on the smooth cheek of mother nature. White and pure, they are heaped up on each other as if after some plan, and look exactly like a huge paper-weight from the writing-table of a Titan. We saw them when we were half-way from the town. They appeared and disappeared with the sudden capricious turnings of the river; trembling in the early morning mist like a distant, deceitful mirage of the desert. Then we lost sight of them altogether. But just before sunrise they stood out once more before our charmed eyes, floating above their reflected image in the water. As if called forth by the wand of a sorcerer, they stood there on the green bank of the Nerbudda, mirroring their virgin beauty on the calm surface of the lazy stream, and promising us a cool and welcome shelter. . . And as to the preciousness of every moment of the cool hours before sunrise, it can be appreciated only by those who have lived and travelled in this fiery land.

Alas! in spite of all our precautions, and our unusually early start, our enjoyment of this cool retreat was very short-lived. Our project was to have prosaic tea amid these poetic surroundings; but as soon as we landed, the sun leaped above the horizon, and began shooting his fiery arrows at the boat, and at our unfortunate heads. Persecuting us from one place to another, he banished us, at last, even from under a huge rock hanging over the water. There was literally no place where we could seek salvation. The snow-white marble beauties became golden red, pouring fire-sparks into the river, heating the sand and blinding our eyes.

No wonder that legend supposes in them something between the abode and the incarnation of Kâlî, the fiercest of all the goddesses of the Hindu pantheon.

For many Yugas this goddess has been engaged in a desperate contest with her lawful husband Shiva, who, in his shape of *Trikûtishvara*, a three-headed lingam, has dishonestly claimed the rocks and the river for his own—the very rocks and the very river over which Kâlî presides in person. And this is why people hear dreadful moaning, coming from under the ground, every time that the hand of an irresponsible coolie, working by Government orders in Government quarries, breaks a stone from the white bosom of the goddess. The unhappy stone-breaker hears the cry and trembles, and his heart is torn between the expectations of a dreadful punishment from the bloodthirsty goddess and the fear of his implacably exacting inspector in case he disobeys his orders.

Kâlî is the owner of the Marble Rocks, but she is the patroness of the *ex-Thugs* as well. Many a lonely traveller has shuddered on hearing this name; many a bloodless sacrifice has been offered on the marble altar of Kâlî. The country is full of horrible tales about the achievements of the Thugs, accomplished in the honour of this goddess. These tales are too recent and too fresh in the popular memory to become as yet mere highly-coloured legends. They are mostly true, and many of them are proved by official documents of the law courts and inquest commissions.

If England ever leaves India, the perfect suppression of Thugism will be one of the good memories that will linger in the country long after her departure. Under this name was practised in India during two long centuries the craftiest and the worst kind of homicide. Only after 1840 was it discovered that its aim was simply robbery and brigandage. The falsely interpreted symbolical meaning of Kâlî was nothing but a pretext, otherwise there would not have been so many Mussulmans amongst her devotees. When they were caught at last, and had to answer before justice, most of these knights of the *rumâl*—the handkerchief with which the operation of strangling was performed—proved to be Mussulmans. The most illustrious of their leaders were not Hindus, but followers of the Prophet, the celebrated Ahmed, for instance. Out of thirty-seven Thugs caught by the police there were twenty-two Mahometans. This proves perfectly clearly that their religion, having nothing in common with the Hindu gods, had nothing to do with their cruel profession; the reason and cause was robbery.

It is true though that the final initiation rite was performed in some deserted forest before an idol of Bhavânî, or Kâlî, wearing a necklace of human skulls. Before this final initiation the candidates had to undergo a course of schooling, the most difficult part of which was a certain trick of throwing the rumâl on the neck of the unsuspecting victim and strangling him, so that death might be instantaneous. In the initiation the part of the goddess was made manifest in the use of certain symbols, which are in common use amongst the Freemasons—for instance, an unsheathed dagger, a human skull, and the corpse of Hiram-Àbiff, "son of the widow," brought back to life by the Grand Master of the lodge. Kâlî was nothing but the pretext for an imposing scenarium. Freemasonry and Thugism had many points of resemblance. The members of both recognized each other by certain signs, both had a password and a jargon that no outsider could understand. The Freemason lodges receive among their members both Christians and Atheists; the Thugs used to receive the thieves and robbers of every nation without any distinction; and it is reported that amongst them there were some Portuguese and even Englishmen. The difference between the two is that the Thugs certainly were a criminal organization, whereas the Freemasons of our days do no harm, except to their own pockets.

Poor Shiva, wretched Bhavânî! What a mean interpretation popular ignorance has invented for these two poetical types, so deeply philosophical and so full of knowledge of the laws of nature. Shiva, in his primitive meaning is "Happy God"; then the all-destroying, as well as the all-regenerating force of nature. The Hindu trinity is, amongst other things, an allegorical representation of the three chief elements: fire, earth and water. Brahmâ, Vishnu and Shiva all represent these elements by turns, in their different phases; but Shiva is much more the god of the fire than either Brahmâ or Vishnu: he burns and purifies; at the same time creating out of the ashes new forms, full of fresh life. Shiva-Sankarin is the destroyer or rather the scatterer; Shiva-Rakshaka is the preserver, the regenerator. He is represented with flames on his left palm, and with the wand of death and resurrection in his right hand. His worshippers wear on their foreheads his sign traced with wet ashes, the ashes being called *vibhûti*, or purified substance, and the sign consisting of three horizontal parallel lines between the eyebrows. The colour of Shiva's skin is rosy-yellow, gradually changing into a flaming red. His neck, head and arms are covered with snakes, emblems of eternity and eternal regeneration. "As a serpent, abandoning his old slough, reappears in new skin, so man after death reappears in a younger and a purer body," say the *Purânas*.

In her turn, Shiva's wife Kâlî is the allegory of earth, fructified by the flames of the sun. Her educated worshippers say they allow themselves to believe their goddess is fond of human sacrifices, only on the strength of the fact that earth is fond of organical decomposition, which fertilizes her, and helps her to call forth new forces from the ashes of the dead. The Shivaites, when burning their dead, put an idol of Shiva at the head of the corpse; but when beginning to scatter the ashes in the elements, they invoke Bhavânî, in order that the goddess may receive the purified remains, and develop in them germs of new life. But what truth could bear the coarse touch of superstitious ignorance without being disfigured!

The murdering Thugs laid their hands on this great philosophic emblem, and, having understood that the goddess loves human sacrifice, but hates useless bloodshed, they resolved to please her doubly: to kill, but never to soil their hands by the blood of their victims. The result of it was the knighthood of the rumâl.

One day we visited a very aged ex-Thug. In his young days he was transported to the Andaman Islands, but, owing to his sincere repentance, and to some services he had rendered to the Government, he was afterwards pardoned. Having returned to his native village, he settled down to earn his living by weaving ropes, a profession probably suggested to him by some sweet reminiscences of the achievements of his youth. He initiated us first into the mysteries of theoretic Thugism, and then extended his hospitality by a ready offer to show us the practical side of it, if we agreed to pay for a sheep. He said he would gladly show us how easy it was to send a living being *ad patres* in less than three seconds; the whole secret consisting in some skilful and swift movements of the right-hand finger joints.

We refused to buy the sheep for this old brigand, but

we gave him some money. To show his gratitude he offered to demonstrate all the preliminary sensation of the rumâl on any English or American neck that was willing. Of course, he said he would omit the final twist. But still none of us were willing; and the gratitude of the repentant criminal found issue in great volubility.

The owl is sacred to Bhavânî Kâlî, and as soon as a band of Thugs, awaiting their victims, had been signalled by the conventional hooting, each of the travellers, let them be twenty and more, had a Thug behind his shoulders. One second more, and the rumâl was on the neck of the victim, the well-trained iron fingers of the Thug tightly holding the ends of the sacred handkerchief; another second, the joints of the fingers performed their artistic twist, pressing the larynx, and the victim fell down lifeless. Not a sound, not a shriek! The Thugs worked as swiftly as lightning. The strangled man was immediately carried to a grave prepared in some thick forest, usually under the bed of some brook or rivulet in their periodical state of drought. Every vestige of the victim disappeared. Who cared to know about him, except his own family and his very intimate friends? The inquests were especially difficult, if not impossible, thirty years ago [1879], when there were no regular railway communications, and no regular Government system. Besides, the country is full of tigers, whose sad fate it is to be responsible for every one else's sins as well as for their own. Whoever it was who happened to disappear, be it Hindu or Mussulman, the answer was invariably the same: tigers!

The Thugs possessed a wonderfully good organization. Trained accomplices used to tramp all over India, stopping at the bazaars, those true clubs of Eastern nations, gathering information, scaring their listeners to death with tales of the Thugs, and then advising them to join this or that travelling party, who of course were Thugs playing the part of rich merchants or pilgrims. Having ensnared these wretches, they sent word to the Thugs, and got paid for the commission in proportion to the total profit.

During many long years these invisible bands, scattered all over the country, and working in parties of from ten to sixty men, enjoyed perfect freedom, but at last they were caught. The inquiries unveiled horrid and repulsive secrets: rich bankers, officiating Brahmans, Rajas on the brink of poverty, and a few English officials, all had to be brought before justice.

This deed of the East India Company truly deserves the popular gratitude which it receives.

On our way back from the Marble Rocks we saw Muddun-Mahal, another mysterious curio; it is a house built—no one knows by whom, or with what purpose—on a huge boulder. This stone is probably some kind of relative to the cromlechs of the Celtic Druids. It shakes at the least touch, together with the house and the people who feel curious to see inside it. Of course we had this curiosity, and our noses remained safe only thanks to the Babu, Narayan and the Takur, who took as great care of us as if they had been nurses, and we their babies.

Natives of India are truly a wonderful people. However unsteady the thing may be, they are sure to walk on it, and sit on it, with the greatest comfort. They think nothing of sitting whole hours on the top of a post—maybe a little thicker than an ordinary telegraph post. They also feel perfectly safe with their toes twisted round a thin branch and their bodies resting on nothing, as if they were crows perched on a telegraph wire.

"Salam, sahib!" said I once to an ancient, naked Hindu of a low caste, seated in the above described fashion. "Are you comfortable, uncle? And are you not afraid of falling down?"

"Why should I fall?" seriously answered the "uncle," expectorating a red fountain—an unavoidable result of betel-chewing. "I do not breathe, mam-sahib!"

"What do you mean? A man cannot do without breathing!" exclaimed I, a good deal astonished by this wonderful bit of information.

"Oh yes, he can. I do not breathe just now, and so I am perfectly safe. But soon I shall have to fill up my breast again with fresh air, and then I will hold on to the post, otherwise I should fall."

After this astounding physiological information, we parted. He would not talk any more, evidently fearing to endanger his comfort. At that time, we did not receive any more explanations on the subject, but this incident was enough to disturb the scientific equanimity of our minds.

Till then, we were so naïve as to fancy that only sturgeons and similar aquatic acrobats were clever enough to learn how to fill up their insides with air in order to become lighter, and to rise to the surface of the water. What is possible to a sturgeon is impossible to man, speculated we in our ignorance. So we agreed to look upon the revelation of the above described "uncle" in the light of a brag, having no other aim but to chaff the "white sahibs." In those days, we were still inexperienced, and inclined to resent this kind of information, as coming very near to mockery. But, later on, we learned that his description of the process necessary to keep up this birdlike posture was perfectly accurate. In Jubblepore we saw much greater wonders. Strolling along the river bank, we reached the so-called Fakirs' Avenue; and the Takur invited us to visit the courtyard of the pagoda. This is a sacred place, and neither Europeans nor Mussulmans are admitted inside. But Gulab-Sing said something to the chief Brahman, and we entered without hindrance.

The yard was full of devotees, and of ascetics. But our attention was especially attracted by three ancient, perfectly naked fakirs. As wrinkled as baked mushrooms, as thin as skeletons, crowned with twisted masses of white hair, they sat or rather stood in the most *impossible* postures, as we thought. One of them, literally leaning only on the palm of his right hand, was poised with his head downwards and his legs upwards; his body was as motionless as if he were the dry branch of a tree. Just a little above the ground his head rose in the most unnatural position, and his eyes were fixed on the glaring sun. I cannot guarantee the truthfulness of some talkative inhabitants of the town, who had joined our party, and who assured us that this fakir daily spends in this posture all the hours between noon and the sunset. But I can guarantee that not a muscle of his body moved during the hour and twenty minutes we spent amongst the fakirs.

Another fakir stood on a "sacred stone of Shiva," a small stone about five inches in diameter. One of his legs was curled up under him, and the whole of his body was bent backwards into an arc; his eyes also were fixed on the sun. The palms of his hands were pressed together as if in prayer. He seemed glued to his stone. We were at a loss to imagine by what means this man came to be master of such equilibration.

The third of these wonderful people sat crossing his legs under him; but how he could sit was more than we could understand, because the thing on which he sat was a stone lingam, not higher than an ordinary street post and little wider than the "stone of Shiva," that is to say, hardly more than five or seven inches in diameter. His arms were crossed behind his back, and his nails had grown into the flesh of his shoulders.

"This one never changes his position," said one of our companions. "At least, he has not changed for the last seven years."

His usual food, or rather drink, is milk, which is brought to him once in every forty-eight hours and poured into his throat with the aid of a bamboo. Every ascetic has willing servants, who are also future fakirs, whose duty it is to attend on them; and so the disciples of this living mummy take him off his pedestal, wash him in the tank, and put him back like an inanimate object, because he can no longer stretch his limbs.

"And what if I were to push one of these fakirs?" asked I. "I daresay the least touch would upset them."

"Try!" laughingly advised the Takur. "In this state of religious trance it is easier to break a man to pieces than to remove him from his place."

To touch an ascetic in the state of trance is a sacrilege in the eyes of the Hindus; but evidently the Takur was well aware that, under certain circumstances, there may be exceptions to every Brahmanical rule. He had another aside with the chief Brahman, who followed us, darker than a thunder-cloud; the consultation did not last long, and after it was over Gulab-Sing declared to us that none of us was allowed to touch the fakirs, but that he personally had obtained this permission, and so was going to show us something still more astonishing.

He approached the fakir on the little stone, and, carefully holding him by his protruding ribs, he lifted him and put him on the ground. The ascetic remained as statuesque as before. Then Gulab-Sing took the stone in his hands and showed it to us, asking us, however, not to touch it for fear of offending the crowd. The stone was round, flattish, with rather an uneven surface. When laid on the ground it shook at the least touch.

"Now, you see that this pedestal is far from being steady. And also you have seen that, under the weight of the fakir, it is as immovable as if it were planted in the ground."

When the fakir was put back on the stone, he and it at once resumed their appearance, as of one single body, solidly joined to the ground, and not a line of the fakir's body had changed. By all appearance, his bending body and his head thrown backward sought to bring him down; but for this fakir there was evidently no such thing as the law of gravity.

What I have described is a fact, but I do not take upon myself to explain it. At the gates of the pagoda we found our shoes, which we had been told to take off before going in. We put them on again, and left this "holy of holies" of the secular mysteries, with our minds still more perplexed than before. In the Fakirs' Avenue we found Narayan, Mulji and the Babu, who were waiting for us. The chief Brahman would not hear of their entering the pagoda. All the three had long before released themselves from the iron claws of caste; they openly ate and drank with us, and for this offence they were regarded as excommunicated, and despised by their compatriots much more than the Europeans themselves. Their presence in the pagoda would have polluted it for ever, whereas the pollution brought by us was only temporary; it would evaporate in the smoke of cow-dung—the usual Brahmanical incense of purification—like a drop of muddy water in the rays of the sun.

India is the country for originalities and everything unexpected and unconventional. From the point of view of an ordinary European observer every feature of Indian life is contrary to what could be expected. Shaking the head from one shoulder to another means *no* in every other country, but in India it means an emphatic *yes*. If you ask a Hindu how his wife is, even if you are well acquainted with her, or how many children he has, or whether he has any sisters, he will feel offended in nine cases out of ten. So long as the host does not point to the door, having previously sprinkled the guest with rose-water, the latter would not think of leaving. He would stay the whole day without tasting any food, and lose his time, rather than offend his host by an unauthorized departure. Everything contradicts our Western ideas. The Hindus are strange and original, but their religion is still more original. It has its dark points, of course. The rites of some sects are truly repulsive; the officiating Brahmans are far from being without reproach. But these are only superficialities. In spite of them the Hindu religion possesses something so deeply and mysteriously irresistible that it attracts and subdues even unimaginative Englishmen.

The following incident is a curious instance of this fascination:

N. C. Paul, G.B.M.C., wrote a small, but very interesting and very scientific pamphlet. He was only a regimental surgeon in Benares, but his name was well known amongst his compatriots as a very learned specialist in physiology. The pamphlet was called *A Treatise on the Yoga Philosophy*, and produced a sensation amongst the representatives of medicine in India, and a lively polemic between the Anglo-Indian and native journalists. Dr. Paul spent thirty-five years in studying the extraordinary facts of Yogism, the existence of which was, for him, beyond all doubt. He not only described them, but explained some of the most extraordinary phenomena, for instance, *levitation*, the seeming evidence to the contrary of some laws of nature, notwithstanding. With perfect sincerity, and evident regret, Dr. Paul says he could never learn anything from the Râj-Yogis. His experience was almost wholly limited to the facts that fakirs and Hatha-Yogis would consent to give him. It was his great friendship with Captain Seymour chiefly which helped him to penetrate some mysteries, which, till then, were supposed to be impenetrable.

The history of this English gentleman is truly incredible, and produced, about twenty-five years ago, an unprecedented scandal in the records of the British army in India. Captain Seymour, a wealthy and well-educated officer, accepted the Brahmanical creed and became a Yogi. Of course he was proclaimed mad, and, having been caught, was sent back to England. Seymour escaped, and returned to India in the dress of a Sannyâsi. He was caught again, and shut up in some lunatic asylum in London. Three days after, in spite of the bolts and the watchmen, he disappeared from the establishment. Later on his acquaintances saw him in Benares, and the governor-general received a letter from him from the Himalayas. In this letter he declared that he never was mad, in spite of his being put into a hospital; he advised the governor-general not to interfere with what was strictly his own private concern, and announced his firm resolve never to return to civilized society. "I am a Yogi," wrote he, "and I hope to obtain before I die what is the aim of my life—to become a Râj-Yogi." After this letter he was left alone, and no European ever saw him except Dr. Paul, who, as it is reported, was in constant correspondence with him, and even went twice to see him in the Himalayas under the pretext of botanic excursions.

I was told that the pamphlet of Dr. Paul was ordered to be burned "as being offensive to the science of physiology and pathology." At the time I visited India copies of it were very great rarities. Out of a few copies still extant, one is to be found in the library of the Maharaja of Benares, and another was given to me by the Takur.

This evening we dined at the refreshment rooms of the railway station. Our arrival caused an evident sensation. Our party occupied the whole end of a table, at which were dining many first-class passengers, who all stared at us with undisguised astonishment. Europeans on an equal footing with Hindus! Hindus who condescended to dine with Europeans! These two were rare and wonderful sights indeed. The subdued whispers grew into loud exclamations. Two officers who happened to know the Takur took him aside, and, having shaken hands with him, began a very animated conversation, as if discussing some matter of business; but, as we learned afterwards, they simply wanted to gratify their curiosity about us.

Here we learned, for the first time, that we were under police supervision, the police being represented by an individual clad in a suit of white clothes, and possessing a very fresh complexion, and a pair of long moustaches. He was an agent of the secret police, and had followed us from Bombay. On learning this flattering piece of news, the colonel burst into a loud laugh; which only made us still more suspicious in the eyes of all these Anglo-Indians, enjoying a quiet and dignified meal. As to me, I was very disagreeably impressed by this bit of news, I must confess, and wished this unpleasant dinner was over.

The train for Allahabad was to leave at eight P.M., and we were to spend the night in the railway carriage. We had ten reserved seats in a first-class carriage, and had made sure that no strange passengers would enter it, but, nevertheless, there were many reasons which made me think I could not sleep this night. So I obtained a provision of candles for my reading lamp, and making myself comfortable on my couch, began reading the pamphlet of Dr. Paul, which interested me greatly.

Amongst many other interesting things, Dr. Paul explains very fully and learnedly the mystery of the periodical suspension of breathing, and some other seemingly impossible phenomena, practised by the Yogis.

Here is his theory in brief. The Yogis have discovered the reason of the wondrous capacity of the chameleon to assume the appearance of plumpness or of leanness. This animal looks enormous when his lungs are filled with air, but in his normal condition he is quite insignificant. Many other reptiles as well acquire the possibility of swimming across large rivers quite easily by the same process. And the air that remains in their lungs, after the blood has been fully oxygenated, makes them extraordinarily lively on dry land and in the water. The capacity of storing up an extraordinary provision of air is a characteristic feature of all the animals that are subjected to hibernation.

The Hindu Yogis studied this capacity, and perfected and developed it in themselves.

The means by which they acquire it—known under the name of *Bhastrika Kumbhaka*—consist of the following: The Yogi isolates himself in an underground cave, where the atmosphere is more uniform and more damp than on the surface of the earth: this causes the appetite to grow less. Man's appetite is proportionate to the quantity of carbonic acid he exhales in a certain period of time. The Yogis never use salt, and live entirely on milk, which they take only during the night. They move very slowly in order not to breathe too often. Movement increases the exhaled carbonic acid, and so the Yoga practice prescribes avoidance of movement. The quantity of exhaled carbonic acid is also increased by loud and lively talking: so the Yogis are taught to talk slowly and in subdued tones, and are even advised to take the vows of silence. Physical labour is propitious to the increase of carbonic acid, and mental to its decrease; accordingly the Yogi spends his life in contemplation and deep meditation. *Padmâsana* and *Siddhâsana* are the two methods by which a person is taught to breathe as little as possible.

Suka-Devi, a well-known miracle-monger of the second century B.C. says:

"Place the left foot upon the right thigh, and the right foot upon the left thigh; straighten the neck and back; make the palms of the hands rest upon the knees; shut the mouth; and expire forcibly through both nostrils. Next, inspire and expire quickly until you are fatigued. Then inspire through the right nostril, fill the abdomen with the inspired air, suspend the breath, and fix the sight on the tip of the nose. Then expire through the left nostril, and next, inspiring through the left nostril, suspend the breath . . . ." and so on.

"When a Yogi, by practice, is enabled to maintain himself in one of the above-mentioned postures for the period of three hours, and to live upon a quantity of food proportional to the reduced condition of circulation and respiration, without inconvenience, he proceeds to the practice of Prânâyâma," writes Dr. Paul. "It is the fourth stage or division of Yoga."

The *Prânâyâma* consists of three parts. The first excites the secretion of sweat, the second is attended by convulsive movements of the features, the third gives to the Yogi a feeling of extraordinary lightness in his body.

After this, the Yogi practises *Pratyâhâra*, a kind of voluntary trance, which is recognizable by the full suspension of all the senses. After this stage the Yogis study the process of *Dhâranâ;* this not only stops the activity of physical senses, but also causes the mental capacities to be plunged into a deep torpor. This stage brings abundant suffering; it requires a good deal of firmness and resolution on the part of a Yogi, but it leads him to *Dhyâna*, a state of perfect, indescribable bliss. According to their own desctiption, in this state they swim in the ocean of eternal light, in Âkâsha, or *Ananta Jyoti*, which they call the "Soul of the Universe." Reaching the stage of Dhyâna, the Yogi becomes a seer. The Dhyâna of the Yogis is the same thing as *Tûriya Avasthâ* of the Vedantins, in the number of whom are the Râj-Yogis.

"Samâdhi is the last stage of self-trance," says Dr. Paul. "In this state the Yogis, like the bat, the hedgehog, the marmot, the hamster and the dormouse, acquire the power of supporting the abstraction of atmospheric

air, and the privation of food and drink. Of Samâdhi or human hibernation there have been three cases within the last twenty-five years. The first case occurred in Calcutta, the second in Jesselmere, and the third in the Punjab. I was an eye-witness of the first case. The Jesselmere, the Punjab, and the Calcutta Yogis assumed a death-like condition by swallowing the tongue. . . How the Punjabi fakir (witnessed by Dr. McGregor), by suspending his breath, lived forty days without food and drink, is a question which has puzzled a great many learned men of Europe. . . It is on the principle of *Laghimâ* and *Garimâ* (a diminution of one's specific gravity by swallowing large draughts of air) that the Brahman of Madras maintained himself in an aërial posture. . . ."

However, all these are physical phenomena produced by Hatha-Yogis. Each of them ought to be investigated by physical science, but they are much less interesting than the phenomena of the region of psychology. But Dr. Paul has next to nothing to say on this subject. During the thirty-five years of his Indian career, he met only three Râj-Yogis; but in spite of the friendliness they showed to the English doctor, none of them consented to initiate him into the mysteries of nature, a knowledge of which is ascribed to them. One of them simply denied that he had any power at all; the other did not deny, and even showed Dr. Paul some very wonderful things, but refused to give any explanations whatever; the third said he would explain a few things on the condition that Dr. Paul must pledge himself never to repeat anything he learned from him. In acquiring this kind of information, Dr. Paul had only one aim—to give these secrets publicity, and to enlighten the public ignorance, and so he declined the honour.

However, the gifts of the true Râj-Yogis are much more interesting, and a great deal more important for the world, than the phenomena of the lay Hatha-Yogis. These gifts are purely psychic: to the knowledge of the Hatha-Yogis the Râj-Yogis add the whole scale of mental phenomena. Sacred books ascribe to them the following gifts: foreseeing future events; understanding of all languages; the healing of all diseases; the art of reading other people's thoughts; witnessing at will everything that happens thousands of miles from them; understanding the language of animals and birds; *Prâkâmya*, or the power of keeping up youthful appearance during incredible periods of time; the power of abandoning their own bodies and entering other people's frames; *Vashitva*, or the gift to kill, and to tame wild animals with their eyes; and, lastly, the mesmeric power to subjugate any one, and to force any one to obey the unexpressed orders of the Râj-Yogi.

Dr. Paul has witnessed the few phenomena of Hatha-Yoga already described; there are many others about which he has heard, and which he neither believes nor disbelieves. But he guarantees that a Yogi can suspend his breath for forty-three minutes and twelve seconds.

Nevertheless, European scientific authorities maintain that no one can suspend the breath for more than two minutes. O science! Is it possible then that thy name is also *vanitas vanitatum*, like the other things of this world?

We are forced to suppose that, in Europe, nothing is known about the means which enabled the philosophers of India, from times immemorial, gradually to transform their human frames.

Here are a few deep words of Professor Boutleroff, a Russian scientist whom I, in common with all Russians,

greatly respect: ". . . All this belongs to knowledge; the increase of the mass of knowledge will only enrich and not abolish science. This must be accomplished on the strength of serious observation, of study, of experience, and under the guidance of positive scientific methods, by which people are taught to acknowledge every other phenomenon of nature. We do not call you blindly to accept hypotheses, after the example of bygone years, but to seek after knowledge; we do not invite you to give up science, but to enlarge her regions. . ."

This was said about spiritualist phenomena. As to the rest of our learned physiologists, this is, approximately, what they have the right to say: "We know well certain phenomena of nature which we have personally studied and investigated, under certain conditions, which we call normal or abnormal, and we guarantee the accuracy of our conclusions."

However, it would be very well if they added:

"But having no pretensions to assure the world that we are acquainted with all the forces of nature, known and unknown, we do not claim the right to hold back other people from bold investigations in regions which we have not reached as yet, owing to our great cautiousness and also to our moral timidity. Not being able to maintain that the human organism is utterly incapable of developing certain transcendental powers, which are rare, and observable only under certain conditions, unknown to science, we by no means wish to keep other explorers within the limits of our own scientific discoveries."

By pronouncing this noble, and, at the same time, modest speech, our physiologists would doubtless gain the undying gratitude of posterity.

After this speech there would be no fear of mockery, no danger of losing one's reputation for veracity and sound reason; and the learned colleagues of these broad-minded physiologists would investigate every phenomenon of nature seriously and openly. The phenomena of spiritualism would then transmigrate from the region of materialized "mothers-in-law" and half-witted fortune-telling to the regions of the psycho-physiological sciences. The celebrated "spirits" would probably evaporate, but in their stead the living spirit, which "belongeth not to this world," would become better known and better realized by humanity, because humanity will comprehend the harmony of the whole only after learning how closely the visible world is bound to the world invisible.

After this speech, Hæckel at the head of the evolutionists, and Alfred Russel Wallace at the head of the spiritualists, would be relieved from many anxieties, and would shake hands in brotherhood.

Seriously speaking, what is there to prevent humanity from acknowledging two active forces within itself; one purely animal, the other purely divine?

It does not behove even the greatest amongst scientists to try to "bind the sweet influences of the Pleiades," even if they have chosen "Arcturus with his sons" for their guides. Did it never occur to them to apply to their own intellectual pride the questions the "voice out of the whirlwind" once asked of long-suffering Job: "where were they when were laid the foundations of the earth? and have the gates of death been opened unto them?" If so, only then have they the right to maintain that *here* and not *there* is the abode of eternal light.

THE END.